Reconceiving Decision-Making in Democratic Politics

American Politics and Political Economy Series

Edited by BENJAMIN I. PAGE

BRYAN D. JONES

Reconceiving Decision-Making in Democratic Politics

Attention, Choice, and Public Policy

The
University
of
Chicago
Press

Chicago
&
London

AWZ 0957-2/2

RYAN D. JONES is the Charles Puryear Professor of Liberal Arts and Professor of Political Science at Texas A&M University. With Frank R. Baumgartner, he is the author of *Agendas and Instability in American Politics*, published in 1993 by the University of Chicago Press.

The University of Chicago Press, Chicago 60637
The University of Chicago Press, Ltd., London
© 1994 by The University of Chicago
All rights reserved. Published 1994
Printed in the United States of America
03 02 01 00 99 98 97 96 95 94   1 2 3 4 5
ISBN: 0-226-40650-4 (cloth)
        0-226-40651-2 (paper)

Library of Congress Cataloging-in-Publication

Jones, Bryan D.
    Reconceiving decision-making in democratic politics : attention, choice, and
public policy / Bryan D. Jones.
        p.   cm.—(American politics and political economy series)
    Includes bibliographical references and index.
    1. Political planning—United States.   2. Social choice—United States.   3. Democracy—
United States.   4. United States—Politics and government—Decision making.   I. Title.   II.
Series: American politics and political economy.
JK468.P64J66   1994
320'.01'9—dc20   94-16608
                                                                    CIP

The paper used in this publication meets the minimum requirements of the American National Standard for Information Sciences—Permanence of Paper for Printed Library Materials, ANSI Z39.48-1984.

TO DIANE

"And we are here as on a darkling plain"

C O N T E N T S

FIGURES

P R E F A C E

Writing a book means carrying a theme. But carrying a theme implies the explicit exclusion of aspects of a topic that might interfere with the argument. One learns the classic four-sentence paragraph: the theme; the elaboration of the theme; the qualification (Of course . . .); and the punch line ignoring the qualification.

The hard part is to be fully aware of what you are deliberately omitting, especially when you trample across as many fields as I have in writing this book. And lots of people have helped me to be fully appreciative of what I was leaving out. Frank Baumgartner, Clarence Stone, Alex Mintz, Nehemia Geva, Tom Hammond, Shanto Iyengar, Bill Graziano, Dorothy Olshafski, and Mark Schneider read and commented on all or parts of the manuscript. In addition, I benefited from discussions with Mel Hinich, Charles Elder, Roger Cobb, John Kingdon, George Edwards, and Arnie Vedlitz, as well as with the individuals who read and commented directly on the manuscript. Frank Baumgartner graciously allowed me to use data that we had collectively assembled for our continuing project in American policy agendas, and ideas that we probably developed collectively. Ben Page and the University of Chicago Press reviewers were helpful with both the themes developed here and the details supporting the themes.

Several graduate assistants at Texas A&M helped me immeasurably in working through the data and analysis presented here. Foremost is Billy Hall; also providing time to an occasionally demanding professor (regularly from their view) were Jeff Talbert and Mike Rosenstiehl. A faculty development leave during the fall of 1993 provided by Texas A&M allowed me to read deeply into the information-processing literature and to draft my initial ideas for the project. The Center for Presidential Studies at Texas A&M and the Roper Center at the University of Connecticut provided data for the analysis of mass attention described in chapter 5. But Texas A&M as an institution caused me to ponder the differences between productivity and creativity; with its culture that demanded quantifiable output, it seemed to push out creativity.

John Tryneski of the University of Chicago Press was not only an able editor; he was a critic of the development of the ideas presented here. By forcing me to sharpen my presentation from the initial prospectus to the final letter indicating what I should do with the comments of the reviewers, he required me to understand my subject better.

Introduction:
A Nonmarginalist Approach for
Political Science

One needs to write an introduction only because the full understanding of what one has done comes late in the conduct of a project. Doing the work frames it. And it was late in this work that I realized how captive our approaches in political science have been to the marginalist model of information acquisition; and how wrong that model is for the study of politics.

Political science has reached somewhat of an impasse. It is an impasse that is mostly unrecognized, primarily because of the open and eclectic nature of the discipline, but it is an impasse nevertheless. It is a consequence of our implicit understandings of decision-making in democratic political systems. The problem stems from our use of preferences as the "crutch" of our analyses. In current visions, democracy has to do fundamentally with the communication of citizen preferences to policymaking elites and the subsequent matching of public policies to those preferences. Yet much of politics concerns the communication of structure rather than the communication of preferences.

A quarter of a century ago, models of democracy and democratic decision-making were simple. Three basic forms existed: the populist, the pluralist, and the elite-competition models. The populist, or overhead democracy, model assumed that elected officials would enact mass preferences and then would control the bureaucracy during the implementation stage. The pluralist model, growing out of group theory, found democratic rule in the struggle among organized interests. And the elite-competition approach saw competition among parties (groupings of elites seeking power) as the prime source of democracy, with parties offering packages of programs for voters to judge during election periods.

All of these models are based fundamentally on preference satisfaction. And for all the quibbling and qualifications about the impact of the institutions of government, none offers much of a role for them. The minimalist approach to democratic rule required only regular, open elections. Political scientists, following the lead of Robert Dahl, called the American system of divided powers "Madisonian," all the while quoting Madison's argument that institutions would not preserve liberty but that a republic of diverse interests would. Even with the suspicions about the minor role for specific governing institutions, political scientists have

1

conducted numerous empirical studies of political institutions, most at the state and local level, where substantial institutional variability exists. The results have been mixed and have not yielded serious political theory about the role of institutions. Interestingly, the study of democracy as preference satisfaction *has* unlocked a theory of institutions, the so-called new institutionalism. It was stimulated by the work of economist Kenneth Arrow, who concluded that *no* mechanism of preference aggregation (short of a dictator) could yield equilibrium policy solutions except under restrictive assumptions (the "single-peaked preference" assumption). Where preferences were not single-peaked, however, policy outcomes were dependent either on the manipulation of the rules by leaders ("agenda-setters") or by the establishment of "structure-induced equilibria," which forced preferences along a single dimension of conflict and hence caused them to be artificially single-peaked.

Structure now seemed not just an epiphenomenon but fundamental to the exercise of public power—in formal theory as well as in the minds of political activists. And unlike economics, with its denial of the importance of institutions in the long run (outside of the minimalist competitive market structure that would ensure dynamic equilibrium), political science seemed fundamentally about institutions. But if institutions are important, modeling them correctly is critical. Some political scientists turned to "game theory" to model institutions, and theorist Peter Ordeshook (1986) asserted that political theory *must* be founded on game theory. But what game models politics? Do participants shift games? And how do they communicate the structure of the game? It is not properly recognized, but the importance of structure means that preferences are less important and that democracy has at least as much to do with the communication of structure as with the satisfaction of preferences. And here is the impasse: much of politics involves the setting of the structure, but we continue to base our analyses on preference satisfaction models.

So we move toward a fuller appreciation of the role of institutions in politics hobbled to models that are not capable of integrating structure into analysis. Even when structure is the focus of analysis, it is treated as if it were as fixed as the firmament. It would, of course, be convenient if all structure were set in the written rules and constitutions, but all of us who have participated in any kind of organization know that is not the case. Norms evolve, culture is critical, and strategic actors can shift the understanding of a situation. So it is by no means self-evident that participants are playing the same game that analysts think they are playing, especially where analysts rely on the written rules to understand the game.

The implication I draw from this is that political scientists must ground theory in a model of individual decision-making that emphasizes the communication of structure among participants. That is, any theory of democratic decision-making must be more about information processing and less about preference maximization. Furthermore, the communication of structure *must* be episodic and not incremental. One structure must be *substituted* for another and cannot be changed through the adding of more information in small increments. So in this book I propose a model capable of integrating information processing with preference maximization.

Even this is not enough. Systems of human action, including political systems, also must acquire and act on information. So in the second part of this book, I attempt to link the information-processing capacities of humans with the information-processing capacities of democratic political systems—in particular, the U. S. political system. To the extent that they behave analogously to individuals, political systems, even the most open and democratic ones, must also behave in an episodic, disjointed manner.

Models of preference maximization generally allow only for gradual change in public policy, because preferences are generally regarded as reasonably stable. Of course, exogenous shocks—Pearl Harbor—may cause great changes, but in more "normal" times, public policy would be more stable. This is definitely *not* the pattern that Frank Baumgartner and I documented in our study of nine public policy issues across an extended time span. Rather, we observed considerable lurching, at least at the subsystem level. To us, change, even major disruptive change, often seemed driven endogenously. What sort of information-processing model could account for these changes? This is actually the question that stimulated this research.

Models of rational decision-making that have been useful in the preference satisfaction approach are implicitly grounded in a theory of information processing known as the *marginalist* model. Individuals will acquire information in increments, until the added benefits that are estimated to accrue from the acquisition of information just balance the added (marginal) costs of acquiring more information. The marginalist model denies even the possibility of *exhaustive* search; such search just isn't rational, because of the declining marginal benefits of continuing to acquire information. In politics, however, the marginalist model won't work much better than the exhaustive search assumption. Information doesn't just shed light on options, controlled through one of those dimmer switches many of us have in our dining rooms. Much of the time we can't rotate the knob until just the proper amount of illumination floods the room. No, sometimes information frames. It colors the very understanding of a problem, affecting what Herbert Simon called the *design problem*. In other words, information can communicate structure.

Rational theorists typically assert that their decision-making model requires only that people are able to make pairwise choices transitively; nothing more is required. The marginalist model fits with this approach, because decision-makers continue to make pairwise choices: to acquire information or to go back and make the decision. If, however, information reframes, then what I term *choice reversals* may occur as people come to understand the problem in a different light. Moreover, as I show, choice reversals can occur *even if preferences are constant.* The possibility of choice reversals in effect marginalizes preference maximization. Rational decision-making in the face of a marginalist information model tells us everything. In the face of a changing information structure, it tells us almost nothing. The downplaying of preferences in democratic decision-making also helps us resolve Arrow's paradox, without having to rely on the completely fluid preference arguments put forth at various times and places by James Q. Wilson, Aaron Wildavsky, and Clarence Stone. The critical observation is that democratic institutions aggregate *both* preferences *and* attention to information. I shall return to this point in the final chapter.

The reader of this book will see that I have by no means rejected the preference maximization model; I think that people do a pretty good job of "approximately optimizing," *given a design.* But I fully reject the marginalist model as a complete explanation of how people acquire and act on information on politics. In some circumstances, they behave according to the marginalist model. But in others, they do not; the acquisition of information causes them to reframe a decision. And the reframing is particularly critical in the conduct of democratic politics. Can we determine when decision-makers are subject to reframing a problem? I think we can, but we will find only empirical, not logical, answers.

One might ponder how to design a political system that would encourage a polity to be open to reframing yet would discourage the hysteria that can emerge when people "convert" to the new understanding. My own answer would be decentralized government with the active "meddling" of the central government. Frank Baumgartner and I somewhat audaciously termed this "governing through institutional disruption" (Baumgartner and Jones 1993). In the second part of this book I explore this thesis in some detail, explicitly linking it to individual-level information processing. But I recognize the need to be open to a reframe.

PART ONE

The Paradox of Temporal Political Choice

In ordinary life people do not weigh beforehand the result of every action.

— ALFRED MARSHALL

Most models of choice treat decisions as if they occur but once. But people are continually making choices, and often they are asked to make similar choices at different times. It is not unusual to find *choice reversals,* in which a choice made at one time is reversed at another. Even if choice reversals do not occur, because exactly the same choices seldom recur, great inconsistencies in choice across time are readily observable. To explain such inconsistencies, we must postulate either a rapid change in preferences or irrationality (not making a choice based on one's preferences). The five chapters in this part of the book explore a third alternative: that preferences are multidimensional and that attentiveness to preferences can shift abruptly as the decisional context changes. It is shifts in attentiveness that often account for choice inconsistencies rather than instability in preferences or irrationality.

It is entirely possible that one may make perfectly rational decisions at one point in time, in the sense of always choosing the best alternative among those considered and being able to impose transitive ordering on all alternatives compared. But if attention shifts, one may nevertheless make glaringly inconsistent choices across

time. This leads to the *paradox of temporal choice:* preferences remain constant even as choices change. So inconsistent decision-making does not imply irrationality, nor
does consistent decision-making imply rationality. Moreover, rational decision-making does not imply consistency
and nonrational decision-making does not imply inconsistency. In a logical sense, nothing about the nature of
decision-making can be inferred from the path of choices
across time, and a rational model of decision-making implies very little about the path of decision-making across
time.

To illuminate the paradox, we must examine how
decision-makers process information concerning the relevance of their preferences in concrete decision-making situations. That is, how do they decide what is relevant to a
choice? This implies that preferences are less important
in understanding temporal choice than is the structure of
the situation within which preferences are activated.

1   Attention and Agendas in Politics

The act of seeing is discontinuous. We see only things we are interested in seeing, although we may suddenly develop an interest that makes us discover something we have been familiar with for years. — PAUL NOUGE'

It is commonplace to note that no individual can pay attention to all things of importance at once, and this obvious limit in the processing capacity of humans has been intensively studied in laboratory situations. It is perhaps less noted, but nevertheless just as true, that even the most democratic political systems occasionally lurch from issue to issue as demands dictate, not always a pretty sight. This book has as its major focus exploring whether these two observations are linked. How do characteristics of human decision-making affect the conduct of democratic public policymaking? And how do the structure and organization of democratic institutions direct the attention of policymakers to issues?

These questions loom large in theories of democratic policymaking. They are as old as Plato and as new as President Clinton's difficulties with the White House press corps. That is because the quandary put forward in the above paragraph is really, How does "human nature" affect politics? Political scientists, along with sociologists, psychologists, and economists, have in the last several decades developed new theories and examined fresh data that make it worthwhile to explore the issue of human nature and politics anew. I do not pretend here to provide a comprehensive treatment of this issue. Rather, I wish to look at two critical aspects of human decision-making, aspects that have important implications for the conduct of public affairs. These aspects are the preferences citizens and policymakers hold and how they decide which among conflicting preferences are relevant for a political decision.

To make the linkage between these aspects of human decision-making and the conduct of public affairs, we must start somewhere. Archimedes of Syracuse claimed that, given a long enough lever and a place to stand, he could move the world. While we won't exactly be doing any world moving in this book, we will, in effect, need a place to stand. That place will be a conception of human decision-making in politics that, as we shall see, stresses *both* the limits in human cognition stemming from the necessity to shift attentiveness *and* the abilities of *homo politicus* to make solidly rational decisions. So this study of decision-making first de-

7

velops a model, an abstraction of the reality of making decisions, that is based on attentiveness to the context of decisions.

The model implies that decision-makers value or weight preferences differently depending on the context in which they are evoked. It treats preferences as relatively fixed, changing only gradually, but views attention to underlying preferences as capable of radical shifts in brief periods of time. Then I will show how actual choices can be affected by this shift—choice reversals in the absence of preference change. This model is more commensurate with current empirical studies of political decision-making, and has the added advantage of incorporating the decision-making capabilities of both elites and mass publics into one framework. Finally, I will show how the type of decision-making depicted by this model is capable of illuminating aspects of collective choice hitherto relegated to the realm of the inexplicable—particularly political mobilization, agenda processes, and punctuated policy change.

In politics, as in other areas of life, preferences get activated by how individuals interpret context, and it is this combination of preferences and context that yields choice. Context is always changing in politics, so that choices are always shifting; but people's preferences aren't always changing. As a consequence, looking at people's choices is often not such a good way to understand their preferences. It is a common, if convenient, mistake in practical politics when politicians claim a "mandate" for a particular policy direction based on the vote totals. Knowing vote totals (the decision) tells little about the rationale for the decision.

Most people, if asked, would say that democracy has something to do with satisfying the "will of the people." Political scientists are uncomfortable talking about some sort of collective "will." Instead, they think in terms of the satisfaction of preferences. Of course, there are some critical rules of the game that ensure the expression of preferences (and the weighting of preferences according to how strongly people feel), such as the right to assemble and circulate ideas freely. But in all conceptions of democracy, the satisfaction of the preferences of the public through the policy actions of government plays a key role. If I am correct in arguing that the activation of preferences is so strongly affected by attentiveness to context, then we must conclude that the standard view of democratic politics as a method for assembling and satisfying citizen preferences is somewhat misleading. So the approach advocated here gives us a new direction on the fundamental problem of linking individual decision-making with activities of the broader political system.

It would not be consistent with the facts to imply that citizens restlessly shift their attentiveness to different aspects of the multifaceted political reality that faces them. Yale political scientist Robert Dahl (1963) coined the aphorism "politics is a sideshow in the circus of life" to indicate just how little attention the average citizen devotes to politics. Because of the relatively scant attention most citizens devote to politics, they employ "standing decisions" about how they understand what is going on in the public arena at any one time. The phenomenon of standing decisions means that it is not always easy to get citizens to shift their decision premises; but candidates, groups, and citizen activists spend inordinate time and money in trying. When there is a shift, however, it tends to be abrupt, for reasons we will trace out in this book.

The existence of choice reversals in politics does not imply that politics is continual chaos. Most of the time, both preferences and choices are stable or, perhaps more correctly, preferences change gradually with choices following. Sometimes, however, choices change too abruptly to be attributed to underlying preference changes. When such a change occurs, it can happen because there are new decision-makers that are involved or because old decision-makers are making different choices. Strictly speaking, only the latter could be counted in favor of the thesis developed here. Yet sometimes leaders are replaced because followers, often activated by competing leaders, are focusing on new issues that the old leaders have failed to articulate. So the phenomenon of choice reversals may be more pervasive than could be estimated by examining direct changes in choices by existing leaders.

It may be useful to indicate a few examples of the phenomenon of choice reversals in the absence of more fundamental preference changes in politics. Some changes in context that lead to choice reversals are easy to grasp. Could any citizen or politician view military expenditures in the same light before and after the end of the Cold War? Favoring national security is not enough to predict support for increases in military spending. This seems so simple as to be trivial, but it is quite overlooked in approaches to politics that view preference satisfaction as the key component of democracies. Another, very concrete, example occurred when the vote of every Republican in the New Jersey Senate on a ban on assault rifles changed within a week in early 1993. Could it be possible that these astute politicians all shifted their positions on the regulation of guns almost overnight? This is not likely; what happened was a shift in focus, not preferences, as citizens made their displeasure with firearms known. Or take the recent reversals in fortune of "big science" projects: both the superconducting supercollider and the space station have lost supporters as deficit reduction has come into focus as a primary organizing principle of American politics.

This book makes the case that all of these shifts, and many more like them, occur because decision-makers become attentive to aspects of the decisional situation that were previously ignored. They don't change their minds, in the sense of changing preferences, but they change their focus, in the sense of attending to preferences that they had previously eliminated from being relevant to the choice situation. This is not a trivial distinction. It is important to distinguish changes in attentiveness from more long-run changes in preferences. It is easy to show that Americans support gun control. It is even easier to observe that New Jersey's Republican senators were inattentive to that preference. What happened was preference activation, not preference change; and it was both fast and complete.

The shifts in attentiveness that characterize individual decision-making have an analog at the level of the policymaking bodies of government. Agendas of governments change, often abruptly. This abrupt shift is caused by three individual-level tendencies in decision-making. The first tendency is, quite naturally, shifts in attention to preferences. The second is path dependency in individual decisions, wherein a particular understanding and evaluation of an issue is semipermanent once adopted. The final link in the chain of causation between individual decision-making and democratic public policymaking is communication: the contagion among individuals of a change in attentiveness. There is evidence that new frames of reference may float around for some time before they "catch on" (Kingdon 1984), but when they do, they affect people almost at once.[1] Or so it seems; actually it may be that the media and what V. O. Key called the "activist strata" shift their attentiveness and that this shift is interpreted as a sea change in the mass public. In any case, the outcome at both the individual level and the policymaking level is a pattern of reasonable stability punctuated by rapid changes.

1. Actually, looks can be deceiving. An idea gradually growing can captivate a polity because nobody pays attention to the gradual growth when it still has few converts. Such is the case for nondamped contagion effects. Let us assume that in a polity of 100 people a policy entrepreneur begins circulating a new notion. Let us further assume that every period, say, every month, the policy entrepreneur and each convert are able to convert one more individual while losing none. Then the number of converts would be $y_{(t+1)} = 2^t$. In the first month, the policy entrepreneur converts one citizen. In the second month, each of the two proponents converts two; now there are four (or 4 percent of the population). No one really notices. In the fourth month, 16 percent of the population is converted, still a fairly unimportant minority. But in the next month the idea becomes "dangerous," as almost a third (32 percent) of the population has converted. But the month after that, an overwhelming majority of 64 percent now believes.

A simple-looking growth model can become explosive. This is an example of *positive feedback effects,* because nothing occurs to damp the explosive growth. I have more to say about contagion effects in politics later.

Decision-Making

While there are many different uses of the concept of rationality (March 1978), the model of decision-making that is commonly known by that term is well specified and well understood. It assumes that the best decisions are made when decision-makers factor and optimize. Rational decision-makers break decisions into component parts (factoring, or analysis) and then examine alternatives for each part of the problem, in each case choosing the best, or "optimum," alternative (maximization). The analytical/maximization approach works, at least in theory, because the problem facing the decision-maker allows this "breaking down" and "putting together" process to work.

While most of decision science is directed at making better decisions under the analytical/optimization approach, economics and those parts of political science and sociology using rational decision-making analysis focus on the implications for economic, political, and social systems if decision-makers factor and optimize. Social systems operate optimally only if individual decision-makers optimize. Economies are fully efficient when producers satisfy consumer demands in order to maximize profits. Representation is completely effective when legislators fully explore the preferences of citizens in their policy enactments in order to maximize future electoral success. For these things to happen, rational decision-makers must maximize *overall* satisfaction, or what is called *utility,* or their preferences. People then may be seen as maximizing a comprehensive *utility or preference function,* which is a relationship between satisfaction, on one hand, and objects of choices or decisions, on the other. So they get the most satisfaction possible from their choices in all aspects of life taken together.

Given that decision-makers must operate on one problem at a time, a major underlying assumption of the rational approach is that the goals of decision-makers in each decision-making situation may be easily translated into the individual's overall utility function. Sometimes people act as consumers; at others they are citizens. Decisions may be compartmentalized and worked on one at a time without introducing contradictions because the social world is well behaved; that is, it is fundamentally linear and decomposable. It can be taken apart, worked on by the decision-maker, then put back together. Operating on one part has easily understandable effects on other parts. That allows decision-makers to appreciate the myriad of trade-offs that they face in making decisions, and they can allocate effort accordingly. So by working on one problem at a time, decision-makers are in effect maximizing overall utility. As we shall see, this assumption is problematic.

Critiques of the rational choice approach in social science abound. Attacked as an unrealistic model of actual decision-making, as a misleading norm for making better decisions, as a poor vehicle for theory building (by hiding all sorts of prior factual assumptions about human cognition and institutions), it nevertheless survives and thrives in all of the major social science disciplines (Lane 1991: chap. 2; Cook and Levy 1990). The reason seems clear: the approach is coherent, with strong deductive features, and opponents lack a convincing interconnected body of theory that can challenge rational choice as an integrating perspective in social science. Counterpoised to the rational choice theorists are not only those who see considerable irrational behavior in human actions but also the proponents of "bounded rationality" (Simon 1979) or other kinds of reasonable human behavior that does not involve the analysis/maximization approach (March 1978). From laboratory and field studies the bounded rationalists have accumulated empirical findings on how humans generally make decisions and have loosely linked these findings to observations about organizations and social systems. So, for example, limited search capacities can lead to incremental decision-making and the conservation of information can lead to organizational routines.

There are circumstances which evoke the capacity of humans to make calculating decisions. And people can learn to make better decisions—for example, how to evaluate risk and integrate risk (rather than fear or dread) into their decisional calculations. Choosing an asset mix between stocks and bonds for a retirement account, for example, is an area where one can learn to make better decisions, decisions based on past behaviors of markets for stocks and bonds. Nevertheless, the rational choice perspective seems particularly limited where incentive structures are vague or where situations are quickly changing. If one cannot specify stable, or equilibrium, conditions that provide strong, well-understood incentives to individuals, then the maximization techniques of rational choice are not so useful in predicting their behaviors (Jones 1989). In such situations, shifts of frames of reference may be common. Reversals of preference in actual choice situations can occur when frames shift (Tversky and Kahneman 1981, 1986; Quattrone and Tversky 1988). In political science, agenda studies have suggested the importance of such shifts in ambiguous situations (see chap. 3 of Baumgartner and Jones 1993 for a review).

Such indeterminacy has sometimes been read as an inability of humans to make decisions rationally. Students of politics have studied the irrelevance of campaigns and political advertising to the issues facing the polity; the roles of attachment and identifications, as opposed to that of information, in determining political choice; and the sweep of fads within the political system. A better approach is to view human decision-makers as "boundedly rational" (Simon 1985), that is, as working to achieve a degree of decision-making rationality through various heuristic devices. One critical component of human decision-making is the "bottleneck of attention"—that is, the biological necessity of human decision-makers to process cognitive information serially (Simon 1985).

Attention and Rationality

Within the cognitive limits of serial processing, humans may be capable of a closer approximation to rational decision-making than is sometimes appreciated. But the world may conspire to magnify the decision-maker's shortcomings by being complex and ambiguous. In this book, I will investigate the possibility of relaxing certain assumptions of the rational approach to decision-making in politics by incorporating the decision to attend to political issues in the decision-making model. "Paying attention to attention" leads directly to a focus on temporal choice—the issue of how people make choices over time (Lowenstein and Elster 1992). And when we view choice over time, we observe incredible inconsistencies.

Yet major aspects of the rational model, in particular, fixed, transitive preference orderings (so that individuals can rank alternatives consistently), are not affected by serial processing—at least with a proper understanding of preferences. Changes in choice are caused not so much by changes in preferences as by the "exquisite sensitivity to contextual cues" (Iyengar 1991: 11) exhibited by human decision-makers. Humans are sensitive to context because they are not just preference maximizers; they are also problem solvers, and problem solving is directly related to perceiving changes in the relevant task environment. It is this contextual sensitivity that is not appropriately appreciated in the "dispositional" models of political choice, whether those dispositions are seen as preferences, or attitudes, or basic values, or affective or emotional identifications with groups, parties, or candidates.

Our basic guiding thesis, then, is that preferences generally change only grudgingly but that attentiveness to those preferences can shift rapidly. Because humans generally process the incoming information that causes this shift in a serial fashion, I term the rapid alteration in attention to preferences the *serial shift*. Preferences are multidimensional; we want many things out of life. Often, preferences are also in conflict with one another, as when we want both to consume and to save, or when we want more public services and less taxes. In politics we may like some

aspects of a political candidate but dislike others. Hence choice is fundamentally affected by attentiveness to the attributes that candidates offer
citizens (or, for that matter, that car manufacturers offer consumers). In
one situation (the Cold War is salient), a citizen may attend to one set of
preferences (he or she focuses on national security). In another situation
(a deep recession is in process), he or she may attend to another dimension of evaluation (stimulating the economy). Note that the citizen may
well want *both* economic stimulation *and* increased military security, but
may not be offered this particular package by candidates. Hence the candidates would be differently advantaged by a shift from a national security emphasis to an economic security focus by citizens. Moreover, the
point is entirely general: the *choices* that people face are almost always
underlain by multiple *attributes.*

Before we go any further, it is advisable to clarify some terms. The
terms *preference, goal,* and *dimension of evaluation* all pretty much sig-
nify the same thing insofar an individual decision-maker is concerned.
They of course may not be the same when we discuss the whole political
system; what citizens want and what is advisable policy may differ. The
attributes, or characteristics, of candidates, or other objects of choice,
are also related to goals and preferences. When these attributes are evaluated (in the sense of having worth attached to them), we speak of *preferences.* This may seem a little confusing at first, but we can clarify by looking again at our candidates offering combinations of economic security
and national defense. These policy packages are two (among potentially
many) attributes of the candidates. National security and economic well-
being are preferences that our hypothetical voter has; they are also dimensions of evaluation along which candidates vary.

The introduction of shifts in attention in temporal choice opens up
a much more important role for the *context* of decisions in determining
outcomes. Attentiveness is affected by context, but preferences are not.
Changes in attentiveness to underlying attributes in a situation can lead
to the above-mentioned choice reversals, in which a decision-maker decides very differently in seemingly similarly structured choice situations.[2]

2. I have chosen the term *choice reversals* to contrast this concept with what Kahneman and Tversky term *preference reversals.* Their approach focuses on shifts in preference
orderings that emerge when alternatives are presented in different contexts. My view is
that preferences are more fixed than choices, and that preferences and context interact to
produce choices. Hence preferences may remain constant, context may vary, and nevertheless choices may reverse.

Context is, of course, mediated by attention—that is, people cannot be affected by
context unless they attend to it. Attention to context is generally lumped into preference
structures, with potentially misleading results. Analysts may decry inconsistency in preferences when in fact context has changed so much that different preferences (and perhaps

Faced with the same "vote" or other choice at two different points in time, the decision-maker may reverse an earlier choice without really changing his or her underlying preferences or goals. The mechanism by which this occurs is the selectivity that occurs when one evaluates the relevance of preferences for a choice situation. Attentiveness is not normally seen as so directly bound up with preferences, but it is easy to see that attentiveness *must* affect the relevance of a decision-maker's preference structure for choice. If we use the term *attentiveness* to refer to the appreciation of underlying dimensions or structure of a choice situation (a normal use of the term), and if we note that evaluated dimensions are essentially preferences (something a little different), then the connection becomes clear. Changes in attentiveness to the underlying preferences (which are evaluated attributes of the alternatives that a decision-maker faces) may lead to a reversal of choice, such as the New Jersey gun control reversal. On the face of it, this may seem inconsistent and nonrational, but an understanding of how selective attention to the various underlying attributes of alternatives makes clear what is going on.[3] In effect, the bases of a choice have changed.

This seemingly minor modification not only introduces a strikingly different view of human choice but also brings into question the prevailing view of democratic government as a mechanism for satisfying preferences. The reason is that in temporal choice situations it is unlikely that citizens change preferences rapidly, but they can quickly change the aspects of a situation that they pick out for attention. Hence changes in focus can change outcomes. Democratic governance has as much to do with responding to these changes of focus as with responding to changes in preferences.

Approaches to Decision-Making

One of the great enigmas in social science concerns how individual actions are linked to social, economic, and political systems (Schelling 1978). By far the most elegant linkage has been achieved in economics,

---

contradictory ones—we all harbor inconsistent preferences) are activated. When attentiveness to context changes, analysts can be misled into thinking that preferences have changed. An objective of this book is to urge analysts to divide preference structures into the actual preferences (what people want) and the preferences they are attentive to at any point in time.

3. It should be clear that direct choice reversals do not actually have to occur to be important in politics. It is the shifting focus of selective attention to preferences that is critical.

through a set of assumptions about the system and the rationality of the individual actor. Competitive markets generate predictable incentives for actors, who rationally respond by maximizing a comprehensive utility function. The major critic of the full rationality model, Herbert Simon, notes that whenever one can completely model the incentive structure of the environment and assume what he calls "omniscient rationality," the behavior of individuals is fully determined. Hence the system-behavior linkage can be forged in any sphere (Simon 1979: 498). Simon's alternative view of rationality, *bounded rationality,* appreciates both the limited cognitive processing capacities of humans and the complexity of the environment with which they must deal. As a consequence, decision-makers develop heuristic shortcuts as aids to decisional calculations.

Predictions about decision-making actions from limited rationality models, while more difficult than from full rationality models, are quite possible. Moreover, linking human decisions to the behavior of organizations not only is possible but has been accomplished. The limited search routines and repetitive behaviors that are a centerpiece of the decision-making models of Simon and Lindblom (1959) have been applied to business organizations (Cyert and March 1963), to federal government budgeting (Wildavsky 1984; Davis, Dempster, and Wildavsky 1974), to municipal budgeting (Crecine 1969; Meltsner 1971), to the distribution of services by urban bureaucracies (Levy, Meltsner, and Wildavsky 1974; Jones 1980), and to the influence of politics on bureaucratic service delivery (Jones 1985: chap. 7). It would seem, however, that different decision models may be necessary for routine and nonroutine decisional processes, an issue it is not necessary to address if a rational choice perspective is adopted. So one of the major objectives of this book is to offer a framework that will encompass all types of decisions.

While limits of cognitive capability are often the focus of studies in bounded rationality, the real difficulty comes about when the limited capacity of human information processing interacts with complex social environments (see Simon 1981; Perrow 1979; Cohen, March, and Olsen 1972; Cohen and March 1986). In many well-structured situations, people can and do perform rational calculations, and where cognitive limits do form outer bounds, they are far distant from the immediate problem facing the decision-maker. One might conceive of a continuum of environments, from the most structured (playing a bridge game) to the most unstructured. The most important task of a decision-maker is determining what facets of a complex environment are relevant to the decisional task. Specifying relevant aspects of the complex environment of decision choice in ill-structured situations makes the decision-maker's problem extremely difficult. What is relevant is often not obvious in politics; hence political scientists must study empirically what political actors treat as relevant.

The mass public is sometimes viewed as lacking in stable preferences for policy alternatives as a consequence of low levels of political information. One can nevertheless find some support for the fixed preferences, varying attention model in the public opinion literature, at least if one adopts a broad view of the term "preference"—that is, preferences refer to end states, not specific policy instruments. Popkin's (1991) work on how voters respond to campaigns depicts an electorate capable of making informed choices. Page and Shapiro (1992) and Mayer (1992) construct careful empirical pictures of an electorate that has stable policy attitudes that move in reasoned response to changing circumstances. These pictures of mass preferences are consistent with a model of fixed (or only glacially changing) mass preferences.

If government were to respond simply and directly to these glacially changing mass preferences, then we ought to observe a fundamentally incremental public policy process. Such a picture clashes with the model of policymaking offered by the agenda-setting perspective. If preferences are fixed, then a simple model of mass preference change–public policy response seems problematic, because policy shifts are almost certainly less incremental than mass preference shifts (on this latter point, see Mayhew 1991; Baumgartner and Jones 1993). Hence policy shifts must be explained through some other mechanism than preference changes.

Policy Agendas and Policymaking

Given that political actors occasionally shift the focus of their attention from one evaluative dimension to another, how is the system of policymaking affected? The answer lies in the notion of policy agendas, the items that policymaking institutions address. Actually, the term *policy agenda* is used in three senses. First, an agenda can refer to voting on particular motions before a legislative body. Because the order in which motions are voted on can affect outcomes, an agenda-setter potentially has the ability to bring about particular outcomes by ingenious pairings of motions (Fiorina and Shepsle 1989). Second, the policy agenda can refer to how a political system comes to treat an idea as a serious matter for policy action. Third, the policy agenda can refer to the general set of topics that a policymaking body considers for formal action during a set period of time (say, a legislative session). Cobb and Elder (1983) distinguish between the *systemic* and the *formal* agenda. The systemic agenda consists of matters that are actively entertained by policy elites; the formal agenda consists of items scheduled for consideration by a policymaking body—specific bills have been introduced, committees have held hearings, and so forth. Hence the Cobb-Elder formulation of agendas must precede the more specific pairings of motions in particular meetings of bodies. In this book, I will use the term *policy agenda* to refer to the formal agenda of a policymaking body.

Agenda setting is episodic. Something is there (on the agenda) that wasn't there before. While many items on the agenda of any public body are routine (like the consideration of the minutes of the last meeting), many substantive items are discordant—in the sense of involving new policy alternatives for consideration and thus diverging from routine business. Just how these new proposals come to be taken seriously (and thereby get put on the formal agenda of a policymaking body) is the central interest of political scientists studying agenda change.

Gradualism versus Punctuation

On the title page of every one of the eight editions of the great late-nineteenth-century economist Alfred Marshall's influential textbook, *Principles of Economics,* is the Latin phrase *Natura non facit saltum:* nature does not make leaps. The aphorism encapsulating the belief that nature is well behaved can be traced at least to the biologist Linnaeus in 1750, but Marshall may have been the first social scientist to popularize it (Gould 1980: 179). This was not surprising; Marshall and the other so-called marginalists analyzed the economy using the tools of equilibrium analysis and its associated mathematics. Marshall's explicit aim was to make economics more like physics and less like history and biology.[4]

In political science, *Natura non facit saltum* comes in various guises, perhaps most easily seen in group theory, where actions always beget reactions, and in the incremental decision-making models, in which decision-makers make only minor adjustments from the status quo. Cycle models, in which actions beget reactions over extended periods of

---

4. The dialogue on the nature of change has a long history in biology. Incremental change was a fundamental part of Darwin's ideas of natural selection; this view of nature has been vigorously defended by Richard Dawkins (1986). Niles Eldredge and Stephen Jay Gould reinvigorated the debate with their notion of *punctuated equilibria* (Eldredge and Gould 1972; Eldredge 1985; Gould 1980; see also Somit and Peterson 1989). There has been considerable sloppy thinking about the nature of punctuated equilibria since Gould and Eldredge developed their model. Specifically, both the standard Darwin approach and the punctuated equilibria approach (which most emphatically does *not* deny Darwinism) postulate well-defined dynamics. That is, in biology and paleontology the ideas of gradual and punctuated change both have causes; they are not solely descriptions.

time, are also popular. Empirically, many political time series look incremental. James Stimson claims that "if we observe almost any phenomenon at regular intervals over time, we will see change produced by the cumulation of small and irregular increments. If we do this for a while ... the idea of change occurring as discontinuous jumps becomes increasingly an idea of oddball irregularities" (1991: 6). Stimson (1991: 21) sees changes in public opinion as "a meandering river"—not a river rushing through mountain passes, across boulders, and down waterfalls but a river drifting lazily across the plain.

Counterpoised to Stimson's "oddball irregularities" is Stephen Krasner's punctuation approach to political development and state building: "A basic analytic distinction must be made between periods of institutional creation and periods of institutional stasis" (1984: 240). Krasner argues that different causal processes may be associated with crisis periods than with calmer periods. He writes that "the state as an administrative apparatus and legal order will not smoothly adjust to changes in its domestic environment. Once institutions are in place they will perpetuate themselves" (1984: 234). For Krasner, discontinuous jumps are a natural result of a disjunction between dynamic domestic social and economic changes and the conservative drag of state institutions. Models of abrupt change have also been prominent in the literature on political parties, as scholars have examined data in a search for the beginnings and ends of party "systems" interspersed with rapid "realignments."

Agenda politics is about the temporal policy choices made by whole political systems. Models of agenda setting are punctuated models, by their very formulation (Baumgartner and Jones 1993). Tracing the flow of new ideas and conceptions into the political discourse invariably involves discontinuous shifts in ways of doing things. Agenda theorists are concerned with shifts in collective attention in policymaking bodies from one constellation of policy issues to another. The agenda approach may be contrasted with the more standard representational approach to democratic governance, in which citizen preferences are translated into public policies by representatives. Agenda processes are so abrupt when viewed from a proper time scale (and this is simply in years rather than days) that agenda conceptions of policy formulation are simply not consonant with traditional representational models—at least if we view preferences as relatively fixed. Something moving gradually and incrementally cannot, acting alone, cause something that is moving discontinuously.[5]

5. Except when there are certain kinds of interaction effects—such as those modeled in catastrophe theory (Thom 1975).

Preference Satisfaction as a Standard for Democratic Performance

Prevailing models of governance in liberal democratic political systems center on the fundamental notion of preference satisfaction. While a variety of models have been developed to analyze the performance of democratic governance, almost all of them concern how mass preferences influence the development of public policies. In an important variant of the basic model, many democratic theorists have incorporated the notion of "interest" into their models. There exist considerable differences of opinion concerning the correspondence of preferences and interests, but at least one theme unifies these approaches: how democratic governments respond to interests or preferences. Because the actual range of policies is far narrower than the variability of preferences or interests in a society, a focus on preference or interest satisfaction leads to an attempt to understand how preferences or interests are aggregated and articulated when they are presented to policymakers.

Some examples will illustrate just how pervasive this approach is. The language of preference satisfaction is prevalent in studies of legislative representation, where the policy activities of representatives are compared to the preferences or attitudes of their constituents on issues of the day (for a review and critique, see Bernstein 1989). The concept of "collective representation" has been used to capture the correspondence between the policy positions of a legislative body and the mass public (Weissberg 1978). It is the foundation of Stimson's work on the role of national moods on what he terms "longitudinal representation" (Stimson 1991: xxi). The question of preference satisfaction characterizes studies of spatial voting, both in mass publics and in legislative bodies. In a one-dimensional policy space, the positions of political parties or candidates are determined by the distribution of voters along that dimension. In more complex situations, the concept of preference aggregation is critical, because where the policy space is multidimensional, the cycling of preferences is a possibility (Riker 1982).

Pluralist theorists have been less interested in the match between mass publics and public policy, focusing instead on the role of organized groups in influencing the policy process. Nevertheless, their fundamental understanding of the policy process is similar to "populist" conceptions of democracy (Riker 1982) in one major respect: their focus on the correspondence between preferences (here, organized preferences) and policy outcomes. Normative evaluations of pluralist systems have differed greatly, ranging from E. E. Schattschneider's complaint that "the flaw in the pluralist heaven is that the chorus sings with an upper-class accent"

(1960: 35) to Mancur Olsen's indictment that groups, by satisfying parochial preferences, cause a decline in economic growth (1982).

Olsen's complaint is a variant of a common charge against pluralism: that its responsiveness to articulated interests causes a divergence from the common good. Group theorist David Truman (1951) thought carefully about this problem, finding a role for potential group mobilization in circumstances in which interests unrepresented in the pressure group system were sufficiently threatened. So one undercurrent in the pluralist approach to understanding democratic government focuses on the degree to which overall public interests are realized in a system in which government responds mostly to the organized. There are really two different questions here: whether mass preferences are realized through the system of group representation, and whether the collective interest is realized. Here there is explicit reference to the possible divergence between collective group preferences (perhaps conceptually aggregated across policy subsystems), mass preferences, and the collective interest.

One can see from these examples that many complex and important issues emerge from a focus on a comparison between government policies and citizen preferences, however they are articulated and aggregated. But there is a second, less well developed approach to open, democratic systems. This is the notion that democracies respond to problems and that their openness allows the expression of problems more efficiently than do closed systems of governance. Now, in one sense there do not have to be any monumental differences between a preference-satisfaction model of democracy and a problem-solving model. One can simply assume that citizens wish governments to solve problems, a sensible enough assumption that can be verified empirically. But the framing of the issue is sufficiently different that it leads to an entirely different empirical focus and a different enough model of decision-making that it is well worth treating these approaches as separate.

Problem-Solving Models

Models based on problem solving emphasize the processing of information both by individuals and by governing institutions. In the preference-satisfaction approach, preferences are most important and the issue of limited information is treated as somewhat of an afterthought (or as a "relaxation" of the basic assumption of a rigorous model to see if the model is robust—that is, whether it can survive when information is limited). Because information is at the core of problem-solving models, the presentation of information, particularly ambiguous information, becomes a central concern. So do mechanisms for selecting what information is processed by political systems—that is, what problems they attend to. Information is not really scarce; there is a wealth of it. The major issue concerns what information is selected for input into the policy process. Herbert Simon has noted that considerable mistakes were made in the design of management information systems through the assumption that information was scarce in policymaking, whereas in point of fact "the scarce factor is attention" (Simon 1981: 167).

For simplicity, we may divide the problem-solving models into two categories: cybernetic, or learning, models and agenda-setting models.

Cybernetics. The cybernetic models stress the adjustment of the political system to economic, technological, or social trends. They incorporate learning and feedback at the systems level, and at least some of the models suggest discontinuities in the process. This idea underlies the political modernization literature in comparative politics, where democratization was thought to follow economic development. (For a brief, pointed summary, see Fukuyama 1992: 55–70). Recently, Dodd has developed a cybernetic approach to American politics that emphasizes the pressures of economic and social change, on one hand, and the world views of political participants, on the other. As the epistemologies (world views) of participants get out-of-date, tensions in politics develop that lead to lurches as the epistemologies of participants move toward correspondence with changing circumstances (Dodd 1991, 1992). Individuals have relatively stable world views that do not respond to small changes in information. In the long run, however, they must adjust, and this leads to a disjointed, jerky adjustment process. Both the modernization literature and Dodd's transformational politics approach move beyond the issue of preference satisfaction (or, more correctly, see preference satisfaction as secondary to the process of adjustment). Among public policy scholars, Sabatier (1987, 1988) has incorporated both system-level learning and political conflict in his "advocacy coalitions" approach.

Agendas. More entrenched in the literature on American politics is the agenda-setting approach. Here the focus is on political issues: where they come from, how they are selected for serious consideration, how they are framed to attract support, and how they influence the policy process. It is, of course, clear that groups and individuals must articulate issues, so a focus on preferences and a focus on issue processing are not at all incompatible. But there are differences: an issue-based approach leads one to try to understand the role of information and its presentation in politics, and away from the question of the linkage between preferences and policies.

One of the contributions of the agenda literature is to force a conception of the political world that is far more dynamic than that implied by the preference-satisfaction approach. Locked into a preference approach, one must assume either rapidly changing preferences or rapidly changing mechanisms for aggregation to account for change. Politics, of course, is characterized both by considerable stability and by remarkable changes, but in the preference-satisfaction approach one is almost forced to stress stability. For example, most formal models are based on rational choice axioms and the satisfaction of preferences. Analysts try to prove analytically the existence of an equilibrium between preferences and policies given the institutions (the "rules") for aggregating the preferences. Although some public choice theorists have become uncomfortable with the implicit equilibrium assumption (Riker 1982), it nevertheless remains a defining characteristic of the approach.

In the agenda-setting approach, information is viewed as inherently ambiguous, so that there is a very important role for leadership and policy entrepreneurship in the framing of issues to garner support for a policy position. That is, the manipulation of information plays a key role in forcing governmental attention to problems. Because attention can shift very rapidly (especially in comparison to preferences), policy action can also shift very rapidly. In preference models, information is viewed as neutral and costly, and hence subject to the laws of declining marginal returns. To the extent that attention is important in these models (and it almost never is), it is treated as a transaction cost, part of the costs of collecting information. In agenda models, information primarily causes heightened attention to an issue, and attention to an issue carries with it a valence (D. Stone 1988, 1989; Baumgartner and Jones 1993). That is, information is never neutral in the policy process, and that is why it is so fundamental.

While both cybernetic and agenda models stress information in the policy process, downplaying preferences, they differ in an important respect. Cybernetic models emphasize the connectivity of political activity to changes in other aspects of the economic and social system, whereas agenda-setting models tend to view politics in isolation. The important point is that these approaches have more in common than either does with preference satisfaction as a performance standard.

Policy Agendas

In the agenda-setting approach, the focus is on political issues: where they come from, how they are selected for serious consideration, how they are framed to attract support, and how they influence the policy process. Substantial progress has been made by agenda theorists in the last twenty years in understanding how new ideas infuse the political system. The focus of interest in agenda studies has been the translation into public policies of perceptions of problems and ideas about how to solve them (Eyestone 1978; Polsby 1984; Beecher, Lineberry, and Rich 1981; Nelson 1984; Waste 1989; Hoppe 1991; Rushefsky 1991). While most research has concentrated on American domestic policy, the approach has been used as well in studying foreign policy (Durant and Diehl 1989) and in analyzing the domestic policies of other nations (Baumgartner 1989; Foley 1991; Studlar and Layton-Henry 1990).

At the risk of oversimplifying, I suggest that the following propositions are fairly well accepted. *First,* the entry of new participants in politics and the "drawing power" of new ideas are related. It is a matter of some controversy whether the ideas draw the participants or whether the participants bring with them new ideas, but the relationship seems well established. (Cobb and Elder 1983; Cobb, Ross, and Ross 1976; Baumgartner 1987, 1989; Baumgartner and Jones 1991; Best 1990). Agenda setting is closely linked to conflict expansion (Schattschneider 1960; see also Bosso 1987). That is, conflict attracts new participants (in the sense that a new set of individuals express political demands). Often a period of "softening up" occurs before an idea draws its full potential of adherents (Kingdon 1984).

Second, the definition of issues is critical in attracting new participants to politics (D. Stone 1988, 1989; Bosso 1989; Brown 1990; Foster 1977; Schoenfeld, Meier, and Griffin 1979). The role of issue definition in politics is related to a broader concern with the use of symbols in political debate (or in forestalling debate). While there was a tendency to see image making as elite manipulation of mass preferences in the earlier literature, current thinking stresses the use of symbols in pluralistic political conflict (see Boulding 1956; Elder and Cobb 1983; Edelman 1964, 1989; Bachrach and Baratz 1962; Crenson 1971; Gusfield 1963, 1981; Majone 1989; Weart 1988). The redefinition of issues can also allow political entrepreneurs to prevail where fighting the battle within the old framework leads to a loss (Riker 1986; see also Fingarette 1988).

Third, the role of the media in defining public problems and communicating policy ideas has been highlighted. Numerous studies emphasize the role of the media in calling attention to existing controversies and helping to frame issues (Bosso 1989; Hilgartner and Bosk 1988; Iyengar 1990; Manheim 1987; Protess et al. 1985; Rothman and Lichter 1982; Rubin 1987; Molotch and Lester 1984; Cook et al. 1983; Protess et al. 1987; Rogers and Deering 1988). In the case of scientific controversies, the role of a handful of journalists who use broad and symbolic conceptions of science, generally "progress" versus "danger," has been noted

(Mazur 1981a, b; Nelkin 1971, 1984, 1987; Nelkin and Fallows 1978; Nelkin and Pollak 1981; McGowan 1986; Rubin 1987; Cohen 1981; Friedman et al. 1987). The media is important because of its communication capacity, but much of the discussion of new policy proposals does not attract the interest of the national media (Kingdon 1984).

Fourth, policy entrepreneurs are critical in defining ideas and shepherding them through the policy process (Schneider and Teske 1992). Ideas are, of course, purveyed by political actors; they are not self-sustaining without advocates. Kingdon (1984) shows how purveyors of policy solutions can attach these solutions to problems by defining the problem as one amenable to their preferred solution. They also can interject new dimensions of conflict into a policy debate, thereby shifting the outcome (Baumgartner and Jones 1993; Schneider and Teske 1993). Policy entrepreneurs, like leaders anywhere, are not motivated solely by the rewards that will stem from the policy itself; they also seek the recognition that stems from accomplishment and enjoy the intrinsic rewards of fighting the good fight (Chong 1991).

Fifth, as new ideas enter the political arena, often new dimensions of evaluation are stressed in policy argumentation (Riker 1982, 1983, 1984, 1986, 1990, 1993). That is, agenda shifts frequently come about because people become aware of new aspects of old problems, and this shift in attentiveness causes changes in choice. As the public debate develops, a process of noncontradictory argumentation occurs, with each side stressing different attributes of a problem. As individuals move from one dimension of evaluation to a second dimension that is being stressed (for example, from equity to growth), their policy choices often change. If these changes are communicated broadly, a shift in the prevailing climate of policymaking can occur.

Finally, there is a complex interaction between political institutions, on one hand, and the processing of new ideas and the entry of new participants, on the other (Carmines and Stimson 1986, 1989; Baumgartner and Jones 1991, 1993; Jones 1975; Jones and Strahan 1985). Milward and Laird (1990), in reviewing five cases of agenda setting, find that issue definition, policy knowledge, and opportunity interacted to yield agenda success. Interaction effects are common findings in agenda research; such effects are often accompanied by contagion and positive feedback effects that result in unforeseen outcomes (Baumgartner and Jones 1993).

These agenda dynamics lead to lurches in public policymaking (Baumgartner and Jones 1993). Because change in attention (or, in systemic terms, agenda access) is associated with change in issue definitions, whole new ways of understanding policy problems can be associated with agenda access. That is, changes in issue definition constitute one critical method for attracting the attention of policymakers to a policy problem. In essence, the function of the policy entrepreneur is to frame an issue so as to move it over the threshold of attention of policymaking institutions. For the most part, agenda theorists do not deny that problems generate policy activity; it is just that many problems exist, and the choice of problems is linked to how political systems recognize and attend to problems. Nor do they want to imply that traditional political forces such as party and interest group activity are irrelevant; clearly these forces are related to how problems are recognized. These two conceptions of the policy process (the role of problems and solutions versus the role of political institutions) are not very well integrated in current research in political science.

There are clear connections between issue definitions and policy change in a quantitative analysis of nine public policy issues undertaken by Frank Baumgartner and myself (Baumgartner and Jones 1993). So long as general attention is low in a policy area, the area tends to be dominated by experts and directly affected groups. When attention is broadened, almost invariably through issue redefinition, the macropolitical institutions intervene in subsystem politics, fundamentally altering them. Redford (1969) noted this possibility some years ago, and it has been supported by subsequent studies. Frank Baumgartner and I described these processes as punctuated equilibria. Work by Peters and Hogwood (1985) showed quantitatively that within policy areas there were periods of intense activity (in establishing new governmental agencies) that corresponded to Gallup poll data showing public concern with the same problems. Each policy area they studied had one such peak. However, activity following the peak did not decline to pre-peak levels. (See also Casstevens 1980.) Apparently a short period of intense interest can leave a substantial institutional legacy. Mayhew's (1991) study of major legislation passed by Congress supports a view of periods of intense policy activity interspersed with periods of less innovation. This line of research vitiates Downs's (1972) claim that attention cycles do not yield substantive public policy outcomes. Real policy change often occurs after collective attention shifts, and these new levels of policies form the base for the next wave of activity.

All of this suggests that what needs to be explained at the level of the political system is a considerable degree of policy lurching. This lurching may be due to cycles of government activity. Historian Arthur Schlesinger (1986) depicts periods of rapid progressive governmental action interspersed with pragmatic retrenchment, rest, and renewal. Huntington (1981) infers cycles of "creedal passion" that overwhelm the system.

McFarland (1991) sees cycles of business subsystems and reaction to them based on consumer protection and democratic egalitarianism. On the other hand, agenda models are more evolutionary (Kingdon 1984; Baumgartner and Jones 1993; Dodd 1992). Cycles are not inconsistent with agenda models, but the agenda approach implies that the history of a system is critically important.

Attention and Representation

The findings from agenda studies indicate that political change is very much driven by changes in the definition of problems and the consequent activation of previously apathetic citizens. Problem definition is far more than abject manipulation; in an open debate, the struggle over definition is how political systems decide what problems to address. Hence we ought to explore the viability of altering the focus of studies of responsiveness in democratic policymaking from preference satisfaction to problem solving. The vehicle for doing this proposed in the present book is linking the decision to attend by political actors to agenda processes at the aggregate or system level.

Many studies of empirical representation have been directed at the connection between constituency policy attitudes and the voting behavior of representatives (Miller and Stokes 1963; see the review by Bernstein 1989). As noted above, collective representation captures the notion that an entire legislative body responds to changes in the policy attitudes of the whole political unit (Weissberg 1978). According to Hurley (1982, 1989) the extent of collective representation in Congress hinges on the congruence between congressional voting and the attitudes of the strongest partisan identifiers ("partisan representation") and the convergence of policy attitudes between partisans and independents in the mass public. It is at least possible that collective representation has more to do with policymakers' discerning varying attention patterns among their constituents and responding accordingly, and less to do with responses to changing preferences. Of course, attention shifts may not occur universally; different groups may become attentive to different aspects of politics (such as Hurley's partisans). Hence *whose* attention shifts are the basis of responsiveness by policymakers is a critical question.

The Four Sources of the Serial Policy Shift

I used the term *serial shift* above to denote the episodic change from one set of preferences to a second in decision-making. Now we see that governments are subject to analogous serial shifts in policymaking. At this point we can at least tentatively identify the conditions under which such serial policy shifts occur. There are four broad conditions, two of which might be called exogenous to the political system and two of which are endogenous. The four sources are often intertwined empirically, but they are analytically distinct. First, serial policy shifts may occur when exogenous shocks affect the system—the "Pearl Harbor" syndrome. Critical events shift the attentiveness of policymakers from one dimension of conflict to another—from peace to war or, in the case of the Arab oil embargo of the early 1970s, from redistributive domestic policies to inflation and scarcity. Abrupt changes in objective circumstances lead to abrupt changes in policymaking. These might be called *event-driven* policy changes.

Exogenous changes may affect political systems in a second way, however. Gradual, cumulative change may be ignored for a long period of time, until some focusing event results in a rapid shift of attentiveness to the new objective conditions. This is the situation described by Dodd's cybernetic model. These are the *process-driven* changes in policymaking.

We may note two endogenous sources of changes in collective attention to problems. The first is a *representational* linkage. The political system responds to changes in the attention of the mass public to facets of the political environment. Legislators and other policymakers, perceiving the change, move to enact policies that reflect the changes. The second source of endogenous policy shifts occurs via E. E. Schattschneider's mechanism of *conflict expansion*. In this mode, an elite consensus breaks down and the losing party seeks to expand the conflict to bring in new allies, particularly the mass public. Schattschneider (1960) reasoned that political parties, by wishing to exercise power, always had motive to exploit elite conflict by trying to engage the mass public.

Clearly these modes are intertwined, and one might try to deny their analytical independence by stressing that representation or conflict expansion might just reflect changing objective circumstances. The problem with this argument is that public policymaking itself affects "objective" circumstances, and hence is creating reality as it occurs. Aaron Wildavsky (1979) termed this very strong feedback aspect of policymaking "policy as its own cause." Because policy is its own cause, history matters—that is, the course of policy cannot be determined solely by some postulated set of exogenous factors. This would be especially true in the conflict expansion mode, where policymaking elites are continually trying to introduce new dimensions of evaluation into the public debate in order to attract new participants into the fray.

Structure of the Book

The basic objective of this book is to explore the possibility that episodic shifting in individual attention dictated by cognitive limits on information processing is related to shifts in the agendas of governments, which often move nonincrementally. That is, the issues selected for serious policy attention by government may be related to the serial processing capacity of decision-makers, voters, or attentive publics.

To note that both individuals and systems are subject to disjointed behavior is insufficient. It is also necessary to show that both individuals and policymaking systems are affected by the serial shift, abrupt changes in attentiveness due to information-processing "bottlenecks." Hence the book has two parts. The first details the model of individual political choice that is based on shifts in attentiveness. The preference structures of decision-makers have two components. The first component is what they want. The second component is what parts of what they want they focus on. So the first part is preferences, the second, attention.

Chapter 2 discusses rational decision-making and its critics, focusing on the implications of constrained choice for the model. Chapter 3 discusses the concepts of attentiveness and decision-making showing that shifts in attentiveness can occur without changes in preferences. A change of focus does not necessarily imply a change of mind. Chapter 4 presents an example of how this can work, using a case study of congressional voting on the superconducting supercollider. Chapter 5 offers evidence from surveys of mass politics that attentiveness (assessed as Gallup's "most important problem" question) often shifts without a corresponding change in preferences. In mass publics, preferences change glacially but focus changes rapidly.

The second part of the book links decision-making based on attentiveness to policymaking. Chapter 6 analyzes the "paradox of issue evolution"—the paradox that issues change and evolve, often abruptly, but frames of reference that order these changes are often recurrent. The resolution of the paradox comes from the tendency of participants to shift evaluative focus as issues develop. Hence the serial shift is consistent with certain cycle theories of politics. Chapter 7 presents an overview of current models of policymaking that are rooted in negative feedback, and shows how those models can become *path dependent,* or locked into a single definition of a policy problem when others are available. Chapter 8 depicts agenda access as a serial shift between the parallel (all-at-once) processing of issues within policy subsystems and the serial processing of legislative institutions. That is, accessing the agenda of a policymaking body means that the body has allocated attention to it; hence the parallel processing of the issue (within subsystems or without the interference of government at all) shifts to serial processing.

Chapter 9 views such systems as general adaptive systems. Attentiveness to a limited number of political topics often gets "fixed" in institutions. That is, policy agencies developed to deal with a single problem in a given manner end up ignoring other aspects of the problem. I explore how a policy system characterized by path dependency and a maladaptive policymaking mode can leap to a better (or in some situations worse) policymaking mode via the serial shift. Such leaps are necessary because "locked-in" participants cannot (or will not) solve the problem of inferior performance on their own. Hence the serial shift at the system level is analogous to Redford's distinction between subsystem politics and macropolitics, and his notion that macropolitical institutions interfere in policy subsystems.

The concluding chapter reassesses the model of choice based on attentiveness shifts in light of the discussion of adaptive systems. The major point is that open, democratic systems are indeed mechanisms for preference satisfaction. Democratic governments respond to changes in citizen preferences. But they are more: they are mechanisms for problem solving. Democracies respond to shifts in attentiveness, and it is this aspect of both system and individual-level behavior that allows governments to shift the focus to new problems (or new understandings of old problems). In the end, one cannot understand democratic government without understanding the serial shift.

2 Rationality in Political Choice

Time is a chief cause of those difficulties which make it necessary for man with his limited powers to go step by step, breaking up a complex question, studying one bit at a time. — ALFRED MARSHALL

Human behavior is not compartmentalized. — GARY BECKER

As Herbert Simon (1985) notes, *homo politicus* is not irrational. Political "man" seems to behave purposefully, adopting strategies that are relevant to general goals, given the limits of cognitive capacity and the complexity of the political world. But these facets make it impossible to maximize, and often inappropriate to try to maximize. *Homo politicus* seems, to Simon, to operate according to the model of *bounded rationality*, that is, by adopting means that are relevant to goals within environmental and cognitive processing limits.

Compare this approach to that of Nobel Laureate economist Gary Becker. He first defines the economic approach as "the combined assumptions of maximizing behavior, market equilibrium, and stable preferences, used relentlessly and unflinchingly" (1986: 110). Becker goes on to argue that "the economic approach is one that is applicable to all human behavior"(p. 112). Markets really operate everywhere, not just where they are regulated by prices. For Becker, and other economists, information is just another good. As such, it is subject to scarcity and declining marginal utility—implying, "for example, greater investment in acquiring information when undertaking major rather than minor decisions" (p. 111).

This chapter first lays out some fundamental issues concerning the nature of preferences, then examines selected aspects of analyses of political decision-making relying on assumptions of full rationality, and finally sets forth some of the behavioral objections to the assumption of fully rational decision-making. As we shall see, the major objections of the "behavioralists" has been that the postulates of comprehensive rationality do not describe human decision-making very well. The response of rational choice analysts has been to defend Milton Friedman's (1953) "as if" assumption—that is, so long as decision-makers approximate the full rationality assumptions (act *as if* they are comprehensively rational), then linkages can be made between individual decisions and system-level behavior. We focus on those parts of both approaches, comprehensive rationality and bounded rationality, that bear on the issues of shifting attention by individuals and shifting agendas by political systems. In doing this, we will particularly examine constrained choice situations, which are choices where objects of choice, or means, goals, or preferences, that underlie the objects of choice are such that no alternative allows decision-makers to achieve their goals completely. Attention shifts have particularly severe consequences for these very common choice situations.

Rationality and the Behavioral Critique

The proponents of bounded rationality are comfortable with many of the concepts of rational behavior, including utility functions, supply and demand, response to incentives, and purposive behavior. The bounded rationalists, however, part company with the rational theorists on what is at the very heart of the theory of rational action—maximizing behavior, market equilibrium, and stable preferences. But their critique has been empirical, a kind of blunderbuss approach to undermining the rational choice perspective. Again and again studies in psychology, sociology, and political science show the weaknesses of the economic approach "used relentlessly and unflinchingly," yet the rational choice edifice stands.

By juxtaposing the rational and the behavioral approaches so starkly, Simon anticipated two general approaches to the study of politics before they fully flowered. Simon viewed his contributions on decision-making as directed primarily toward economics and organizational theory, perhaps because of his education at the University of Chicago, which developed the behavioral school of political science during the 1930s (Simon 1985). So it is ironic that political science, more than any other social science discipline, has developed in parallel the two approaches to decision-making. On the one hand, a vigorous analytical social choice literature has developed, focusing on voting behavior in mass publics; decision-making in committees of Congress; the formation of interest groups; urban service delivery arrangements; and the behavior of bureaucrats. On the other hand, most empirical studies of political behavior and institutions have as underpinnings some form of bounded rationality, either made explicit or left implicit.

One might puzzle how a scientific theory so at odds with observations of human behavior could stand. Perhaps the major reason is that much predictability stems from the noncontroversial aspects of the economic approach—that behavior is purposive, that incentives matter, and that scarcity affects incentives. And, as Alfred Marshall noted over a century ago, in economic life the rationality assumptions work best—habit and custom reinforce incentives to reward calculation; they also act to reward those who follow habit and custom rather than independently calculate things out rationally (Marshall 1961: 20).[1]

Few theorists of the bounded rationality camp have paused to consider exactly how assumptions of the economic approach might be relaxed to incorporate bounded rationality assumptions without undermining the whole edifice. In the next few chapters, I will develop a model of choice that keeps the assumptions of stable preferences and maximization, but drops the assumption of equilibrium—making the model of choice highly dependent on context. But first I review the use of rational decisional analysis in context-independent situations.

The Difficult Issue of Preferences

Models of rational choice embody the assumption of *fixed preferences*. The assumption of fixed preferences has been used in two senses: fixed for the purposes of analysis (that is, the analyst has no business exploring preferences, only how people realize those preferences) and fixed in the sense of unchanging. Hence economics concentrates on understanding how consumer demands (tastes backed up by money) are satisfied and political scientists focus on the satisfaction of citizen political demands (politically expressed tastes for policies).

Several political scientists have attacked the assumption of fixed preferences in both of its manifestations. James Q. Wilson (1980) and Clarence Stone (1992), among others, have argued that in politics preferences cannot be taken as fixed, because much of the political process concerns persuasion about preferred courses of action. Hence analysts must examine the molding of political preferences, because this process is more important for politics than the issue of how these tastes are satisfied through government. A once-vigorous research program in political socialization concentrated on the acquisition of political values and dispositions across the life span. Inglehart (1990), among others, has examined broad changes in value structures that affect the conduct of politics. So there has been considerable interest among political scientists in understanding how tastes and values are formed and how they are altered.

1. He notes that "the side of life with which economics is specially concerned is that in which man's conduct is most deliberate . . . And further it is that side of his life in which, when he does follow habit and custom, and proceeds for the moment without calculation, the habits and customs themselves are most nearly sure to have arisen from a close and careful watching the advantages and disadvantages of different courses of conduct" (Marshall 1961: 20–21).

There would seem to be little doubt that preferences change, in politics, in economics, and in other domains of life. I once bought a certain Scandinavian automobile, convinced that the higher quality I anticipated was worth the higher price I paid. But the quality was such that the only "utility" I received for my dollars was the camaraderie of the nice people whom I met in the service waiting area. My beliefs about the quality of the product changed through experience. Similarly, public administrators may learn that a policy is no longer working to achieve its desired goal, and thus modify their preferences for the policy. So one question in the issue of changing preferences is how experience modifies preferences.

Michael Cohen and Robert Axelrod (1984) have developed a decision-making model that is based on such an experiential update of a utility function. To understand their approach, let us assume that a public sector manager wants to achieve an outcome, y. He or she believes that a policy, x, is related to the outcome according to some *production function* (that is, $y = f(x)$). Cohen and Axelrod assume that decision-makers have two types of preferences: extrinsic (that is, they want more y) and intrinsic (that is, they like x independently of how much y they get). "Our model is in essence a kind of learning process in which the manager comes to ascribe additional value [to the policy] if such assignments are associated with pleasant surprises, and comes to assign less value to the level of x when it is associated with negative surprises" (Cohen and Axelrod 1984: 34). The Cohen/Axelrod model allows the adjustment of "beliefs" about the production function relating the policy to the outcome through the mechanism of intrinsic preferences: one likes the policy better if it performs better *even if* one is not sure exactly why it is working better. Just add more when it is working better than expected and add less when it is working less well. Because the Cohen/Axelrod model doesn't question the value of the outcome, y, to the decision-maker, it really is consistent with fixed preference models. Intrinsic preferences are but a proxy for the ill-understood relationship between the outcome and the policy.

One may, however, actually *discover* new preferences through experience, and that experience may be direct or vicarious (through the process of instruction). Cohen and March (1986: 222) call this "goal-finding behavior." As social and political institutions put citizens in contact with one another, they may learn new perspectives and approaches that are fundamental to their value structures. Take the example of political tolerance. One may be tolerant because one cannot have one's way without tolerance and compromise—that is, tolerance may be a means to a goal. But one may also be tolerant because one has learned to value tolerance intrinsically. Unlike the Cohen/Axelrod intrinsic preferences, which seem to be a proxy for ill-understood relationships between ends and means, intrinsic preferences may also imply more fundamental goals or values.

Now we seem to have two kinds of intrinsic preferences: those that seem to be proxies for an inability to specify means-ends relationships and those that take on value independently of their relationship to other goals. Naturally enough, success with the Cohen/Axelrod type of intrinsic preferences can lead one to value them independently. But negative surprises lead to less value for their intrinsic preferences. Would negative surprises lead one to abandon tolerance? Maybe, but would not the conditions of change be different? Hence this distinction is important and leads directly to an examination of the issue of fixed preferences.

Two Kinds of Preferences

Exactly what is it that is "fixed" in the rational decision-making model? One may think of two different kinds of preferences, one centering on the actual objects of choice, the other on the individual's goals that are to be realized as a result of the choice. In essence, a goals-based conception of preferences underlies the work of George Stigler and Gary Becker, two economists who have developed a framework that will allow economic analysis of all sorts of human behavior. They argue that we ought to interpret the rationality maxim of fixed preferences to mean unvarying: "Tastes neither change capriciously nor differ importantly between people" (Stigler and Becker 1977: 76; see also Becker 1976). In their model of consumer choice, Stigler and Becker conceive of consumers as "maximizing a utility function of objects of choice, called commodities, that they produce with their own time, their skills, training, and other human capital, and other inputs" (p. 78) rather than "a utility function of goods and services bought in the marketplace" (p. 78). In this approach, individuals can be viewed as maximizing self-esteem, style, or other intangibles as well as economic well-being. So it is easy to see that these economists have in mind the general goals that people harbor when they refer to fixed preferences. Stigler and Becker go on to argue that markets can be found anywhere that things of value are exchanged and will respond to "shadow prices" for the inputs that will produce those commodities. That is, the costs in time, effort, and resources that must be expended to obtain the "commodity" are balanced against the value of the "commodity" that the individual wishes to acquire.[2]

2. Sociologists have treated much of human interaction as involving some kind of exchange, and the area of study was termed "exchange theory" (see Blau 1964). So the

We may distinguish between two kinds of preferences. The first, call them *direct* preferences, are desires for particular goods and services in the marketplace, or for particular public policies in politics. The second, which we might term *Stigler-Becker* preferences, refer to the underlying attributes that structure the particular choice. While Stigler and Becker would likely disagree, I would insist that learning and experience can modify basic goals, but would also suggest that such basic goals probably change most glacially. Hence one could adopt the premise that Stigler-Becker preferences change little in the short run. The "intrinsic" preferences of Axelrod and Cohen are quite definitely of the direct type.

People seem to harbor a mixture of both kinds of preferences. Sometimes they seem capable of working through the various attributes underlying a choice (the trade-off between more square feet and expense when building a house, for example); at other times, they seem to reify the choice object ("I want that car"). If preferences are of the Stigler-Becker type, they are unquestionably multidimensional. In acquiring an automobile, people may want thrifty transportation and a comfortable ride and "status." If they are of the direct variety, they generally may be ordered along a single dimension.

So long as we treat preferences as referring solely to the objects of choice (direct preferences), two implications follow. First, changing preferences seems natural and could account for substantial changes in choice over a limited time span. The Axelrod/Cohen model is very effective in showing how one might shift one's preferences for a policy over a fairly short time span because the policy is either successful or not in affecting a more basic goal (their output criterion). Second, comprehensive utility functions referring to those objects seem plausible. Surely people can rank the cars they like, or the political candidates, and can presumably rank the cars with the political candidates (which is what a comprehensive utility function would do).

Unfortunately, examining only direct preferences suggests considerable choice inconsistency across time. When alternatives are described in different terms, people have different preferences (Kahneman and Tversky 1985). They make different choices when considering the same objects at two times. They apply wildly varying discount rates to the future in different domains, sometimes strongly valuing present satisfaction over future satisfaction (they smoke), at other times only weakly valuing the present over the future (they fear low-level nuclear waste sites

---

conception of all sorts of human behavior being rooted in exchange is not new with Stigler and Becker. What they have done is to add the rational maximization decision-making axioms to this line of thought.

in their communities) (Lowenstein and Elster 1992). Some of these inconsistencies are not really inconsistencies. For example, the law of diminishing marginal utility suggests that the desired trade-off between apple pie and Alka-Seltzer will change with the consumption of apple pie. Others, such as the nuclear waste versus smoking example, are not so explicable.

Realizing that underlying attributes of the objective choice are often what concern people can help make sense of an otherwise chaotic and unpredictable situation. When the underlying attributes of an object of choice become valued, the resulting preference is of the Stigler-Becker type. But when we introduce Stigler-Becker preferences into the equation, the existence of comprehensive utility functions becomes problematic. The reason is that *all objects of choice are multidimensional in their attributes, but people don't incorporate all those attributes into any particular choice.* Trying to evaluate multiple alternatives all structured by multiple attributes is overwhelming; oftentimes people just don't do it. Considerable research shows that they tend to pick out the attributes they view as important, ignoring the rest. Unfortunately, what is not important now may be important tomorrow.

Now, if we view the consumption of Stigler-Becker "commodities" not in an economic paradigm but in one of political choice, and add the common assumptions of complexity and ambiguity in the environment, then we can postulate a model of choice that emphasizes the selectivity of attention in the determination of action. The selectivity of attention is critical in two respects: (a) in the selection of which among multiple goals to emphasize; and (b) in the selection of which among the possible means to adopt in trying to realize these goals. That is, decision-makers may share the desire for a productive, orderly, and just society, but may differ in the attention they pay to these goals and in their evaluation of the means that will achieve those goals. The means-goals distinction corresponds to the difference between direct and Stigler-Becker preferences.

Rational Decision-Making in Politics

There are quite a few variants on what has been termed *the* model of rational choice. Nevertheless, most models of decision-making under comprehensive rationality are based on three fundamental assumptions. First, all possible states of the world facing decision-makers can be ranked in regard to desirability. Second, decision-makers know the connection between the strategies they may choose from and desired goals, or evaluated states, of the world. Third, decision-makers optimize. That is, they choose the strategy that brings about the largest total amount of satisfaction to them (which is the best state of the world discounted by the cost of the strategies that can be used to bring it about). Two other assumptions seem necessary in most situations. The first concerns search: in some sense, search for alternatives ought to be exhaustive. Actually an exhaustive search among alternatives would itself be irrational in a cost/benefit sense: such a search would consume more in resources, such as time, than could be expected from the probable benefits that would accrue from the newly discovered alternatives. So most decision theorists assume that information in a search process is subject to the law of declining marginal returns. That is, the information becomes less valuable in illuminating choices (both the alternatives uncovered and the relationship between the alternatives or strategies and those outcomes that the decision-maker wishes to achieve) as more information is acquired. This *marginalist* conception of information essentially incorporates information acquisition in the comprehensively rational decision-making mode. A final common assumption is that complex decisions may be factored, or broken down into components, without doing any violence to the basic model. In effect, this means that maximizing the solutions to the parts is the same as maximizing the whole.

Naturally it will be objected that the means-ends relationship in the real world may not be so simple. Decision theorists have studied three separate situations: *certainty*, where each and every means is known to lead to specific outcomes; *risk*, where each strategy leads to one of a number of ends, each with known possibility; and *uncertainty*, where outcomes are known but probabilities associated with the outcomes are not (see Luce and Raffia 1990: 19–40.) In certainty models, there is a known function that relates means to ends, and hence to satisfaction (or utility). Hence the problem is to maximize the utility function. In situations of risk and uncertainty, scenarios are developed which go under the general rubric of *game theory*. Table 2.1 provides a brief overview of some of the salient facets of the rational approach to decision-making.

One implication of the overview of the rational choice approach in table 2.1 is that preferences refer to *outcomes*, or end states, and not to the strategies themselves. Now, it may happen that strategies become valued in themselves, as when a voter becomes attached to a candidate independently of (or in conjunction with) the outcomes that the candidate's election may accomplish. This is what happens in the Cohen/Axelrod model, for example. Such "brand loyalty" may be incorporated as an outcome of the choice of strategies. As we shall see, treating alternatives as strategies rather than ends in themselves is important, because decision-makers tend to evaluate alternatives attribute by attribute

TABLE 2.1 Outline of the Rational Decision Model

In the rational decision model, the decision-maker is faced with

1. a set $\{S\}$ of strategies, s;
2. a set $\{X\}$ of states of the environment, x;
3. a set $\{R\}$ of outcomes or results of the interaction between strategies and the environment;
4. a function, R, the outcome function, that associates each strategy-environment pairing (s, x) with an outcome $r = R(s, x)$.

The sets $\{S\}$ and $\{X\}$ are mutually exclusive and exhaustive. The problem for the decision-maker is to choose a strategy, s, that is optimal in some respect.

Optimality is defined relative to the decision maker's *preference ordering*, which orders outcomes according to the principles of *completeness* (all elements in R are included in the ordering); and *transitivity* (if the decision-maker prefers a to b or is indifferent between them, and he or she prefers b to c or is indifferent between them, then he or she either prefers a to c or is indifferent between them).

It is not enough for the decision-maker simply to rank outcomes. He or she must actually rank outcomes relative to the costs of the strategies. So what must actually be ranked is the set $\{R\} = r(s, x)$, that is, the results conceived as pairs of outcomes and the strategies that achieve them.

Because the world is fraught with uncertainty, the decision-maker assesses the *expected utility* of each strategy-outcome pair. That is, he or she weights the desirability of the outcome by the probability that it will occur given the chosen strategy, so that

$$E(u_s) = (u_r)\, p(r|s),$$

where u_r is the utility derived from outcome r and $p(r|s)$ is the probability of outcome r *given that* strategy s was pursued. What is optimized, then, is the expected utility from pursuing strategy s.

---

rather than globally, across attributes. Hence the salience of the attribute (or goal-state) is an important component of how people actually make decisions.

Decision theory is supposed to be neutral with regard to assumptions about what satisfies decision-makers. That is, there is no notion in the theory itself about what goals decision-makers pursue. This, as it turns out, will not take us very far in analyzing the political world, so that most students of rational choice make assumptions about self-interest. (See Mansbridge 1990 for a critique.) One example of the use of this assumption is the classic collective action problem. Here the puzzle is why individuals will ever join together to achieve collective aims, because individual incentives will cause them to defect from the collectivity and allow the public good to be produced without their efforts. That is, they will "free ride" on the efforts of others. If everyone defects, then the collective good will not be produced, making everyone less well-off. Clearly rational actors have become self-interested actors in this model and specific goals have been postulated.

Spatial Theory and Constrained Choice

Broadly speaking, political scientists working in the rational choice tradition have produced two important bodies of literature that illuminate politics. The first is in analyzing the collective action problem. The second is in understanding the voting choice, both in mass publics and in legislative chambers and committees. The dominant approach in this latter body of work involves geometric analysis; hence it is known as the *spatial theory of voting* (Davis, Hinich, and Ordeshook 1970; Enelow and Hinich 1990).

While it has been directed at understanding voting choice, the spatial theory of voting is actually a general theory of *constrained choice*—or, rather, spatial theory is a major application of a general geometric choice theory. Since all decisions are constrained in one way or another, spatial theory can be used to understand a large class of decision-making situations. In the case of elections, voter choice is limited to the candidates offered by the parties. Other applications of the general geometric choice theory come in the theory of consumer behavior under budget constraints and the allocation of public funds to objectives.

In the spatial theory of voting, it is assumed that both individual voters and the alternatives they consider can be ordered in space such that the further away an alternative is from the voter's *ideal point,* the less preferred is that alternative. "Further away" is defined relative to the voter's *indifference curves,* which demarcate those alternatives among which the voter is indifferent. Indifference curves can hypothetically take on a variety of forms (Radner 1964), but it is generally assumed that indifference curves monotonically decline from the voter's ideal point. This is the so-called single-peaked assumption.

Figure 2.1 illustrates this approach in a one-dimensional choice situation. There the X-axis orders the actual choices, while the Y-axis indicates the utilities that individuals will receive under the various choices. $I(a)$ is voter a's ideal point; similarly $I(b)$ is voter b's ideal point. If the choice is simply one involving a decision between two candidates, or between a yes and a no vote in a legislature, then the distance between the ideal point of a voter and the alternatives is an inverse indicator of how much it is preferred. Hence the voter will choose the alternative that minimizes the distance between his or her ideal point and the alternative.

In figure 2.1, voter *a* will choose alternative P while voter *b* will choose alternative Q.

Now, if we assume that there are a number of decision-makers, such as might compose a legislature or an electorate, then we could picture them as falling along the line representing the choice dimension, perhaps sometimes in clumps, perhaps sometimes in bare regions. If there is an agenda-setter, or a candidate, with complete freedom to position an alternative before the whole set of decision-makers, then the winning point will be at the *median*. No alternative can be put before the electorate that is closer to a larger number of voters than the median, the point that divides the set of decision-makers into two equal numbers of individuals. So if (and this is a big if) an agenda-setter or candidate can get an alternative (or a platform) before the voters at the median, then no one else can defeat that alternative. The choice system is at equilibrium.

The problem with the above approach is that it can be used only for what we have termed *direct preferences*—that is, where the objects of choice (the means) are directly and simply related to preferences (or goals). In most situations in politics, the alternatives cannot be placed simply in a one-dimensional space, because goals are multidimensional. This is another way of saying that the voters are forced to choose between two alternatives consisting of multidimensional attributes. Voters may perceive that presidential candidate Q is a better choice on domestic policy but that candidate P is a better choice for leadership in foreign affairs.

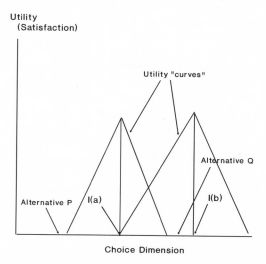

Fig. 2.1. A one-dimensional choice system with two alternatives and two decision-makers.

Or they may like the appeal of candidate Q because he appeals to working class interests, but not like him because he includes blacks and other minorities in his coalition. This implies that underlying any political choice are general goals that cannot be achieved without trade-offs. In the political science literature, these general goals are known as *dimensions of conflict* because individuals differ on their desirability; hence political conflict occurs over them. Often the objects of choice are essentially multidimensional, but sometimes the choices are deliberately made multidimensional. This often happens in legislatures, when leaders incorporate diverse policies in a single bill to try to appeal to a broad coalition of supporters.

Figure 2.2 depicts a situation in which two dimensions of conflict structure a choice situation. To make the situation more specific, let us assume that the choice involves whether to try to stimulate economic growth through government spending, which can be the Y-axis, or through limited government intervention in the economy, the X-axis. At first glance, this might seem to be one dimension of preferences, having to do with government intervention at one end and the lack of it at the other. However, legislators and citizens can prefer either investment-based spending by government (on, for example, highways or "big science" projects), or they can prefer redistributive or ameliorative spending (for health care or unemployment payments, for example). So it is possible for a decision-maker to favor more spending for investment but not for redistribution. Here we deal only with a two-dimensional example to make things reasonably simple. In figure 2.2, the voter, I(a), now has an ideal point defined by two dimensions, so that ideally (that is, without any constraining circumstances) the voter would like Y(a) amount of dimension Y, government spending, and X(a) of dimension X, less government intrusion. The further away from the ideal point an actual choice presented to the voter is, the less that voter will like it.

Now, we still think of utility as a third dimension in the space; that is, we can think of spikes going up from the page such that the higher spikes are at the ideal point and decline away from that point. This is difficult to draw (and to comprehend), so we may simplify by depicting this declining utility as a series of concentric circles or ellipses such that the utility for the voter is equal along a single curve but is higher on curves closer to the ideal point than on curves further away. The figure depicts two alternatives, P and Q, with alternative P offering more of goal Y and less of goal X than does alternative Q. In this example, the hypothetical decision-maker will choose alternative P, because it lies on a higher indifference curve than does alternative Q (that is, it lies on an indifference curve that is closer to the decision-maker's ideal point).

Figure 2.2 implies that decision-makers evaluate choices through straightforward *trade-offs*. That is, a decision-maker completely understands the trade-offs between the two dimensions. If the decision-maker is offered alternative P, then he or she performs a calculation that involves a trade-off between goal Y and goal X, and decides whether that trade-off is superior to the trade-off implied by alternative Q. So the decision-maker sees that the choice situation incorporates two underlying dimensions, or goals, that he or she would like to see realized (at the ideal point, the perfect combination of the two goals for the decision-maker). And the decision-maker chooses by a comparison of the trade-offs by comparing the distance between the ideal point and the alternative. The shape of the indifference curves depicts the decision-maker's weighting of the goals, with circular curves representing equal weighting and elliptical curves indicating that one goal is valued more highly than the other.

As in the one-dimensional example, we may view decision-makers with their indifference curve as occupying various positions in the space. Some parts of the two-dimensional space will have "clouds" of decision-makers, whereas other parts of the space will be bare. Now, in certain situations the choice system can reach equilibrium, but these situations are rare. It's like the old adage that threesomes, in love as in power, are instable. Two can always gang up on one, but there is no alliance that is stable over all alternatives in two-dimensional space. Hence our hypothetical agenda-setter may never find an unassailable position within a

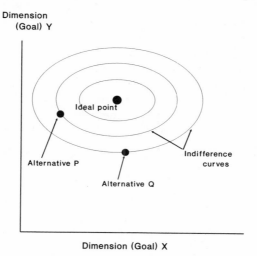

Fig. 2.2. A two-dimensional choice system with two alternatives.

policy space that contains two or more dimensions in many situations. This is the "aggregation of preference" problem. If there is more than one dimension of evaluation involved in a choice situation, then there may be no way that the preferences of the voters can be aggregated to yield a single, overall equilibrium outcome. Any position consisting of a combination of x and y (the two issues or policies) can potentially be destabilized by some other combination.

If there are several alternatives within this two-dimensional space, then agenda-setters can offer the voter a variety of "packages" of X and Y. In many cases, however, the choices offered the voter are highly constrained. For example, in any two-candidate election, the choices can be placed on a single choice dimension, even if the dimension exists in multiattribute space. That is, candidates each offer one (and only one) package of X and Y, of government growth spending and limited government. Moreover, in many cases, even where there are a number of alternatives, they may be ordered on a single choice dimension. This means that the situation is already structured with regard to the basic dimensions of conflict.

For example, a legislative committee may get to decide how much money to spend for highway construction and other transportation projects, understanding that the more that is spent, the more government is stimulating economic growth through fiscal policy and through infrastructure building. But the government is also intruding on the private sector, through taxation to raise money for the enterprise. But another structure of choice, say, spending on education, could (hypothetically) be both more stimulative and less intrusive. The structured choice situation is depicted in figure 2.3.[3] (Note that as we move left on the X-axis, we get more limited government—not more government.)[4]

Figure 2.3 shows how strongly constrained choices affect goals. Note that as a committee moves toward more spending, it is increasing growth spending but not at a one-to-one ratio. That is because there will always be an imperfect relationship between the means, or policy, and the goal, or dimension of conflict. Note that moving in the "more" direction of

3. What we have is a structured choice dimension that is embedded within a policy or outcome space. This carries the assumption that the relationship between means (the choice dimension) and ends (the outcomes, or dimensions of conflict) is known. This knowledge would be summarized by the function relating the choice dimension to the dimensions of conflict.

4. In the example, education does better on both dimensions, thus offering a better choice altogether. That would not have to be the case, of course. Were choices not segmented by policy area through the operation of the legislative institution, such global comparisons might be made. The structure of choice, however, generally prohibits such global comparisons.

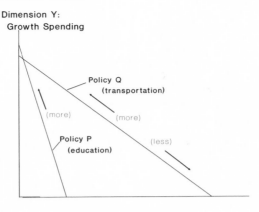

Fig. 2.3. A structured choice situation with two underlying dimensions of evaluation.

policy P, education in our hypothetical example, is more efficient in that a marginal dollar of spending on education yields more growth than does a marginal dollar of transportation spending.

Given the constrained choice situation, in which a single policy dimension is inserted into the goal or conflict space, how does the individual decision-maker decide what level of the policy to support? Examining figure 2.4, we see that the level of the policy supported by the decision-maker is the point at which the line representing the policy is tangent to an indifference curve. That will be the point that is closest to the decision-maker's ideal point, taking into consideration the dimensional weightings represented by the elliptical shapes of the indifference curves.

Of course, our example is hypothetical. Moreover, we are assuming the relationships between the policies and the goals are known; in the real world they will be infused with uncertainty. But we will see that depicting the political decision-maker as harboring conflicting goals and as facing strong constraints on reconciling those goals models politics better than either omniscient rationality models or bounded rationality models that often tend to be too ad hoc.

Bounded Rationality

The model of decision-making discussed above imposes high demands on the calculational abilities of decision-makers. Legislators or voters must be able to conceive of the structure of conflict as consisting

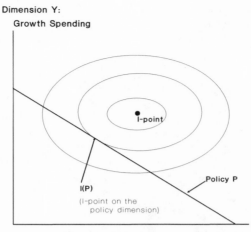

Dimension Y:
Growth Spending

I-point

I(P)
(I-point on the
policy dimension)

Policy P

Dimension X: Limit Government

Fig. 2.4. Making a decision with one choice dimension and two underlying dimensions of evaluation.

of multiple dimensions of basic attributes, or goals, that they wish to see implemented. In effect, that means that decision-makers are able to rank order alternatives along separable dimensions. Second, voters or legislators must be able to make comparisons among the various dimensions that structure the situation. If the situation is previously structured by a choice dimension, then voters or legislators must be able to understand the relationship between the choice structure and the basic dimensions of conflict underlying the choice structure. These requirements may be well beyond the normal calculating capacity of humans (Herstein 1981). Moreover, the decision-making environment may not be as well structured as the spatial approach suggests; ambiguity often leads to considerable rhetoric in politics.

Herbert Simon (1983) developed his bounded rationality approach to provide a model of choice that is more in tune with empirical studies of decision-making. Simon's dissatisfaction with the full-blown rationality assumptions is that they are highly unrealistic and seldom yield accurate predictions about human behavior. His bounded rationality approach is founded on two premises, each of which is contrasted with the "omniscient rationality" approach. First, Simon argues that limits on cognitive abilities of humans cause them to take a number of decisional "shortcuts" in contrast with what would be predicted in the rationality model. "Humans are information-processing systems operating largely in serial fashion, and possessing very modest computational powers" (Simon 1981:

173–74). In the second premise, Simon indicates that the environment is far more complex, ambiguous, and uncertain than proponents of rational choice are willing to grant. Because of this complexity, much of human problem-solving activity is a problem of design, or generating alternatives, rather than of decision, or choosing among these alternatives. In political science, major contributions were made by Charles Lindblom (1959) and Aaron Wildavsky (1984), who stressed the role of incremental adjustments to avoid major mistakes in decision-making in complex, multifaceted environments. Bounded, or limited, rationality models are more consonant with empirical analyses of human information processing and decision-making than full rationality models. Students of human cognition continually stress the limited processing capacity of the human brain and its effects on decision-making (Allport 1989; Schacter 1989). Social psychologists have found strong contextual and social effects that interact with the limited information-processing capacities of humans (see Lane 1991 for a review and discussion).

Rationality and Preferences

James March (1978) notes that there are actually a variety of competing notions of limited rationality, but all share assumptions about the limits of decision-makers and about the complexity of the world they face. He warns against trying to construct a model of choice based on observed choices and assumptions about preferences, because choices may or may not reflect preferences (see also Sen 1991). The world within which the decision-maker operates forces compromise; moreover, preferences are not fixed but, rather, shift according to circumstances. People "know that no matter how much they may be pressured both by their own prejudices for integration and by the demands of other, they will be left with contradictory and intermittent desires partially ordered but imperfectly reconciled" (March 1986: 156).

There is nothing in the rational approach to decision-making that prohibits contradictory preferences, however. Indeed, much of the approach is directed at decisions under scarcity; hence it is based on contradictions. The comprehensive utility function is primarily a mechanism through which people resolve the trade-offs they face. Becker (1986: 114) shows how rational analysis can be used to understand the contradictory preferences of the satisfaction gained from smoking versus the wish for a long and healthful life. To Becker, there is just a tradeoff: the joy of smoking versus the probability of living longer if one doesn't. "The life-span forfeited is not worth the cost to him" (p. 114). The acquisition of information is a part of the model; the optimal decision-maker treats information as a scarce good, which therefore is subject to the same trade-offs as any other good; the rational individual will acquire information until it is too costly given the decision.

Becker is clearly not wrong to note the contradictions, but he seems misguided in thinking these contradictions are ordinarily integrated. Most people don't integrate preferences that way; rather, they tend to fix on one goal to the exclusion of the other. This aspect of decision-making has been termed *mental accounting* to denote the tendency of people to compartmentalize decisions that are logically parts of a whole. Thaler (1991:92) notes that households develop mental accounts, such as dividing their assets into "wealth" and "income," and display less temptation with wealth. Such compartmentalization is so fundamental to human decision-making that it ought to be treated as an effect. So preferences are often contradictory, and that offers no problem to rational analysis, but because of mental accounting, preferences are ill integrated into an overarching utility function. In Becker's approach, there is no room for mistakes or *regret;* no room for smokers who wish they had quit as their health deteriorates, or workaholics who are pained that they did not choose to spend more time with their families. Becker thinks that the smoker had optimal information and hence made an optimal choice. Is the smoker now behaving irrationally by becoming depressed? Becker (1986: 114) says that "most deaths are . . . 'suicides.'" I would say that some deaths may be a result of focusing on one facet of preferences in a multifaceted world.

So one of the most important differences between conceptions of limited, or bounded, rationality, and comprehensive rationality concerns the extent to which people integrate the decisions they make into a comprehensive preference function. At some level, most social scientists would agree that people factor—that is, break down—their totality of activities into component parts and work on the parts sequentially. One of the founding fathers of maximization and marginalist models in economics, Alfred Marshall, saw economic decisions as themselves factored but as integratable later. Writing in 1890, he says that

> It [is] necessary for man with his limited powers to go step by step; breaking up a complex question, studying one bit at a time, and at last combining his partial solutions into a more or less complete solution of the whole riddle. In breaking it up, he segregates those disturbing causes, whose wanderings happen to be inconvenient, for the time in a pound called *Ceteris Paribus*. The study of some group of tendencies is isolated by the assumption *other things being equal:* the existence of other tendencies is not denied, but their disturbing effect is neglected for a time. The more the issue is thus

narrowed, the more exactly can it be handled: but the less closely does it correspond to real life (Marshall 1961: 366).

The question is whether decision-makers can and do integrate these parts into some comprehensive whole, and, as Marshall makes clear, that has much to do with how the world works. Marshall apparently believed that the ceteris paribus assumption would operate to vindicate, at least in the normal course of events, the factorization common in human decision-making.[5] That is, factorization will work as intended only in a linear and decomposable world, one approximately at equilibrium.

The Role of Information

Perhaps nowhere does the rational model of political choice diverge from boundedly rational understandings of politics than in the role of information. For most rational choice theorists, information is a "good" like other goods; hence it is subject to the rules of utility maximization. The more one values a decision, the more one will invest in acquiring information; but the more information one acquires, the less valuable it is in illuminating a decision. At base, this is a marginalist conception of information: information, like other goods, is subject to declining marginal utility. A decision-maker will stop acquiring information when the marginal cost of acquiring more offsets the marginal gain from the new information.

Political scientists, however, note that it is always irrational to acquire information about voting in almost all elections, because the probability of influencing the outcome is infinitesimal. Hence considerable analysis has been directed at "the puzzle of informed citizens" (Fiorina 1990: 336). It seems rational to be ignorant; the marginal cost of acquiring information is always more than the marginal utility of information. At the very least, one must postulate satisfaction that is received by informed citizens that is quite independent of the probability of influencing the electoral outcome. Because this paradox is at the very heart of political participation, political scientists have been far more suspicious of treating information as a neutral good than have economists.

The problem goes even deeper. Information often provides a social definition; people often make statements about themselves by their knowledge about politics, stance on the issues, and attitudes toward candidates and parties (Fiorina 1990: 340). Because information provides social definitions, political communities of interest are made and unmade

5. Marshall (1961: 17–19) also viewed the price system as critical in forcing utility comparisons; that is, the institutional structure provided the incentive for rationality.

during the exchange of information.[6] Policy issues are not just illumi-
nated by information; they are framed by it. When issues are reframed,
often through the highlighting of a previously ignored dimension of evaluation, our basic understanding of an issue shifts. Because information
sometimes restructures, a marginalist approach to information can be
misleading in politics.

Political Behavior: From Irrationality to Bounded Rationality

Early studies of political behavior tended to emphasize the nonrational facets of political life. For example, political scientists studying the
political attitudes and behaviors of mass publics empirically tended to
stress the roles of affective facets of social life—emotional attachments,
the role of symbols, and the limited capacities of voters for abstract political thought (Campbell et al. 1960; Lane 1969; Milbrath and Goel 1977;
Converse 1964). The major cause of voting choice was partisan attachments, attachments which formed early in life and which were reinforced
in group contexts. There is scant hint in the early voting studies of even
boundedly rational choices.

However, considerable recent work has reoriented political behavior research into a bounded rationality framework. Sniderman, Brody,
and Tetlock (1991) stress the use of heuristics in making political decisions within mass publics, and they back up their arguments with
numerous well-designed studies based in survey research. They note
that the combination of low levels of information, limited interest, and
limited processing capacity may lead to the use of heuristic devices—
such as observing an important reference group and finding out what
issues it supports. They also point explicitly to the role of emotion,
calling much political reasoning "affect-driven." Popkin (1991) develops
a theory of campaigning based on "low-information rationality" that
stresses the informational shortcuts that voters use (and that successful
campaigns cue into) but that rejects nonrational theories of voting
choice.

Recent work in the use of political schemata emphasizes cognitive
aspects of the organization of political stimuli rather than the traditional
emotion-cognition nexus that was the focus of earlier voting behavior research (Conover and Feldman 1984, 1991; Kuklinski, Luskin, and Bolland 1991; Lodge and McGraw 1991; Miller 1991). Schema studies have

---

6. I am only slightly rephrasing Alfred Marshall (1961: xiv) here.

stressed cognitive shortcuts in dealing with complex political stimuli; as such, they are firmly rooted in the bounded rationality approach.[7]

Design and Choice

Complex environments imply that one may not know at all what strategies are relevant to what goals. Hence considerable analysis is required to decide just what the problem is and just what kinds of solutions might be relevant. We may think of decision-making as consisting of problems of choice and problems of design (H. Simon 1977). "Design is concerned with devising possible means for ends" (p. 160). Choice, on the other hand, involves the selection of means once they are specified. Design issues arise because a decision-maker is faced with a problem. Now, a decision-maker has essentially two ways to approach a design problem. First, he or she may adopt traditional patterns; that is, the problem can be seen as one capable of being solved using known means. But if no known means will work, then the decision-maker must employ heuristics: "weaving together the fabric of means, coming from the left with the fabric of ends, coming from the right, requires exploration of new alternatives" (p. 165). The distinction between design and choice has been viewed as the difference between "understanding" and "search": "The understanding process generates the person's internal representation of the problem, whereas the search process generates the person's solution" (VanLehn 1989: 530).

The less familiar the problem, the more likely the necessity of using heuristics in generating the choice frame. But any strategy for trying to understand a problem is costly; the least costly is for the decision-maker to choose a standard approach, or frame of reference for understanding the problem, and proceed to the choice phase directly. Of course, if the frame of reference is wrong, then the problem will not be solved correctly. Hence the costs of search (for a better design) and the costs of making an incorrect decision can be in conflict. In so-called "knowledge-rich" task domains, tasks are complex, and expertise and familiarity with the nature of the problem are important in solving it (VanLehn 1989:

7. There is, however, nothing in schema theory that in principle is contrary to rational decision-making. In solving problems, psychologists and cognitive theorists have noted the learning of schemata to fit classes of problems. According to VanLehn (1989: 545), schema-driven problem solving "seems to characterize experts who are solving problems in knowledge-rich domains." In politics, however, which we might characterize as an information-rich, knowledge-poor environment, the use of inappropriate schemata and the emotive attachment to schemata seem to be common.

528). In such task domains, experts often use "schema-driven" problem solving, in which they first choose a "problem schema" and then use known solutions to the general type of problem to solve the problem (pp. 545–53).

Ill-Structured Problems

A very important class of problems, and indeed the typical problem in politics, involves "open constraints." These are those constraints that develop as problem-solving proceeds (Reitman 1964: 292–93). Reitman asks us to consider such problems as "writing a fugue," which is similar in form to "designing a health-care system" or "producing an intergovernmental block-grant system" or "cutting the federal deficit." The end is specified; other constraints are "generated from one transformation of the problem to the next" (Reitman 1964: 296).

The emergent solution is *path dependent,* in the sense that one step in the process of finding a solution is dependent on prior decisions. Most critically, the design problem, the whole range of choices that exist at any point in time, is strongly constrained by earlier decisions. If one has started on a path that is leading to a poor fugue (or deficit reduction plan or health care system), he or she is going to find a suboptimal solution that will be extremely difficult to change. In problem solving and decision-making, history matters.[8]

Finally, it may be noted that ill-structured problems with emergent constraints focus the attention of decision-makers on a limited number of attributes of the problem. Indeed, one characteristic of the suboptimal solutions that can emerge in solving ill-structured problems is the ignoring of essential dimensions of evaluation that later appear to be important. This is a major reason that "no solution to an ill-defined problem can count on universal acceptance" (Reitman 1964: 302).

The Complexity Catastrophe

Critiques of rational decision-making have tended to center on the empirical: people can't do it in complex environments. The implication is that if the genetic makeup of *homo sapiens* had been different, perhaps they could have. But humans are great learners and clearly can learn to

8. Paul Schulman (1980) characterizes large-scale policymaking as dominated by the issue of sunk costs: "We've gone this far; we can't turn back now without wasting the resources spent." Strictly speaking, a concern with sunk costs is not rational (Thaler 1991). But path dependence implies far more than sunk costs; it means that a whole new design will have to be fashioned in solving the problem.

make better decisions. The question is whether they can learn to be fully rational, in the sense of maximizing overarching utility functions.

Biologist Stuart Kauffman (1993) has developed a model that implies that optimizing in decision-making is simply not possible in complex situations. Whereas he developed his model to study evolution, it is quite general in its implication—applying to so-called combinatorial optimization problems. Kauffman (1993: 53) writes that "as systems with many parts increase both in the number of those parts and the richness of interactions among the parts, it is typical that the number of conflicting design constraints among the parts increases rapidly. Those conflicting constraints imply that optimization can attain only ever poorer compromises." Optimization can occur when systems are not complex (that is, when they are additive and not interactive; or when they contain few elements). Optimization cannot occur as a matter of the nature of the conflicting constraints when systems are complex—that is, where there are many elements and they interact.

The implications are powerful. Even if people could learn to overcome their cognitive limitations, they could only maximize in simple worlds. If the world is complex, they must make compromises, and the more complex the world, the poorer their compromises are likely to be. It is the nature of the world more than cognitive limits that imposes the limits on optimization. Moreover, the complexity catastrophe and the consequent occasional failure of factoring as a decisional approach also affect many behavioral reconstructions of decision-making. The Cohen/Axelrod model discussed above relies implicitly on factorization: only the relationship between x, the policy, and y, the outcome, matters. There is no room for multiple effects from the policy; hence the implicit assumption is that factorization works.

Simon thinks that generally good decisions can be made by factorization—that is, ignoring the irrelevant parts of the environment. He writes that we live in a "nearly empty world—one in which there are millions of variables that in principle could affect each other but that most of the time don't" (Simon 1983: 20).[9] Simon is right in one sense: at any one point in time, probably not too many variables affect a choice. But the world has a way of changing, bringing in previously ignored facets that act to undermine a choice that seemed perfectly respectable a little bit earlier. Evaluating choice means that we must attend to the temporal

---

9. I am struck by how closely the thrust of the work on decision-making by Herbert Simon parallels the thought of Marshall—as opposed to some of Marshall's more direct intellectual descendants, such as Gary Becker. Of particular interest is the similarity of their thoughts on factoring decisions.

dimension, because over time more variables have the opportunity to undermine a compromise (path-dependent) solution.

Temporal Choice

How do political (and other) actors make choices over time? This is a question that has been studied empirically but has attracted surprisingly little theoretical work.[10] The omission is most glaring in rational analyses of political choice, where the "fixed preference" approach has led to studies of strategies of leaders as "agenda-setters" who offer proposals to followers (who could be voters or legislators in a chamber or members of a committee). The followers have fixed preferences, so that agenda proposals can move around in a fixed space (Fiorina and Shepsle 1989). The only change comes from the manipulation of the proposals; the recipients of the proposals don't change their minds (Riker 1990).

Economists have employed the *discounted utility (DU) model* to explain intertemporal choice. This model claims that decision-makers maximize some function of current and expected future consumption, with the latter subject to a discount rate (that is, decision-makers prefer present to future consumption, so that the same benefits now are worth more than they would be sometime in the future). The model thus integrates decisions whose benefits occur now with decisions whose benefits must be deferred to the future. The problem is that "when scrutinized through the lens of DU, intertemporal choices appear hopelessly inconsistent" (Lowenstein and Elster 1992: x).

One major problem with the DU model is its inability to account for differing time preferences (discount rates) across domains of action. That is, domains are not well integrated with respect to the application of time discount factors. Decision-makers appear willing to delay consumption in some domains but not in others. The same individual who visits the dentist regularly underinvests in energy efficiency. The same lack of consistent discounting occurs at the societal level: "We construct shoddy highways, refuse to switch to the metric system, even type on a keyboard that was designed to slow the typist down to a rate that 19th-century typewriters could accommodate. But we also invest in basic research whose payoff is remote and eschew nuclear waste disposal sites because they may cause problems centuries hence" (Lowenstein and Elster 1992: x). There is great variance in concern for the future across domains of action at both the individual and societal levels.

10. For example, political scientists and sociologists have studied changes in attitudes and behaviors across time and within age cohorts (see Mayer 1992; Page and Shapiro 1992).

Studies by psychological decision theorists Tversky, Kahneman, and Quattrone (Kahneman and Tversky 1985; Quattrone and Tversky 1988) also call into question the ability of people to make consistent choices temporally. These scholars have conducted experiments that imply *reversals of preference* when choice objects are described in different (but entirely consistent) terms. For example, people may choose different medical treatments depending on whether outcomes are described in terms of deaths avoided or lives saved. This violates the rational choice criterion of *invariance,* the notion that different descriptions of equivalent outcomes should not influence choices. Quattrone and Tversky (1988: 734) write:

> Although there is no universally accepted definition of rationality, most social scientists agree that rational choice should conform to a few elementary requirements. Foremost among these is the criterion of invariance . . . which holds that the preference order among prospects should not depend on how they are described. Hence no acceptable rational theory would allow reversals of preference to come about as a consequence of whether the choice is based on rates of employment or rates of unemployment, crime commission statistics or law obedience statistics . . . We have seen [in experiments], however, that these alternate frames led to predictable reversals in preference.

The clear implication of this work is that the same decision, described differently at two times, can lead to different choices. These experimental findings have been used to question the entire concept of preferences itself. People seem to make different decisions depending on situational framing. Can something so instable be a meaningful concept? Frisch (1993) has taken an important step in unifying preferences and context in the face of instable decision-making across time. She distinguishes between "decision preference," or the actual choice, and "experience preference," the preference one would actually find more desirable. Frisch's approach implies that people can make decisional mistakes, and thus runs quite counter to the economist's assumption that preferences can be inferred from choices. As we shall see, considerable confusion can be eliminated if we distinguish between preferences and attentiveness, with the latter being influenced by context.[11]

That rational models of decision-making have so thoroughly failed to account for temporal choice is not surprising. The seeming inconsisten-

---

11. Frisch's approach actually confuses mistakes in decisions with attentiveness to context. I would not deny the possibility of mistakes. But preferences can be inconsistent across time without the decision-maker committing errors—at least direct preferences.

cies in choice are not hard to understand, at least within a bounded rationality framework. First, cognitive capacities are limited, and hence are strongly affected by the structure of the situation. Both the strength of the incentives and the character of the information act to structure the situation. Second, any choice that is made in a complex world is automatically suboptimal, just because optimal solutions don't exist. As time passes, what was once a pretty good approximation may look like a poor choice. But it will be hard to change, because most decisions, in politics at least, operate on ill-structured problems. Problem definitions unfold as the problem is worked on. Hence they are path-dependent in the very definition of the problem.

For example, this kind of suboptimal path dependency characterizes U. S. environmental policies today. There is strong consensus that much of environmental regulation is misdirected (in the sense of neither working on the most important problems nor alleviating problems in a cost-effective way). Environmental "superfund" cleanups of toxic waste sites are directed at the worst, and hence most expensive, waste sites rather than at the easily restored sites. Some chemicals are highly regulated, whereas other, potentially more dangerous, chemicals are haphazardly controlled. Courts have ruled that liability for cleanups is "joint and several," which means that any one polluter where there are many can be held responsible for the entire cost of restoration. This has led to debilitating legal actions. The reason for this is understandable: environmental groups were initially working in a hostile political world and used every "horror story" of pollution to gain acceptance of an approach that was antithetical to prevailing understandings of economic growth. Policymakers, having little familiarity with the problem and reacting to political pressures, acted to ameliorate the immediate situation with whatever policy tools could be used. The result was a jerry-built environmental policy, one that is seemingly irrational but completely understandable as a path-dependent process in a complex world offering no optimal approaches.

Conclusions: Optimality Redux

Economist Gary Becker (1986: 119) claims that "all human behavior can be viewed as involving participants who maximize their utility from a stable set of preferences and accumulate an optimal amount of information and other inputs from a variety of markets." Empirical studies show that people don't—at least lots of times they don't. The reasons are twofold: they can't because they are cognitively unable to, and they can't because the world won't let them. I would view humans as great learners;

potentially they could learn to behave according to Becker's model, even if they don't do so now.

The next chapter will explore a major heuristic for struggling with cognitive limitations: shifting attentiveness. But the major message I want to convey here is that people are boundedly rational because a multifaceted decision-making environment won't allow them to be omnisciently rational. Kauffman's complexity catastrophe places strong limits on rational decision-making because it denies optimization in complex systems. Infinite calculational power will not change that. James March (1978: 583) has termed this *contextual rationality*: "the extent to which choice behavior is embedded in a complex of other claims on the attention of actors and other structures of social and cognitive relations." At least in the early stages of the development of the quantitative approach to economics, the claim was *not* one of omniscient rationality by decision-makers. The claim of Alfred Marshall and the other marginalists had to do, rather, with the appropriateness of factoring as a decisional strategy—the world was basically linear and decomposable in the "normal" course of events. People could work on one thing at a time; then if anyone wanted to add all of these things up, they would approximate a decisional equilibrium: effort and utility would exist in a nice balance. So things worked out all right in the end; the infamous "as if" assumption (the world operates *as if* people maximize) does no damage.

What if the world is not so nicely decomposable? What if domains affect one another in complex patterns? Now cognitive limits intervene. Decision-makers are going to have to compare across decisional domains, because they are not divisible. They could try to balance the facets in some sort of average. But they often don't. Rather, they tend to pick out facets that are most relevant at the time and make decisions based on those facets. They continue to compartmentalize and factor, behaving as if the world is linear and decomposable. It is not misleading to suggest that they maximize within compartments. But when the context changes, bringing in new facets, they can be left with poor past choices. If they now make new choices based on the changed context, they will look inconsistent.

3 Attention and Temporal Choice in Politics

Great inconsistencies in choice may result from fluctuating attention. — HERBERT SIMON

Interesting things happen when the complexity of the political world interacts with the serial processing capacity of human decision-makers. The political world is multifaceted, not offering any stable overall equilibrium. And human decision-makers deal with complex decision-making circumstances by factoring, that is, by compartmentalizing decisions and making them on only "what's relevant." They process information serially, examining one facet at a time, and this serial processing is why humans must factor. Herbert Simon (1983) sees serial processing as a key component of his "behavioral model" of decisional choice. That implies that decision-makers will attend to only a limited part of the environment when making a decision. As we shall see, attentiveness is a prime component of Simon's approach, albeit the aspect of his theory that has been most overlooked in political science.

In general, attempts to unify behavioral rationality with omniscient rationality have been desultory and ineffective.[1] In this chapter, I will develop an approach to decision-making that allows for the operation of the full rationality model within decision domains, but will offer shifting attention as a major mechanism for moving between domains. Although this undermines the comprehensive utility approach in the rational model, it holds to rational analysis within domains. This simplifies matters by refusing to allow ad hoc behavioral findings to compromise maximization within domains. Factoring allows rational decision-making to work pretty well within domains, but the world won't let factoring work to integrate across domains. An advantage of this strategy lies in its ability to account for important systems-level behavior through the operation of

---

1. Mainly because rational choice proponents have been unwilling to consider relaxing the comprehensive utility function thesis for something more realistic. However, William Riker (1984, 1990) has worked to put the rational choice model in a more realistic political setting, giving great room for rhetoric and what he calls "heresthetics" (where the issue frame is changed to convince). He was roundly attacked for giving ground by Peter Ordeshook (1984), who objected to the diminished ability to predict in Riker's model. Riker's work is discussed in chapter 4.

individual decisional processes. To understand the shifting nature of policy agendas, one must understand the interaction between a complex and interdependent political world and the tendency of humans to factor.

The Decision to Attend

In the last chapter, we visited the dilemma of temporal choice: across domains of action, humans seem remarkably inconsistent. This apparent dilemma may be resolved once we recognize that people are not attentive to all domains of action simultaneously and that they normally fail to integrate the domains of action into a coherent whole. In other words, people lack an overarching utility function that serves to integrate the various facets of their lives. Because they generally fail to integrate utilities across domains of action, the decision to attend must become a fundamental component of decision analysis.[2] Simon has noted that "one requirement for a comprehensive logic of decision is that it should handle the attention-directing decisions that determine when particular kinds of action should be initiated" (Simon 1977: 157). This is so critical because for humans "most behaviors requiring significant participation of the central nervous system must be performed serially" (p. 157).

Serial processing implies a certain degree of lurching, or episodic shifting, in the kinds of things that are selected for action. "Attention can, in general, be invested in only one activity at a time" (Thorngate 1988: 250). Simon has suggested that facing one kind of decision, say, buying a car rather than contemplating a job change, "will probably focus your attention on some aspects of your life to the relative neglect of others . . . Hence, it is unlikely that a single comprehensive utility function will watch over the whole range of decisions you make. On the contrary, particular decision domains will evoke particular values, and *great inconsistencies in choice may result from fluctuating attention*" (Simon 1983: 18, italics added). Selective attention to decisional domains implies that preferences may be relatively easy to rank within domains but relatively difficult to rank across domains. Iyengar (1990: 161) writes that "most aspects of politics pass by unnoticed most of the time . . . under ordinary circumstances, political attention is discretionary." Because some domains of politics are more relevant to some people than others, "information about public affairs is, therefore, likely to be domain-specific."

Attention may be incorporated into rational choice models as a "cost"

2. The term "domains of action" is somewhat ambiguous. As will become clear, "maximization within domains" works well only when those domains are structured by a very limited number of dimensions, to which actors attend. Where a domain of action is delimited by multiple dimensions, the problem of serial processing will often reemerge.

of decision-making. Moreover, in well-structured environments, such as competitive markets, actors can establish routines for monitoring those aspects of the environment that are most relevant to the major goals of the organization (H. Simon 1977). The price system elegantly forces market participants to monitor relevant aspects of the environment and easily allows comparisons among these aspects. For example, it is conceptually simple for a firm to compare the relative roles of costs and sales on profits. The question is whether we understand politics by trying to force the decision to attend, as well as other aspects of bounded rationality, in the more complex and less quantified environment of politics. Understanding the demands of serial processing on both decision-makers and policymaking organizations is fundamental to politics, and hence the relegation of attention-directing mechanisms to the realm of rational decision-making is misguided. In particular, it directs our attention as analysts to structure and institution in politics, and away from change. On the other hand, models of limited rationality force analysts to examine both stability (through the commonly understood mechanisms of routines and limited search) and change, even nonincremental change (through the mechanisms that are responsible for the decision to attend).

Components of Design Decisions

A design decision precedes an actual choice; it involves imposing structure on a situation so that alternative solutions may be listed. Any design decision can be factored into two components. The first component encompasses the dimensions of evaluation that are used to structure the decision. These evaluative dimensions are actually *goals;* they are what the decision is supposed to contribute to. In politics, the goals of actors and the goals of the collectivity can diverge; this is the famous "collective action problem" (see Sandler 1992 for a recent review and analysis). Hence we must be careful to specify the level of analysis upon which the goal is supposed to operate. To take a simple example, it is normally assumed that politicians are motivated primarily by the desire for reelection. But that cannot be a collective goal, and the satisfaction of individual goals of reelection may or may not maximize the general good. More troublesome is the fact that all participants in politics have multiple goals, and the alternatives that can be listed once the situation is structured are likely to affect these goals differently and not necessarily in the same direction. Hence trade-offs are necessary.

The second facet of design is the structure of attention: the aspects of the problem situation that the decision-maker attends to. That is, many evaluative dimensions may be relevant to a particular decision, but the decision-maker has no ready way of making comparisons among these dimensions. Hence one of the great heuristics of decision-making is the elimination of evaluative dimensions that do not seem to be relevant at the moment. Attentiveness to a limited number of evaluative dimensions, or goals, is similar to the concept of factorization in decision-making. In the complex world it is often justifiable to proceed by focusing on one aspect of a problem at a time, and then "breaking down the aggregate of possible solutions, be they limited or unlimited in number, into percepti-bly smaller mutually exclusive sets" (Kauffman 1968: 13). Nevertheless, there are trade-offs, so that just how and why some dimensions of evalua-tion get attended to, and others get ignored, is fundamental.

Let us return for a moment to the spatial choice model presented in chapter 2. The model as presented allows us to associate the interposition of the choice dimensions (policies P and Q) with Simon's design prob-lem—that is, with decisions on the appropriate means for achieving goals. Then the level of spending along a single choice dimension is Si-mon's choice problem. That is, once means are specified, the decision-maker must determine the proper level of action—knowing full well that trade-offs among goals are involved. "The same behavior may have as consequence more than one value—it may be a member of more than one means-end chain" (H. Simon 1977:75).

Noncompensatory Decision-Making

A major issue in the study of decision-making concerns how people make trade-offs among attributes underlying a choice situation. When these attributes are valued, they may be termed preferences. The previ-ous chapter introduced the idea of multidimensional preferences, termed Stigler-Becker preferences, which underlie the more direct pref-erences that relate to the actual choice a decision-maker faces. Stigler and Becker, along with most economists, contend that people can make the trade-offs among attributes in a reasonably straightforward manner. One way in which people may deal with trade-offs among attributes of a choice situation is to use a *compensatory* strategy of decision-making. "According to this model, in choice situations, if a certain alternative is low on a given dimension, then a high score on another dimension can compensate for it" (Mintz 1993: 4). Decision-makers combine the vari-ous attributes of a multidimensional choice situation into a "total score," such as "net gain" (p. 5).

Compensatory decision-making describes some choice situations, but in others decision-makers may use noncompensatory methods. Amos Tversky and his collaborators note that "because it is often unclear how to trade one attribute against another, a common procedure for resolving conflict in such situations is to select the option that is superior on the more important attribute" (Tversky, Sattath, and Slovic 1988: 372). Selection on the prominent attribute both reduces the cognitive strain of trying to compare dimensions and provides "a compelling argument for choice that can be used to justify the decision" (p. 372). In decisions regarding foreign policy, oftentimes attributes are eliminated because they are deemed "politically unacceptable" (Mintz 1993). For example, for the Clinton administration, the horrors of "ethnic cleansing" in Bosnia in the early 1990s could not compensate for the political unacceptability of committing American ground forces. It would seem that *no* "score" on the moral issue could compensate for the perceived political problems. In effect, decision-makers have set a threshold on one dimension (political difficulties) and any strategy that exceeds that threshold will be eliminated, regardless of its justification on other dimensions—a strategy known as *elimination by aspects* (Tversky 1972; Mintz 1993).

There is nothing in noncompensatory decision-making that logically counters the classic rational decision-making model. The best alternative is still being selected among those presented. Moreover, the ignoring of less important dimensions underlying the choice can be viewed within a marginalist information framework: it is rational for a decision-maker to utilize those dimensions most relevant to choice because the cost of examining all potential dimensions would be very high. In the decision-making strategy of elimination by aspects, discussed above, the comparisons among dimensions are explicit and weights assigned. In effect, the indifference curves of decision-makers are elliptical rather than circular, and the ellipses have very small minor axes (see chap. 2). Indeed, a noncompensatory decision-maker is just a compensatory decision-maker when all attributes save one have null weights.

Once again, however, the model gets into trouble when examined across time. The problem is that the prominence of a dimension of evaluation (or Stigler-Becker preference) is contextually contingent. As Tversky and his colleagues have shown, the weighting of the prominent dimension is affected by the structure of the choice situation. One might make a choice through *comparison* (choosing between two political parties) or through *matching* (comparing the positions of the two parties on a criterion measure or comparing the prices of two brands of soap). Psychological experiments suggest that the more prominent dimension weighs more heavily in comparisons than in matching, the so-called *prominence hypothesis* (Tversky, Sattath, and Slovic 1988: 372). In matching in a multidimensional situation, one must assess each relevant dimension explicitly (for example, scores and grades in an admissions decision). In direct comparisons, on the other hand, people tend to focus on a single dimension of evaluation. This suggests that where metrics are available, more dimensions of evaluation can be compared than when they aren't available. However, focusing on what is measured in a multidimensional choice situation can lead to Bauer's (1966) famous social indicator problem: once an attribute is measured, it becomes overly prominent in decision-making. If measurement validity is exact, then there will be no problem. But if it is inexact, or if it measures one dimension of performance and excludes others, then incentives will exist for decision-makers to maximize on a single dimension in a multifaceted situation.

There is a broader point here. The ability to deal with multiple attributes in decisions is very much related to how clearly defined the structure of decision-making is. In situations where the decision-making structure is well understood and relatively static (that is, at equilibrium), human decision-makers are generally quite capable of comparing strategies across dimensions. Think of a comparison of baseball pitchers. While there are many dimensions of performance and several intangibles, most . of the relevant variables regarding pitching have been quantified and assessed over the years: strikeouts; earned-run averages; innings pitched; and so forth. Pitchers and managers employ different strategies—fastball versus curveballs being the most important. But these are strategies and are related to the measures of outcomes in pretty standard ways (an eighty-mile-an-hour fastball won't win many games).

When problems are ill structured, participants bring structure with them. They can do so by rule writing, that is, by specifying the decision-making structure and getting everyone to agree to it. Unlike in baseball, in most domains of life this is not enough to fix permanently the dimensions of evaluation that decision-makers use. In economics, one might see the rules of competition as relatively fixed. But the preferences that consumers bring to the marketplace may shift radically—from, say, price to quality. In politics, the preferences of voters may shift from an emphasis on economic growth to one of social control. This may not change the rationality of politicians—they may still try to maximize their electoral potential. But if they miss the shift, they may be maximizing on the wrong dimension. If they pick it up, they will look terribly inconsistent. Great disruptive changes in policy can occur even within the constraints of the institutional rules of democracy, and within a maximization model of political action.

Finally, note that the marginalist concept of information in making decisions works well in baseball. At some point, it just doesn't make any sense to keep acquiring information about pitchers. But a marginal approach to information is insufficient to account for shifts in decisional frames—that is, the shift from one set of attributes that underlie a particular choice to another. So marginalist information models will work better in some realms of life (baseball) than in others (politics).

The Concept of Attention

All decisions must involve selectivity, because they all involve factoring out the unimportant. How we decide what aspects of the decision-making environment are relevant and ought to be attended to is thus fundamental to decision-making. Attention, however, implies more: it is the mechanism through which attribute prominence is brought into the decision-making structure. Because attributes are preferences when they are valued (as they always are in political choice situations), selective attention is the manner in which preferences are brought to bear on choice. This would matter little if attentiveness to preferences were constant in time; but clearly it is not. When the structure of choice changes, attribute prominence (and thereby salient preferences) changes. Hence the very values on which decisions are based shift when attentiveness shifts. A decision-maker may maximize under one structure and then maximize under another, but if attentiveness shifts then choices can shift.

Attention refers to "processes or conditions within the organism that determine how effective a particular stimulus will be" (Berlyne 1974: 124). Hence attention has always been synonymous with selectivity. Moray (1970: 6) details seven uses of the term, including mental concentration, in which a person tries to exclude irrelevant stimuli in order to concentrate on a particular task; vigilance, in which a person is paying attention in order to detect something; selective attention, in which a person is receiving numerous messages and wants only to respond to one; search; activation, where a person is ready to deal with what happens next; and set, where a person exhibits a readiness to respond in a certain way. Underlying all of these meanings is a selectivity of some aspect of the environment for further processing.

The concept of selectivity of stimuli has had a checkered history in philosophy and psychology. Turn-of-the-century psychologists viewed attention as a process of moving into consciousness, a view that American behaviorists viewed suspiciously (Berlyne 1974: 128). Indeed, under the doctrine of "response selection" of the behaviorists, attention was scarcely studied (Berlyne 1960). Serious study of attention returned to psychology in the 1950s. Most important, Broadbent (1958) developed his "filter theory" of attention. In this approach, information enters the perceptual system of the organism through a number of parallel sensory channels. The channels were in actuality several simultaneously arriving signals (Berlyne 1974: 140) or functional channels (Moray 1970: 28), not simply the auditory and visual pathways. Because the brain features a limited-capacity channel to process inputs, the parallel signals must be translated into serial inputs. Broadbent postulates a short-term memory store at the end of the parallel signals, followed by a filter. The filter selects one of the inputs and sends it into the limited-capacity channel. In effect, the filter translates the parallel signals into serial ones. Hence "overloading of the limited capacity channel is prevented by serializing the input to it" (Moray 1970: 29). Broadbent also provided for retrieval of stimuli into the short-term memory store and for access from long-term memory.

Following Broadbent's path-breaking work, several psychologists further developed the mechanisms associated with the "bottleneck of attention." (See Moray 1970: chap. 2 for a review of the work immediately following Broadbent's; see Allport 1989 for a summary of more recent work.) The filter was conceived by Treisman (1964) as attenuating signal strength rather than as acting to exclude nonselected inputs altogether. Considerable research was directed at the issue of whether the selectivity of stimuli occurred early or late in cognitive processing (Allport 1989: 634–37). The idea of the relationship between limited cognitive processing capacity and the bottleneck of attention has survived as a key component of cognitive processing (Allport 1989).

Arguing that the concept of attention and selective processing is crucial for understanding human psychology, Neisser (1967) has emphasized the active and cognitive components of attention. The selection of functional channels for processing is characterized by Neisser as "preattentional selection"; attention refers to the complex, active process of analysis by synthesis (Moray 1970: 37).[3] Neisser notes the ability to attend to one's own thoughts, and for him attention "amounts to matching stimulus sequences with processes that the subject can construct" (Berlyne 1974: 141). If there exists a "bottleneck of attention" in political decision-making, it surely exists at the higher levels of processing described by Neisser.

In later work, Neisser is highly critical of the passive filter theories that are supposed to protect the brain from being overtaxed. For Neisser,

> the cognitive structures crucial for vision are the anticipatory schemata that prepare the perceiver to accept certain kinds of information rather than others . . . because we can see only what we know

3. Ohman developed a more complete model of cognitive processing based generally on the filter approach and utilizing Neisser's ideas of preattentional processing (see Spinks and Siddle 1983: 246–48 for a discussion).

how to look for, it is these schemata (together with information actually available) that determine what will be perceived . . . Because schemata are anticipations, they are the medium by which the past affects the future; information already acquired determines what will be picked up next (Neisser 1976: 21–22).

Hence for Neisser there is a *perceptual cycle,* in which schemata (internal cognitive organization) affect what is perceived and what is perceived affects internal schemata: "We cannot perceive *unless* we anticipate, but we must not see *only* what we anticipate . . . perception is directed by expectations but not controlled by them" (Neisser 1976: 43). Schemata have become central to linguists and psychologists studying the human processing of information: "Research in information processing strongly supports the notion that we use some type of plan or blueprint to interpret, store, and recall information" (Fitch-Hauser 1990: 77). And the plan or blueprint may vary according to level of generality. Neisser's perceptual cycle implies that, for normal people at least, "schemata exert their effects by selecting some kinds of information rather than others, not by manufacturing false percepts or illusions" (Neisser 1976: 43–44). One cannot avoid selectivity, but the check of reality can bring other elements of reality into the perceptual field.[4]

Most theories of attention have been developed in laboratory situations on very simple auditory and visual stimuli. Hence for the most part information processing as generally studied involves a very limited conception of information. Thorngate, however, offers a broader view of attentiveness, which he terms *attentional economics* to stress the role of attention in allocating processing capacity in an information-rich world. "Attention is exactly what we 'pay' for information" (1988: 249). At the individual level, then, attention serves to allocate processing capacity to topics.[5]

Pattern Recognition and Attention

Howard Margolis (1987) has developed a complete theory of cognition based on pattern recognition. Margolis depicts cognition as a spiral,

4. Neisser's perceptual approach receives support in studies in social psychology that indicate that individuals tend to seek out information favorable to a choice they have made (position they hold) but that they do not exclude unfavorable information (see Jones and Gerard 1967 for a review and discussion). If this is generally true, then individuals, while selecting information that does not fit their decisional frameworks, nevertheless are open at some level to information that challenges that framework.

5. Kahneman (1973; see Spinks and Siddle 1983 for a discussion) originally developed the notion of a central processing "allocational policy" for examining stimuli.

in many ways similar to Neisser's perceptual cycle: "At the top of each cycle a pattern (the arrangement of features in a room, phonemes in a word, for examples) is prompted by cues in context. That pattern itself then becomes part of the environment which cues the next pattern" (1987: 2).

Given a judgment (that a pattern fits a situation), there is a tendency to hold to that judgment, which gives stability to cognition. Pattern recognition incorporates attention because it implies that the decision-maker attends to environmental cues (which may be an earlier pattern) that evoke a pattern. Moreover, pattern recognition is an episodic, disjointed event: a person must decide (often unconsciously) whether a pattern fits a situation. Margolis details four basic subprocesses in pattern recognition: "jumping" (reaching a response); "checking" (taking a closer look); "priming" (a predisposition to make a certain jump); and "inhibiting" (a predisposition to refuse to make certain jumps). He notes that all organisms must find a balance between jumping too soon and checking too long (1987: 28)

Commenting on the episodic nature of pattern recognition, Margolis (pp. 136–37) writes that "as with seeing an ambiguous picture, a point is reached where modest tilting of the cues to favor one pattern rather than another can decisively tilt the perception . . . from one that supported the traditional view to one that supported its adversary." But the tendency to hold on to a cue—pattern association means that "challenging entrenched networks [bundled patterns] will be resisted, never absolutely, but on a scale with how deeply entrenched the network has become by intensity of unproblematical use" (pp. 139–40).

Margolis's study of pattern recognition as the basis for cognition, like Neisser's use of perception as a basis for thought, involves a cycle in which a dominant association between a perception (or a pattern) and a cue is treated as a standing decision unless something problematic about the association is detected. Then a rapid shift from one pattern or perception to a second can occur. Cognition, then, is fundamentally episodic, and we should expect such patterned shifts in more complex situations.

Cognitive polarization, or "twoness," is an outgrowth of the tension between "jumping" and "checking." It is "the ability to see a field of perception in two ways, but rarely in more than two ways" (Margolis 1987: 275). Cognitive "twoness" is particularly in evidence in social judgments that transcend the experiences of ordinary life. "It is hard (for example) to see the efficiency and equity sides of an economic issue as simultaneously in focus . . . We can arrive at what we feel is a balanced judgment by switching back and forth between the two gestalts, but it is hard to merge the two into a single gestalt" (p. 275).

Even in situations where cognitive polarization does not hold, research has shown that people do not often judge alternatives separately across attributes and then compare the alternatives (in essence, they do not sum across attributes). Instead, they tend to focus on salient attributes of the alternatives—sometimes attending to only one attribute of the alternatives (Herstein 1981; Tversky 1972; Payne 1976). If individual decision-makers do focus on one attribute in comparing alternatives, then a shift in focus from the dominant attribute to a second attribute can shift the choice episodically.

Attention, Selection, and Decision-Making

It is easily seen that attention and the associated perceptual cycle are relevant for the process of decision-making. People cannot make decisions about things they do not apprehend. Hence attention is bound up with decisional action; these are the infamous premises that underpin decision-making. Decisional premises may be held well beyond their usefulness, but a pathogenic attachment to a schema or set of decisional premises in the face of obviously changed circumstances is just that—pathogenic.

Moreover, the perceptual cycle is analogous to Simon's heuristic search procedures for the design stage of problem solving (H. Simon 1977). Heuristic search can be very costly; hence decision-makers tend to settle on solutions that work rather than the best solution for the problem, a process termed *satisficing*. Satisficing may be the best solution to a problem when costs are factored in; it may not be, however. That is because of the tendency to search for solutions "near" the known set of solutions. In particular, reasoning by analogy tends to characterize much policy search (Jones and Bachelor 1993). Should the situation change, decision-makers may be in the position of continuing to apply solutions that once were satisfactory but have become maladaptive.

Because of the costly nature of search, decision-makers tend to select repetitively the same aspects of the environment for input into decision-making. Hence in the process of making decisions, both Neisser's model of a continuously modified interaction between schemata and perception and Margolis's model of interactions between cues and imputed patterns imply the existence of periods of stasis, in which decision premises are not questioned, interspersed with periods of change, in which they are. Decision-makers making repetitive (or very similar) decisions in politics probably redesign their strategies only episodically.

A key question for political analysis, then, is, What makes decision-makers pay attention to selected parts of the environment, all the while ignoring others? What about selectivity in goals, that is, the situation in which the decision-maker focuses on some subset of goals to the exclusion of others?

The Role of Emotions

Many people are passionate about their politics, and emotion infuses the political reasoning of the most sophisticated as well as the least. A major approach to the understanding of voting behavior, the "Michigan model" (so named because it was developed by scholars at the University of Michigan), emphasizes the role of attitudes in determining voting choice (Campbell et al. 1960). Attitudes are conceived to have three aspects: cognitive, evaluative, and affective (emotive); hence feelings toward political objects such as parties and candidates have a major role in the model. That model has been criticized for underestimating the abilities of voters to exercise reasoned (even if not fully rational) judgment (Popkin 1991; Page and Shapiro 1992). For many, feelings "can serve as a calculational crutch," with feelings toward groups, parties, or ideologies dictating support for particular policies (Sniderman, Brody, and Tetlock 1991: 8).

The bounded rationality voting model of Sniderman and his colleagues at Stanford and of Popkin has a critical emotive component. For example, the Stanford scholars understand ideology to involve passions and preference intensities, which can serve to help people identify themselves. "Ideological identification is an expression primarily of people's feelings, not an indication of their belief in a set of political programs or policies" (Sniderman, Brody, and Tetlock 1991: 161).

The public opinion studies emphasize the role of emotion in directly influencing political choice. But affect in politics serves a second function. Simon (1983: 29) ties the role of emotion to attentiveness: "Emotion has particular importance because of its function in selecting particular things in our environments as the focus of our attention." Political symbols such as powerfully written books influence "in large part because [they have] evocative power, the ability to arouse and fix the attention . . . A behavioral theory of rationality, with its concern for the focus of attention as a major determinant of choice, does not dissociate emotion from human thought, nor does it in any respect underestimate the powerful effects of emotion in *setting the agenda for human problem solving*" (Simon 1983: 30, italics added).

In their study of election campaigns, Marcus and MacKuen (1993) have integrated emotion into mechanisms of candidate selection: "Changes in mood constitute a critical part of information-processing mechanisms" (p. 673). They propose a "dual system" of emotional response to campaigns: "anxiety" and "enthusiasm." "Emotional responses are functionally focused, with one system [anxiety] alert to intrusive signals of novelty and threat and the other system [enthusiasm] monitoring the success of current behavior" (p. 674). That is, attention to attributes of the campaign is focused via the dual system, and the two emotions play different roles in the focusing of attention. "People unaroused will safely vote their standing choice, while those pricked by anxiety will perk up, gather new information, and perhaps abandon their old habits" (p. 677). Marcus and MacKuen feel that voters shift from the "standing decision" associated with enthusiasm to a search mode based on "conscious rational choice" when "pricked by anxiety." It seems very plausible that anxiety causes search behavior, but it may be that the search is primarily a shift in evaluative frames that happens suddenly and without the careful search that these scholars imply. Nevertheless, their work is a breakthrough in conceiving emotionality in campaigns within an information-processing framework rather than simply as a "calculational crutch."

Attention in a Social Context

Most psychological studies have focused on the selectivity of very controlled stimuli in laboratory situations, leading Neisser to complain that "contemporary studies of cognitive processes usually use stimulus material that is abstract, discontinuous, and only marginally real. It is almost as if ecological *in*validity were a deliberate feature of the experimental design" (Neisser 1976: 34). This aspect of experimental studies makes the inference from serial processing capacities as assessed in simple laboratory experiments to political decision-making in complex and changing environments problematic.

Clearly a broader view of attention is implied in models of decision-making. Attention, after all, has a variety of connotations, all centering on selectivity of perception. It can involve sublime rationality, as would be the case with a chess master pondering the innovative move of his able opponent. But it can also involve heightened states of emotion generated by threat to life or core values. Humans evolved in a threatening world, one in which hunting for food required intense concentration, and threats to life or the family required levels of high emotion resulting in "fight or flight." (On the role of evolutionary context in modern politics, see Schubert 1989.) Quite clearly, both emotional states are involved in politics; both focus attention but with different consequences.

In contrast to the laboratory experiments on attention, "the confusion of the real world imposes constant attentional choices on people" (Fiske and Taylor 1984: 194). Students of social cognition have examined attention in a variety of social circumstances, most of which are not really relevant to the study of politics. These studies still suffer from overreliance on the laboratory method; nevertheless, they do consider the social context of attentiveness.

Two general findings in this research are important for our purposes. First, the nature of the stimulus matters, with presumably more salient stimuli, which are novel within a context, attracting more attention. Attentiveness seems to guide interpretation and judgment of the salient stimulus (Fiske and Taylor 1984: 199). Second, "the central point underlying the effects of attention on various forms of behavior seems to be that people act on whatever norms are made salient, especially when forced to reflect on themselves" (p. 210).

The psychological experiments on this aspect of attentiveness are too simplistic to make uncritical inferential leaps to political behavior. Mayer (1992: 137) correctly notes that psychological research has focused on how the individual actor "is affected by a clearly defined stimulus . . . with a narrow range of possible responses." Political scientists are interested in how people deal "with an incredibly diverse range of stimuli that may differ substantially among individuals, and with a much larger array of potential options." For example, the psychological studies on attentiveness to norms involve reminding children to take only one piece of Halloween candy and reminding students not to cheat (Fiske and Taylor 1992: 210). Nevertheless, the experiments are important because they suggest that behavior can be changed through shifts in attentiveness to internal states (memory). One can be quite sure that children's preferences for Halloween candy were not altered by the reminder to be well behaved; only attentiveness to the norm was manipulated.

Attention Fixing

Arousing attention and fixing it for a sustained period of time are not as simply related as it may first seem. Getting people to pay attention to a stimulus and getting them to continue to focus on it (for example, until the problem is solved) may be viewed as separate processes. This may not be so much a consideration where ends and means are closely related. Once a person focuses on a particular end (solving a crossword problem, for example) and the means and ends are obviously connected, then the incentives exist to direct attention until the task is completed. This may also occur where, for example, a task force is assembled to solve a particularly severe problem—the problem can be severe enough to arouse and fix attention for an extended period of time.

Situations in which there are many competing goals and where goals and means are not so simply related, or are related through complex chains of action, or where a given strategy is connected to more than one goal (H. Simon 1977: 73–75), can be more problematic for fixing attention—because there are multiple ways of understanding a situation. Attention in politics would seem to involve both the process of attracting attention and the process of fixing it, because attracting attention alone will not result in lasting policy actions.

The approach of Thorngate (1988), who suggests that people develop rules for allocating attention, stands out as an attempt to deal both with attracting attention and with fixing it. The allocation rules cause people to ignore some stimuli and attend to others; they also act to fix attention until a task is completed. Both Neisser and Margolis incorporate such "standing decisions" in their cyclical models of cognition. For Margolis, a cue-pattern association is held until a major failing of the association occurs (that is, the association can't just be "fixed up").

The Accessibility Bias

A number of experiments by social psychologists have attempted to make certain attributes more accessible in an experimental situation in order to examine the hypothesis that accessible attributes will be used more extensively in choice situations. While a number of experimental techniques have been used to heighten accessibility, they all tend to support the principle of differential weighting by accessibility (Iyengar 1991: 132). This research, along with most research in the psychological determinants of decision-making and choice, has as its common denominator "the dominance of intuitive and informal over rigorous and systematic approaches" (Iyengar 1991: 131). Clearly accessibility is strongly related to attentiveness, and in complex situations contextual cues such as those provided by psychological experimenters may simply raise attentiveness to the experimental attributes. The term *accessibility* may suggest more cognitive limits than are observed in many political and economic decisions, especially elite-based decisions. It may be that the concept of accessibility could be subsumed under theories of social attention such as that suggested by Thorngate (1988) or in the present work.

Nevertheless, the notion of accessibility has been critical in the work of Iyengar and his colleagues in studying the reactions of publics to the mass media. This work focuses explicitly on the communication of frames of reference. These researchers have studied experimental and observational evidence for four effects that are related to attentiveness and the principle of differential weighting by accessibility: agenda-setting effects, priming effects, bandwagon effects, and episodic/thematic effects (Iyengar 1991; Iyengar and Kinder 1987). "The well-known agenda-setting effect refers to the tendency of people to cite issues 'in the news' when asked to identify the significant problems facing the nation" (Iyengar 1991: 132). The "priming effect" refers to the tendency of people to use issues prominent in the national news more heavily in making political judgments. Bandwagons may result when the news media report elections as "horse races," thus encouraging people to focus on electability. Finally, episodic reporting by the media tends to encourage people to attribute responsibility to events and individuals, whereas thematic reporting "helps people to think about political issues in terms of societal or political outcomes" (Iyengar 1991: 134).

The general point supported by the research program of Iyengar and Kinder is that the news media tends to communicate frames of reference for political decision-making and that these frames affect the attentiveness of citizens to particular aspects of complex political reality. There are substantial differences in individual susceptibility to framing (Iyengar 1991: chap. 9), but it is the frames that are communicated, not direct choices. As we shall see, politics is often more about the communication of frames of reference (and thereby attentiveness to preferences) than it is about the direct communication of preferences, as is held in the "preference satisfaction" model of democratic decision-making.

Attention and Preferences

We are now in a better position to unify current approaches to selective attention and formal decision theory. First, let us recall from chapter 2 that rational decision theorists in political science have been sensitive to variations among decision-makers in the weighting of attributes. That is, different decision-makers assign different saliences to the underlying attributes, or Stigler-Becker preferences. These saliences have simply been seen as part and parcel of the preference structure. What I propose is to separate the two components and to envision them as varying independently across time.

Now we have a mechanism within the preference structure for the incorporation of changes in context: the salience weights on the dimensions. Context may affect the Stigler-Becker preferences, or what in spatial theory would be the decision-maker's i-point, through changes in the saliences. It seems consistent with what we know about political decision-making to assume that i-points are subject to gradual change but that salience is strongly affected by context. That leads us to an appreciation of selective attention as a mechanism for integrating context into preferences via awareness.

Attentiveness to underlying dimensions and salience in decisions are not the same thing.[6] One can be attentive to an underlying dimension without its being salient in an actual choice situation. There is, however, a necessary and sufficient connection between the two concepts: one cannot incorporate a dimension into a choice without the operation of selective attention. But once one becomes aware of a preference, it is not logically necessary that the new preference be brought into the decision. Hence the connection between selective attention and the salience of preferences is partially an empirical issue. Given the strong human tendencies toward cognitive polarization, it is highly likely that the two are tightly associated. Moreover, it is inappropriate for decision theorists to ignore the empirical connection if they want to make a scientific as opposed to a normative contribution to understanding politics.

A second empirical issue has to do with the number of dimensions or attributes that decision-makers generally incorporate into a decision. It is inconceivable that all potential relevant factors are ever incorporated into a decision. Not only is this kind of comprehensive search unlikely, but most decision theorists would see it as not rational. The reason is that there is a trade-off between search and choice in decision-making. Hence factoring, or eliminating irrelevant attributes, is critical to efficient decision-making. This means that only a limited number of dimensions or factors will ever be incorporated into a choice. If, however, issues are linked in reality but separated in choice, then the choice may be wrong. More probably, what is irrelevant today may be highly relevant tomorrow.

Conclusions: Factoring and Attention

The rational choice model requires that decision-makers combine the various dimensions of evaluation structuring a decisional situation to assay their *net* benefits. Unfortunately, this is an extraordinarily difficult task and there is little evidence that it actually happens.

The problem of establishing ends-means relationships where both multiple goals and multiple means exist leads to *factoring* in political decision-making. Decision-makers focus on a very limited number of

6. This point has been made forcefully to me by Ben Page.

means-ends relationships, ignoring complexity (Simon 1983: 20). This often stems from the fact that many problems, particularly in politics, are ill structured. That is, decision-making constraints emerge as decisions are taken; each decision-making step in trying to solve a problem constrains the domain of possibilities for future steps. So factorization stems both from limits in human decision-making and from the nature of problems, which are often ill structured not because of human limits but because they really are that way. The tendency of decision-makers to reason by analogy when faced with a new problem, thus importing established policy reasoning to new situations, exacerbates the factor problem.

We live within an institutional structure that encourages factorization and does so by "solving" the design problem. In effect, institutions preselect means, leaving decision-makers to exercise choice among the preselected means. We return to this important matter in the second part of this book. As a consequence of the limits of human decision-making, the nature of the problems decision-makers face, and the structure of political (and other) institutions, decision-makers always face constrained choices. Hence the best models of decision-making and choice must explicitly include those constraints. This is well recognized in consumer theory, for example, where consumers must purchase goods subject to a budget constraint.

All problems, including the most constrained ones, are fundamentally multidimensional. Because of the limits on decision-making, however, it is not normally possible for decision-makers to assay net benefits from all dimensions simultaneously. Attention is directed to a limited number of those dimensions at any one time. *Hence the shifting of evaluative priorities from one dimension to another is fundamental to understanding choice.* Table 3.1 offers a summary of the key components of the decision-making model proposed in this chapter. It may be compared with the overview of the rational approach presented in table 2.1.

Attention is episodic. It is critical to political decision-making because of the inability of political actors to handle the multiple goals/multiple means problem. Hence decision-makers tend to focus on one evaluative dimension at a time and to evaluate means accordingly. When attention shifts to previously ignored evaluative dimensions, the whole way of thinking about the ends-means relationship shifts. So outcomes can change. In the next chapter, we examine how shifts in attention to evaluative dimensions can alter political outcomes.

There exist two different decision-making situations: those in which factoring works and those in which it does not. The two situations have different implications for changes in choice. When factoring works, changes in choice across time can be explained in two ways. First, prefer-

TABLE 3.1 Development of A Model of Political Choice

Objective
Develop a model of political choice that is more consonant with the manner in which people make political choices but that does not sacrifice completely the deductive power of rational analyses of political choice.

Criteria
1. Capable of accounting for episodic changes in choice outcomes internally; i.e., within the constraints of the model itself.
2. Elites and masses use the same fundamental mechanism of choice.
3. Rely as much as possible on rational analyses of choice for framework. (Alternative models tend to be too eclectic and ad hoc.)
4. Integrate modern findings on decision-making in politics into the model but without destroying the model's ability to relate individual decision-making to system-level actions.

Characteristics
1. Decision-makers harbor multiple domains of preferences but do not impose a temporally consistent ordering among the domains.
2. Within domains, preferences are ordered and well behaved.
3. Domains are "linked" through episodic shifts of attentiveness to the domains of preferences (the "serial shift").
4. The choice dimension or domain is not identical to the preference (or evaluative or goal) domains. (We must make choices that are only tangentially related to our preferences or goals.)

Implications
1. Utility functions are "broken"—that is, they are well ordered within domains and may be well ordered among domains at any given point in time, but the order among domains is subject to shift.
2. Contradictory preferences are allowed (since preference domains may not be consistently ordered).
3. Direct preference functions are subject to radical reordering.
4. Shifts in attention to domains of preferences can lead to shifts in choice outcomes with no underlying changes in Stigler-Becker type preferences.

---

ences may change *exogenously*. That is, one may change goals as one grows older, or poorer, or when one changes jobs or residential location. Second, preferences may change *endogenously*. If one perceives an activity as not producing the desired results on the dimension of interest, then one may want to engage in less of that activity. This is the situation that Cohen and Axelrod describe.

In some situations, factorization fails. If one is paying attention only to a limited number of dimensions of evaluation, of Stigler-Becker preferences, then at some point it may become obvious that the activity one is pursuing may be satisfactory on the dimension one is attending to but is failing on some other suddenly relevant dimension. Then shifting choice is based not on preference change but on preference activation: that is, one is acutely aware of other preferences that are relevant to the previously factored decisional situation. So the mechanism of choice will be different when factorization works compared to when it fails. Indeed, the failure of factorization may lead to a search for a new design to problem understanding.

4 A Change of Mind or a Change of Focus?

Which do you prefer, angel food cake or a Bach prelude? — PETER ORDESHOOK

Why have political decision-makers made different decisions at two different times on the same choice? Was it a simple change of mind? Was more information present in the second instance? Or did outside pressures interfere with the implementation of preferences? Was the situation so different on the second vote that the choice was, for all practical purposes, different?

This chapter explores the last alternative.[1] We will try to explain changes in actual political choices without inferring changes in preferences, elaborating the ideas developed in the last three chapters in a more complete model, and detailing an example of how the fixed preference, varying attention approach can account for choice reversals in politics. To do this, we observe that a change of choice from one time to another means either that preferences have changed or that the context has changed, activating a different underlying preference. Unfortunately, "context" and "situation" tend to be used as residual categories of explanation; hence they really don't enlighten very much. Understanding politics requires that we must be more explicit about what we mean by contextual changes. The concept of attentiveness to evaluative dimensions (or goals or preferences) is a means whereby context shifts may be understood. Contexts change when decision-makers shift their attention from one evaluative dimension to another. Let us see how this might work.

The Supercollider Vote

On June 17, 1992, members of the House of Representatives voted 232–181 in favor of an amendment by Congressman Dennis Eckart of Ohio to eliminate all funds except shutdown costs for the superconduct-

1. The case for this approach has been made by Enelow and Hinich (1983). They note that "critical features of the voting environment rarely remain the same" (p. 436). They offer the example of a common-site picketing bill that was passed in 1975 by both houses of Congress but vetoed by President Ford. Then, with a Democratic president in office in 1977, the House of Representatives defeated a nearly identical measure.

ing supercollider, being constructed in Texas for an estimated cost of $8.3 billion. The year before, members had rejected a similar amendment to the energy and water projects appropriations bill by 90 votes (*Congressional Quarterly*, June 20, 1982: 1782). Six weeks later, the Senate voted 62 to 32 to restore funding, sending the revised appropriations bill to conference committee (*New York Times*, August 8, 1992). The conference committee chose a funding figure close to the Senate's (Clayton 1992).

Fully seventy-nine representatives voted yes on the supercollider in 1991 and no in 1992. The standard interpretation offered by journalists was that these members changed their minds on the large, expensive project under the pressures of "antideficit fever." Independent presidential candidate Ross Perot had made the deficit the centerpiece of his "grass roots" bid; only one week before, the House had narrowly defeated a constitutional amendment requiring a balanced budget. Texans, and in particular Congressman Joe Barton, in whose district the supercollider was being built, were vigorous supporters of the amendment. Many speculated that some members reacted negatively to such gross displays of hypocrisy. Opponents, in addition, had been able to raise questions about the appropriateness of the technology of the supercollider by invoking expert witnesses, although clearly this was a minority position in the science policy community. By the time of the Senate vote, however, Perot was out of the race (temporarily, at least) and emotions had cooled over the balanced budget amendment. The Senate, moreover, had traditionally been more supportive of the project, having rejected a move by Senator Dale Bumpers of Arkansas to cut the project the year before by a vote of sixty-two to thirty-seven. Senators had not changed their minds about the "big science" project.

It is possible that *none* of the representatives changed their minds on the supercollider vote and that their changed behaviors were caused by a shift in attentiveness to the underlying dimensions of conflict that structured the vote. Following the line of argument developed in the previous two chapters, we may infer that legislators and other political decision-makers select certain facets from a complex environment to attend to and the particulars that command attention can shift behaviors even in the absence of any changes in preferences. Separating attentiveness to context from more fixed preferences is an assumption about how people make decisions. Generally, the rational choice model has lumped the two facets of "preferences" and "attention to preferences" into one, simply treating the attention component as a "preference weighting." The differences in the two approaches is critical to understanding temporal decision-making. If, in the case of the supercollider, choices change, a rational theorist must conclude that preferences have changed. This could be due to more "information." But I would say that attentiveness is what has changed and that there have not really been any changes in preferences.[2]

While it is not essential, in a strict sense, to the model, I also make the conjecture that the dimensions of conflict are fairly stable, in the sense of generally being present, but that the attention directed toward these dimensions is highly variable across time. This presumption is important in trying to understand why political coalitions in legislatures look so stable, whereas issues seem to sprout anew almost continually in democratic politics. The model is thus a hybrid, drawing from rational decision-making in general, but insisting that attention be separated out as a fundamental characteristic of the decision-making process rather than treated as part of the preference "structure" or as a "cost" of making decisions.

The introduction of new dimensions of conflict (and thereby definitions of issues) has been recognized as fundamental to understanding political decision-making. Riker (1982, 1990) indicates that preference cycling can occur when new dimensions of conflict are interjected into a political debate. But he emphasizes the strategic manipulation that can occur through agenda control. Clearly such strategic manipulation can occur, as is the case when agenda controllers offer "packages" of bills that must be accepted or rejected on the floor of the legislature. But strategic manipulation can only go so far.[3]

2. In 1993, the drama was repeated. In June, the House voted 280–150 to end funding; opponents had picked up an additional 50 votes. But the Senate defeated the Bumpers amendment in September on a 57–42 vote. The conference committee would again support the Senate approach. Had representatives found a "free" anti–big science, pro-deficit reduction vote, making a public stand against the collider and then allowing the Senate to save the pork? Maybe, but more important is the fact that the nature of the conflict had fundamentally changed such that support for "investment" spending was perceived as a big negative. Sure enough, the House members of the conference committee on the energy and water projects appropriations bill allowed the Senate language on the supercollider project to be included in the final version of the bill. Then in October the House disproved the "free vote" hypothesis by voting 282–143 to send the conference committee's version of the energy and water projects appropriations bill back to the conference committee with instructions to kill the supercollider funding (Mills 1993). The new dimension really had displaced the pork of investment spending.

3. Considerable strategic agenda manipulation took place on the supercollider vote. The substantive committee report selected the amount for the supercollider to be included in the appropriations bill, an amount lower than the president had requested to appeal to the suspicious. The Eckart amendment selected an alternative amount (essentially zero) from among the possible alternative positions. The Rules Committee set a favorable rule for the committee report, one that was supported in a floor vote. Yet all of

The Serial Shift

The approach developed here rests on two assumptions. First, I assume that decision-makers must select aspects of the decision-making environment that they then treat as relevant for the decision-making situation. Second, I assume that attentiveness evokes frames of reference that are evaluative in nature. This is another way of saying that decision-makers have goals that they view as more or less relevant to the decision in question, and that the realization that those goals are relevant imposes different structures on a situation. Recall from chapters 2 and 3 that selective attention is a critical facet of the model of bounded rationality (H. Simon 1977, 1981, 1983, 1985). Selectivity in attention means that decision-makers can focus on only a limited number of items during a single time span. The limits of serial processing necessitate episodic shifts from one focus of attention to another.

The second assumption, *decision framing*, is a concept developed by psychologists Kahneman and Tversky to describe situations in which decision-makers allow descriptions of outcomes of choice that are seemingly irrelevant to the choice to affect the decision (Kahneman and Tversky 1985; Tversky and Kahneman 1981, 1986). In chapter 3, we noted how framing has affected the ideas social scientists have about decision-making across time and the stability of preferences. Framing seems to be pervasive and affects both the sophisticated and the naive. "In their stubborn appeal, framing effects resemble perceptual illusions more than computational effects" (Kahneman and Tversky 1984: 343).

It is not hard to see how shifting attention to contextual cues often evokes new frames of reference. Indeed, framing only occurs because whole new evaluative frames are evoked by contextual cues (the descriptions of outcomes in the experiments of Kahneman and Tversky). Finally, because humans must process information serially and because frames are raised by contextual cues, it is most difficult for decision-makers to integrate utility functions across frames and be consistent across time. That is, a utility function can be quite coherent at one point in time because it is structured by one frame of reference. Similarly, at a second point in time, the decision-maker's utility function may be quite coherent but structured by a second frame. However, the two functions may be quite different, shattered by a shift between the two frames.

Serial shifting is fundamental to linking decision-making to broader social choices. Agenda theorists have noted that at certain times some

---

these activities were manipulations by House leaders that *ultimately failed* on the House floor vote.

policy topics literally leap from obscurity to the realm of serious consideration (Baumgartner and Jones 1993; Kingdon 1984; Cobb and Elder 1983). But what causes continued attention to one conflict dimension to the exclusion of others? And what causes a shift from one focus of conflict to a second? The individual decision-making model developed in this chapter has critical implications for this aspect of collective choice.

Social Choice and Shifting Attention

The standard social choice approach has assumed unchanging preferences on the part of decision-makers and has focused research attention on the manner in which these fixed preferences are translated into collective choices. Much progress has been made in understanding how political institutions may be manipulated to achieve leaders' ends, both where the preferences of followers are cyclical and no "equilibrium" social choice function exists, and when an equilibrium condition exists (known as the Concordet alternative).

But how does the model deal with change? People don't change their minds very much in the models; otherwise any established equilibrium would be upset. Moreover, if people changed their minds, then the preference aggregation problem would be far less important in democratic theory. Preferences are fixed. But fixed preference decision-makers may not be optimal performers, as Cohen and Axelrod (1984) have shown. Clarence Stone (1993) has argued that the world is so dynamic that fluidity in preferences is a necessity. These theorists, however, have a relatively restricted notion of preference, and a broader view such as that proposed by Stigler and Becker (1977) may avoid the problem of adjustment to changing reality.

In the fluid preference approach, it seems that decision-makers are subject to a change of mind every time the decisional context changes. Since context is notoriously slippery as a concept, we are left with a very difficult situation—unless we can do a better job of specifying "context." Surely context has much to do with decision frames; just as surely, preferences and attention frames are distinct (or at least may be treated as distinct for the purposes of analysis).

Important advantages accrue if we continue to assume fixed preferences but allow attention to those preferences to vary in time. Actually the most realistic approach would allow preferences to vary, mostly incrementally because they are firmly held, and attention to preferences to change sharply in response to changing circumstances. Established models of political choice already allow for variation in salience of evaluative dimensions across decision-makers (Ordeshook 1986: chap. 2). If we view preferences (or goals) as remaining relatively fixed while attention to those preferences or goals varies considerably, we can take advantage of the models developed for the analysis of differences among decision-makers in attentiveness to dimensions of choice.

In the standard rational choice model, conflicting preferences are allowed (and, indeed, assumed). Indifference curve analysis implies trade-offs among competing alternatives. Indifferences can be thought of as reflecting two marketplace goods (apples versus oranges, in the classic Economics 101 example). In politics, it could be applied to trade-offs between two candidates or two policy alternatives. These are what we have termed *direct preferences*. But the trade-offs can also refer to the underlying evaluative dimensions or goals that structure the actual, or realized, choice situation. These are the Stigler-Becker preferences of chapter 2. Conflicts between two direct preferences may often be resolved by the type of comparisons implied by indifference analysis. But for Stigler-Becker preferences, contradictions are often reconciled through selective attention. In the supercollider example, a legislator might like both extensive growth spending and a smaller public budget. The choice situation can force the trade-off, and in such a situation the differential attentiveness of the legislator to the basic dimensions of choice could dictate his or her vote.

Riker's Heresthetics

William Riker has noted that "the formal theorems about equilibrium reveal nothing about moving parts" (1990: 46). That is, formal political theory lacks dynamics. In an attempt to add dynamics, Riker (1986, 1990, 1993) distinguishes between situations where political leaders induce voters (in committees or in general elections) to change their ideal positions in issue-space, which he terms *rhetoric,* and situations where the leader alters the issue-space or other constraints in the voting situation to get voters to change their behavior. Riker terms the latter *heresthetics.* In such situations, leaders redefine issues by making salient dimensions of conflict that were previously latent.

Riker's approach derives directly from the indeterminacy of majority rule where more than one dimension of conflict is involved (1982:182–86). In a choice system composed of a single dimension of evaluation and decision-makers with single-peaked preference functions, the alternative at the median would result in equilibrium. In multiattribute choice systems, global equilibria can exist, but only under special conditions unlikely to be fulfilled in real choice situations. Indeed, McKelvey's agenda theorem proves the possibility of cycling throughout the issue-space

(Riker 1982:186–88). In general, then, there is no point in an issue-space that is guaranteed to provide an equilibrium. Under certain distributions of legislators, equilibrium can result, but these conditions are very restrictive. Because a one-dimensional issue-space does guarantee an equilibrium, if agenda-setters can change a one-dimensional conflict structure into a two-dimensional structure, they can strategically move motions around in the multidimensional space until they achieve a desired end. Therefore, Riker sees more possibilities of manipulation through the transformation of a one-dimensional issue-space to a multi-dimensional issue-space (1990: 53–54).[4]

This approach leads to a somewhat mechanistic view of the issue definition process in which leaders have considerable leeway in the process of definition in order to achieve their (fixed) aims. In the literature on systemic agenda setting, issue definition tends to be viewed as part and parcel of the political dialogue, with no individual having exclusive privilege to define the dimensions along which conflict proceeds, and with considerable indeterminacy and contingent strategic behavior (D. Stone 1988, 1989; Baumgartner 1987, 1989; Baumgartner and Jones 1993; see also Elder and Cobb 1983). Riker moves in the right direction in distinguishing between rhetoric and heresthetics, but he retains a far too mechanistic view of the process of issue definition. Agenda-setters cannot freely manipulate, because of the phenomenon of "cognitive twoness," which implies a complete shift from one evaluative dimension to another. So while it is possible for leaders to introduce a new dimension of evaluation, they may have difficulty controlling the "flow" from one dimension to another.

Issue Cycling and Attention

Riker's analysis of emerging dimensions of conflict stems from the *paradox of voting*, first noted by the French mathematician Concordet in the eighteenth century and rediscovered by Duncan Black in the 1950s.

4. Riker's examples tend to focus on a single move, in which conflict is shifted from one dimension to another, at least for a "swing" group of committee members. He implies that the introduction of a new dimension of conflict is abrupt, causing rapid shifts in outcomes. This would seem to come closer to accepting the serial shift and cognitive "twoness" than his formal analyses imply. He offers the example of the heresthetics of Senator Warren Magnuson in 1969. The issue concerned the transportation of nerve gas from U.S. military supplies in Japan across the state of Washington to a detoxification center in Oregon. The senator demanded Senate prerogatives in treaty negotiations, appendaging the nerve gas issue to the entirely distinct treaty. Because most senators cared little about the nerve gas issue, as their states were not involved, many supported Magnuson. The single move determined the outcome, with ten senators moving to Magnuson's position (Riker 1986).

Fundamentally, any voting scheme lacks an equilibrium with three or more voters in two or more dimensions. (Riker 1982 provides a full discussion.) The paradox appears in a somewhat different guise in Kenneth Arrow's attack on the existence of a general social welfare function. Unfortunately, as Arrow has demonstrated, no method of decision (short of a dictator) can guarantee the aggregation of citizen preferences transitively under all preference configurations, even if each citizen's preferences are transitive (Riker 1982: chap. 5). Table 4.1 gives an illustration of the issue cycling that may result from a majority voting system.

In spatial terms, the voters in table 4.1 do not have "single-peaked" preference functions. Suppose that we were to order the alternatives on a single dimension of choice, from x to y to z. Then voters A and B would have single-peaked preferences but voter C would not. C's preference function would be high for z, low for y, then high again for x; it would be dual-peaked.[5] The "single-peaked" problem can be transformed to a problem in which choice is multidimensional, as developed in chapters 2 and 3. This is certainly the normal state of affairs, at least if we view choices as generally involving multiple attributes (Davis, Hinich, and Ordeshook 1970). The cycling problem translated into a two-dimensional format is depicted in figure 4.1.

The voters may be connected by lines AB, AC, and BC. If the proposals x, y, and z are placed at the median of the lines AB, AC, and BC, then each proposal can attract two voters, thereby achieving a majority. This is because the median is the closest point that is equidistant between the

---

TABLE 4.1 Issue Cycling

Let a system consist of three voters (or voting blocks): A, B, and C. Let these voters choose among three competing alternatives: x, y, and z. Then it is possible that:

Voter	Preference Ordering
A	xPyPz
B	yPzPx
C	zPxPy

Then the willing proposal or alternative depends on the order of presentation. If the presentation is x versus y, then the winner versus z, z is the winner. If the presentation is z versus y, then the winner versus x, then x is the winner. But if the presentation is x versus z, then y, then y wins.

---

5. Of course, the order of x, y, and z is arbitrary. Placing the proposals in a different order just causes a different voter to have multiple-peaked preference functions; it does not change the nature of the problem.

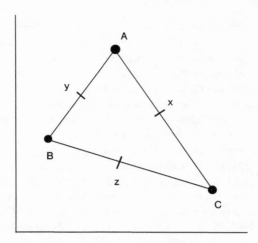

Fig. 4.1. The potential of issue cycling in two dimensions.

endpoints of the line. Hence the construction of majorities in such situations is dependent on the presentation of the alternatives, as before.

Interestingly, it is possible to conceive of the preference-cycling problem as affecting a single individual offered three alternatives which incorporate two attributes that he or she values at some level. Most people have experienced this "cycling in the head" as they try to come to a choice which involves alternatives that incorporate more than one attribute. This would happen if the alternatives all lay about on the same indifference curve in the multidimensional preference space (see fig. 2.2). Note that the noncompensatory decision-making model discussed in chapter 3 would negate such cycling by making one dimension prominent in the choice situation. This suggests that attention to preferences (in the Stigler-Becker sense of valued attributes) might be key in avoiding cycling.

Depicting preferences within a spatial structure involves using cardinal numbers, whereas Arrow's formulation relies solely on ordinal properties. Giving up generality allows for an important insight from the multidimensional framework in comparison to the single-dimensional dual-peaked preference representation. The attribute dimensions can be weighted by attentiveness. If the attribute dimensions are weighted similarly by all or most participants at any one point in time, then the problem of issue cycling can disappear. If a majority is focused on one dimension of choice, then the two-dimensional preference orderings of the voters will be projected on the single dimension, even if their two-dimensional preferences would imply differences, and hence open the possibility of cycling. This is illustrated in figure 4.2.

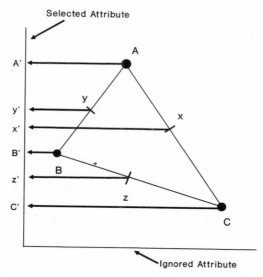

Fig. 4.2. The potential of issue cycling is ended when group attention focuses on one dimension of evaluation.

Note that the original preference orderings from table 4.1 cannot be fit on the one dimension, given the hypothetical distribution of voters and proposals presented in figure 4.1. Being forced to consider only one attribute when in actuality multiple attributes underlie the available alternatives may reorder preferences for the alternatives. In effect, limiting the debate to a single dimension constrains the patterns of choices that are available to decision-makers.[6] This example also shows why students of public choice generally view i-points and dimensional salience (as represented by elliptical indifference curves) as part and parcel of a unitary preference structure. When salience changes, *direct* preferences can change. Shifts in salience alone can cause a reordering of direct preferences. But *Stigler-Becker* preference structures need not change when saliences shift, as will become clearer below.

Collective shifts in attentiveness, which are probably common, can act to force choice along a single attribute dimension. To the extent that

6. Actually, we don't know how the hypothetical decision-makers would respond to the collapsing of their two-dimensional preference structures into one dimension. In figure 4.2, we assume that they would project their i-points perpendicularly onto the selected dimension. That probably would not happen. The selected dimension is actually the constrained choice dimension of chapter 2, with the choice dimension actually corresponding to the y-dimension. The projections would depend on the shape of the two-dimensional indifference curves.

collective shifts of attention occur, the discretion of leaders to alter out-comes by rearranging the presentation of alternatives is circumscribed. Indeed, the tendency of decision-makers to use limited dimensions of evaluation and to shift them episodically implies that much of leadership activity will be concentrated on highlighting the dimension that leaders believe will yield their preferred outcome. Much of the behavior of lead-ers in politics is consumed with changing the focus rather than changing minds. But the aim is not to be able to push proposals around in policy space. Rather, it is to cause a disjointed shift from one alternative to an-other. Moreover, it is not necessary for *all* decision-makers in a collectiv-ity to shift focus in a debate; oftentimes only a small block can alter out-comes. Hence leaders may devote inordinate effort to persuading those most sensitive to shifting frames of evaluation. This, however, reintro-duces the problem of aggregation, only it is attention that is being aggre-gated rather than preferences.

The Choice Dimension

The problem with the above analysis as it stands is that most choice dimensions are constrained, and therefore cannot be shifted to the Stigler-Becker axes, as is suggested in figure 4.2. Chapter 2 shows that the dimension of choice virtually never corresponds to the underlying attributes that structure the choice. In this section, I extend the analysis introduced above to the constrained choice situation initially discussed in chapter 2.

Let us return to the supercollider issue, assuming that an underlying dimension of choice structures the simple yes-no dichotomy that was of-fered legislators on the issue. The postulation of a continuous choice di-mension underlying this vote suggests that other alternatives could have been presented to the House on the supercollider, ranging from more to less supportive of the project. That this was indeed how the issue was perceived can be gleaned from the fact that the Eckart amendment was a vote to cut $450 of the $484 million allocated in the Appropriations Committee recommendation for the supercollider for Fiscal 1993. This was an identical amount to that allocated in Fiscal 1992, even though President Bush had requested $650 million. Hence the committee rec-ommendation was considerably less than the president's, and the Eckart amendment less than the committee's (but even the Eckart amendment left some funds for shutdown; many projects return from the grave when funeral costs are included in a budget bill).

Now we can depict the choice dimension using the tools of spatial analysis discussed in chapter 2 (see Davis, Hinich, and Ordeshook 1970;

Ordeshook 1986). Figure 4.3 is similar to figure 2.1, but now we are focusing explicitly on the supercollider choice. In figure 4.3, the yes and no votes are depicted on the underlying choice dimension but, for convenience in discussion, support for the supercollider has been labeled as the yes vote (even though it was actually a no vote on the Eckart amendment). We know that the seventy-nine legislators were "closer to" the pro-vote in 1991 but were "closer to" the anti-vote in 1992. (Recall that the pro-vote was exactly the same in monetary terms in the two years and that the anti-vote was essentially the same.) The locations of the ideal points for these legislators are arbitrary, because the vote would not suffice to reveal their exact preferences, but the diagram gives an interpretation consistent with the facts of the case. Utilities are depicted on the Y-axis, making the traditional single-peaked assumption. So I(a) can be interpreted as the *average* ideal point for the seventy-nine legislators in 1991 (although, of course, they would range between the origin and one-half the distance between the positions of the yes vote and the no vote). I(b) is the average ideal point on the choice dimension in 1992.

Looking at this diagram, it would seem that the legislators, for some reason, changed their preferences. They voted differently on the same choice set at two different points in time. One might think that they received new "information" that caused them to shift their preferences. This new information, in journalistic accounts, was probably the deficit situation. The problem with this interpretation is that the deficit situation was bad the year before. The objective "facts" of the situation had not

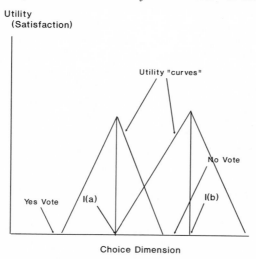

Fig. 4.3. The supercollider vote in one dimension.

changed very much. It is more likely that changes in the political context caused legislators to pay attention to this dimension of conflict.

An Embedded Choice Dimension

Spatial analyses of elections and other structured choice situations have generally assumed that the observed alternatives are drawn from more fundamental underlying choice dimensions (Davis, Hinich, and Ordeshook 1970; Ordeshook 1986). Analyses of electoral choice situations from survey data have confirmed that, indeed, electoral choice is structured by a limited number of dimensions of conflict (Weisberg and Rusk 1970). Dimensional analyses of legislative roll-call voting have also been successful in isolating a limited number of dimensions along which political conflict proceeds (Clausen 1967, 1973; Jones 1973; Poole and Rosenthal 1991).

However, the dimension of choice may not be identical to the dimensions of conflict that structure the legislative body. Indeed, any particular decision is almost certainly likely to be imperfectly correlated to the underlying dimensions of conflict that structure a body. If these dimensions of conflict are thought of as underlying generalized evaluative dimensions or goals, then spatial models of political conflict become general models of decision-making. This is consistent with a suggestion by Riker (1990: 57) to think of an alternative space as distinct from an outcome space. That is, decision-makers are presented with a set of alternatives. Generally, decision-makers are interested not so much in the set of alternatives as in the outcomes these alternatives presumably bring about.

Rather than viewing the choice and outcome spaces as distinct and separate, we might assume that the alternative, or choice, space is embedded in the outcome, or policy, space. The choice space is smaller than the outcome space in dimensionality; hence the alternative space can be defined in terms of the outcome space. This is another way of saying that any choice has multiple dimensions along which it can be evaluated. Generally, the axes of the choice space will be oblique to the axes of the policy or outcome space. This result implies that the choice space is correlated with dimensions of the policy or outcome space. Should the choice space collapse onto the outcome space, the alternatives are perfectly correlated with outcomes, and any change in alternatives will bring about a direct and proportional change in outcomes. Usually, however, by acting on the choice space, decision-makers know that they can affect the policy space, but each unit of change on the choice space will not yield an equivalent change in outcomes. Looking back at figure 2.4, we can see this notion depicted for a two-dimensional outcome space and a one-dimensional policy space.

Given the postulate of two "spaces," we may distinguish two situations. In the first, decision-makers know the relationship between the choice and policy spaces. In the second, they know that there exists a relationship but are unsure of its exact nature. This latter condition introduces an element of uncertainty (the relationship between alternatives and outcomes). It allows for more rhetorical play than the former condition, which is more amenable to the politics of issue definition and heresthetics. For the present, we assume that all actors see the relationship as the same but that they can evaluate the worth of the outcomes differently.

In many cases, the alternative space will be unidimensional, because the choices can be ordered from more to less along a single dimension. This pertains to many budget decisions and amendments to them, since budget decisions involve more or less money for a program or policy. Alternatives would also fall along a single dimension in cases of *structure-induced equilibria,* which impose issue-by-issue voting in a legislative body via the committee structure (Shepsle 1979). Structure-induced equilibria stem from the institutional factoring of decisions, assigning issues to committees such that there can exist no issue cycling. Transportation committees vote for transportation bills, even though mass transit would affect urban sprawl and environmental pollution as well as transit problems.

Predictive Mappings

Adopting the tactic of viewing the choice space as embedded in an outcome space allows us to take advantage of a theory of embedded dimensions developed in a somewhat different context—the *theory of predictive mappings* of Hinich and Pollard (1981) and Enelow and Hinich (1983, 1990; see also Enelow 1984). Enelow and Hinich ask us to consider an election in which multiple issue dimensions are involved and where candidates are placed in the minds of voters along a single ideological dimension. Then the major issue for analysis is how voters predict issue positions from their understanding of ideological differences among candidates.

Now it may be seen that the embedded choice dimension discussed here is completely analogous to the ideological dimension in the Enelow-Hinich theory of predictive mappings. Legislators must make inferences from the choice dimension to the evaluative dimensions in a manner that is mathematically similar to the Enelow-Hinich approach.[7] An important result from this analysis is that where voters have single-peaked preference functions on the issues and there are linear mappings between the issue dimensions and the ideological dimension, preferences on the ideological dimension are single-peaked. For most goals or evaluative dimensions, one adopts but a single position, and as one moves away from that goal-state he or she is less satisfied. But it is not obvious that single-peakedness holds for any actual choice dimension, composed as it is of bits of numerous evaluative dimensions.

This vantage point also underpins the work of Poole and Rosenthal (1991) on the structure of congressional voting. For them, roll-call votes are placed on a dimension that cuts through the ideological space. The ideological space structures conflict that is empirically observed on roll-call votes. If we think of the ideological dimensions as evaluative dimensions and the roll-calls as forced choices, then we are back to the model discussed above. Poole and Rosenthal write that their finding of a stable low-dimensional conflict space structuring congressional voting patterns "says nothing about how specific issues get defined in terms of the structure" (p. 229) and "how specific issues get mapped on the dimensions may change over time" (p. 232). But attentiveness to the underlying structure can also shift over time.

So we can see that there has been considerable work in political science that has viewed the actual choice situation as distinct from the goals that participants in politics have. This work includes studies of the ideological dimensions that separate the parties in elections (the realized choice) and the issues that voters are concerned about (the underlying Stigler-Becker preferences of voters). It also includes Riker's distinction between an alternative space (the actual choices) and an outcome space. Finally, it includes legislative studies where roll-calls are viewed as the alternatives, or realized choices, with the ideological orientations of legislators being the underlying goals. These seemingly diverse examples all can be reduced to the general model of choice we have been developing.

The Supercollider and the Serial Shift

Armed with these tools, let us return to the supercollider vote. There we might assume (with considerable justification from the journalistic accounts of the event) that the choice dimension was embedded in a two-

7. Enelow (1984) has developed a model in which legislative voting is conditioned on earlier votes such that there exists a linear mapping (forecast) from earlier to later votes, thus imposing consistency on legislative choice (also dealing seriously with cognitive limits in legislative choice). Enelow and Hinich (1990) show that this approach is mathe-

dimensional policy or outcome structure, one of which concerned deficit reduction and the other of which concerned public spending to stimulate economic growth. Clearly other considerations intruded, including the benefits generated from supercollider contracts (proponents had carefully constructed a network of suppliers in forty-five states). But the dimensions of conflict postulated here are as old as the debate between Hamilton and Jefferson concerning the limits of government. Nevertheless, it is important to remember that the particular policy content of the dimensions, as important as they are in this example, are not critical for the general analysis.

The choice dimension (funding for the supercollider) embedded in the two-dimensional policy or outcome structure is presented in figure 4. 4. The choice dimension is the same as in figure 4.3, but the figure presents only the situation in 1991. I/D2 (the ideal point in two dimensions) is the hypothesized average ideal point for the seventy-nine legislators who shifted positions in the two-dimensional structure. Now it is clear that the ideal point for the legislators in 1991, I(a), is the point at which the choice dimension is tangent to the smallest utility contour encircling I/D2. This is the closest distance between the choice dimension and the average ideal point, I/D2. Because the point of tangency, I(a), is closer to the yes vote than the no vote, the legislators voted to approve.

The choice dimension is depicted as a negative linear function in relation to the two goals. This indicates that the choice involves a structured trade-off between growth spending and limiting government spending. Hence it is similar to the standard budget constraint from microeconomic analyses of public policy (Stokey and Zeckhauser 1978). In the typical budget simplex situation, decision-makers may choose any point within the triangle formed by the possibility frontier and the two axes. They will choose a point on the frontier because to do otherwise would be a suboptimal choice. There are other reasons that the choice dimension may force a trade-off other than strict budgetary limits, however. Generally, Stimson (1991: 24) notes, "constant values can produce variable value trade-offs over time. In A vs. B we always value both A and B. But changing circumstance might well lead rational electorates to change the A/B cut point, how much A is to be sacrificed to gain how much B." Trade-offs can also be created by the institutional structure and by the manipulation of agendas by agenda-setters. In any model using the dimensions of public spending for growth and limited govern-

---

matically equivalent to the ideological predictive mapping model of Hinich and Pollard (1981).

ment as its outcome structure, a trade-off between the dimensions (and hence a downward-sloping choice dimension) is a strict necessity.

Figure 4.5 depicts a model of the voting situation in which legislators changed their minds. In this instance, they decided to move in the direction of *more* budget cutting, without wishing to sacrifice any growth spending. This would have the effect of shifting the average i-point from I(a)/D2 to I(b)/D2, and the preferred condition under constraint from I(a) to I(b). This moves the preferred position on the choice dimension in the direction of a no vote (and presumably closer to the no vote than the yes vote). Note also that because legislators were unwilling to forgo any growth spending, the position of tangency at I(b) is on a lower indifference curve than I(a) was. That is, their ideal point is further from any point on the choice dimension. By changing their minds, they are worse off than before—but, of course, that does not matter. If they changed their minds, they changed their minds, so that being worse off is a consequence of the real shift in preferences. Other changes of mind could yield a better outcome for decision-makers; the general point is that changing one's preferences in a structured choice situation changes utilities deriving from the choice.

Fixed Preferences, Varying Attention

So one way to account for the shift in vote between the two points in time is a change in preferences. Decision-makers do change their minds,

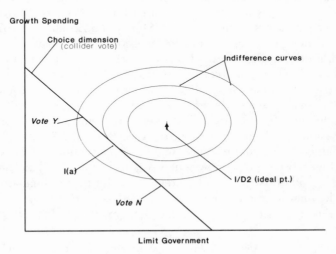

Fig. 4.4. The supercollider vote in two dimensions.

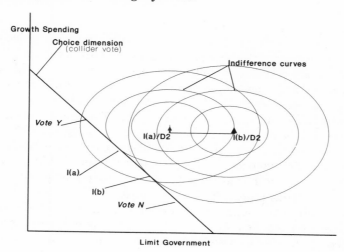

Fig. 4.5. A change of mind.

perhaps when new information is available. But the problem in decision-making is not so much the lack of information as its overabundance (Simon 1981: 167). This suggests that the structure of information is more important than its availability. Put otherwise, what is important is the information that the decision-maker attends to.

In examining shifts in attentiveness to conflict dimensions, the shape of the indifference curves of decision-makers is quite important. Circular indifference contours in multidimensional space imply indifference between the two dimensions, while elliptical curves imply that one dimension is more important or salient to the decision-maker (Ordeshook 1986: chap. 1). It takes a smaller change in the dimension parallel to the minor axis of the ellipse to move a legislator to a higher indifference curve. Hence it is the dimension associated with the minor axis that is more important to a decision-maker.

The axes of the utility ellipses may be parallel to the policy axes, as depicted in figures 4.4–4.6, or they may be oblique to the axes (see fig. 1 of Enelow and Hinich 1983: 438). The latter would imply that the evaluative dimensions are inseparable (or at least linked). The model developed in this chapter requires that evaluative dimensions be separable, and hence requires indifference curves that are parallel to the outcome axes, because preferences are allowed to be contradictory. (See appendix A for a discussion.)

So spatial choice models have been developed that allow for differences in the salience of outcome dimensions among decision-makers.

That is, decision-makers can evaluate some outcome dimensions as more important than others and these evaluations may differ among decision-makers. We are interested here in temporal variations in salience. Let us now explore a model that treats preferences as fixed, as in the social choice models, and allows attention to the conflict structure to vary. This situation is depicted in figure 4.6. There, two sets of indifference ellipses are superimposed on a single ideal point (I/D2). The two sets of indifference curves can be interpreted as the averages for the seventy-nine legislators who voted differently in 1991 and 1992. The ellipses labeled "A" represent the 1991 vote and have their minor axes parallel to the Y-axis, which represents the Hamiltonian position of using public spending to promote economic progress. This implies that the legislators were more sensitive to variations along this dimension than along the Jeffersonian, limited government dimension (the X-axis). At time 2, the legislators have become most sensitive to the limited government dimension; this is represented by the "B" ellipse.

Note that the result of this approach is to shift the ideal point projected on the choice dimension (the point of tangency) from I(a) to I(b). Here this implies a shift from a yes to a no vote. The vote has changed even though the i-point has not, and we have assumed no strategic manipulation such as altering the presentation of alternatives. The only aspect of the standard spatial choice model that we have relaxed is the (unstated) assumption that indifference curves hold their shape for indi-

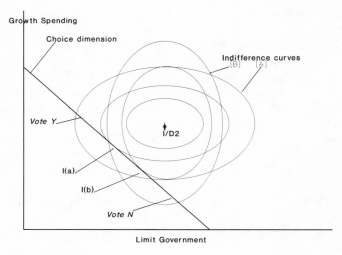

Fig. 4.6. A change of focus.

viduals over time, thus allowing for variation in attention to the structure of the choice situation.[8]

Susceptibility to the Serial Shift

In any group of policymakers, there will exist a different propensity to shift frames of reference during a policy debate. The heresthetic device of attempting to get opponents to focus on a new dimension of conflict may work well with some participants but fail to convince others. Even though there can exist a powerful contagion effect when a new dimension is introduced, not all individuals will be swept away.

In the case of the supercollider votes, most legislators were consistent in their voting patterns. Almost 45 percent voted in favor both times, while 33.6 percent voted against both times. Most of those who shifted moved against the project, but fifteen legislators actually voted in favor in 1992 after voting against in 1991. What are the factors that made some legislators more sensitive to the new issue frame than others? It is easy to examine some standard factors, such as region or party affiliation. Table 4.2 presents the supercollider votes by the region of the district that the legislator represented. Clearly there were regional differences; Southern representatives were both more supportive of the project generally and less likely to shift their votes against the project. But the more dramatic differences were between Texas representatives and their colleagues in other regions; the delegation was both highly supportive and

---

8. The model developed above fits a constrained choice situation where the actual choice falls along a single dimension and the alternatives offered occupy two points on the choice dimension. An underlying assumption of this is that decision-makers prefer the choice point closest to their multidimensional i-point (weighted by the attention or salience coefficients). But what they get is a dichotomous choice on the continuous choice dimension. So a second assumption is added: that a decision-maker will minimize the distance between the preferred point on the choice dimension and the actual offered choice. (See Coughlin and Hinich 1984.)

In the case of circular indifference contours, this is not an important distinction. The choice dimension is perpendicular to the decision-maker's actual i-point at the point of tangency to the indifference circle. This means that the distance between the preferred actual choice positions and the i-point is shorter than the distance between the i-point and the less-preferred alternative. In the case of elliptical indifference contours, however, the assumption is not so trivial, because the preferred position on the choice dimension is not perpendicular; hence the (simple) distance between the i-point and the preferred alternative can be larger than the distance to the rejected alternative. But the weighted distance will be less, and we know that preferences on the choice dimension will be single-peaked where preferences on the basic evaluative dimensions are linear mappings onto the choice dimension (Enelow and Hinich 1990).

TABLE 4.2 **Supercollider Votes and Region**

| | Region of Representative | | | |
Votes[a]	Non-South	South	Texas	Total
Both for	106	63	26	195 (44.8%)
	(35.4%)	(57.8%)	(96.3%)	
Against to for	11	4	0	15 (3.4%)
	(3.7%)	(3.7%)	(0.0%)	
For to against	61	17	1	79 (18.2%)
	(20.4%)	(15.6%)	(3.6%)	
Both against	121	25	0	146 (33.6%)
	(40.5%)	(22.9%)	(0.0%)	
Total	299	109	27	435 (100.0%)
	(100.0%)	(100.0%)	(100.0%)	

Note: Tau-b: $-.27$; gamma: $-.50$; chi-sq. (9 df): 48.94.

[a]Votes indicate support for supercollider funding in 1991 and 1992. The actual votes in both years were on amendments to cut funding. Pairs for or against are tabulated as if the representative actually voted. "South" includes the states of the old Confederacy, less Texas.

virtually inoculated against shifting. The fact that the project would be built in north Texas was not irrelevant to this inoculation. Party affiliation, however, was not predictive of susceptibility to the shift; 18.7 percent of Democrats and 17.4 percent of Republicans shifted, and Republicans were generally only slightly more supportive of the project overall.[9]

In many policymaking situations, the introduction of new evaluative criteria can cause decision-makers to reevaluate the bases of their choices, causing the potential for destabilizing choice reversals. Such re-evaluation need not inflict all involved in a choice. Even where a rela-

9. A somewhat more complete analysis can be performed using regression estimations. First, we may assume that the voting choices can be ordered from most to least supportive. The first vote against and the second for is rated as more supportive than the first for and the second against, because from the supporters' viewpoint, the second pattern was more damaging. Then we regress region and party on the support score, yielding the following regression estimate:

$$Y = 1.63 - 0.35 \text{ REGION} - 0.09 \text{ PARTY} - 1.17 \text{ TEXAS}$$
$$t: (21.38) (-3.14) \qquad (-0.82) \qquad (-4.35)$$
$$R^2 = 0.10$$

It is generally difficult to predict support for the supercollider from the variables included, with explained variance at only 10 percent, but note that regional affiliation and being a member of the Texas delegation are statistically significant while party affiliation is not.

For another study of voting shifts in Congress, see Leogrande and Brenner (1993). These authors report significant conversion of legislators over the very similar votes in the 1980s on aid to the Nicaraguan "Contras."

tively small number reevaluate, however, the outcome can be reversed. Whether such a reevaluation is to be lauded as exemplary of the kind of flexibility needed in open and democratic decision-making, or excoriated as weak and unprincipled depends on one's vantage point. It is sufficient for the present to note important interindividual differences in susceptibility to a decision frame shift in a choice situation.

"Broken" Utility Functions and the Aggregation of Attention

Changes in choice can be a function of shifts in dimensional salience rather than any changes in preferences, which are more fundamental. That is, if one keeps preferences of decision-makers fixed and allows attention to the dimensions of conflict to vary, then voting choices can be changed. This happens because changes in attentiveness shift the point of tangency of the decision-makers' indifference curve and the choice dimension.

There are two major implications of this, one at the individual level and one at the level of the collective decision-making unit. First, attentiveness can destabilize individual preference functions. Along each dimension of evaluation, decision-makers in this model have well-behaved preference functions: they are well ordered and no cycling is possible. At any one point in time, preferences are also well ordered for a constrained choice situation in multidimensional issue-space because of the predictive mapping theorem of Hinich and Pollard. Preferences are complete and transitive (Ordeshook 1986: 12). But between two time points, a shift in relative attentiveness to the dimensions can cause a reordering of preferences. Across time, utility functions may be "broken" by the intrusion of attentiveness. Within the same general preference structure for a decision-maker, choices at two points in time can be quite inconsistent. Decision-makers are not being irrational; in this model they are still maximizers. They are just incorporating new information, and they are doing so without really reevaluating their underlying policy preferences.

The collective implication is this: collective choice may have as much to do with the aggregation of attentiveness as with the aggregation of preferences. The sensitivity of outcomes to agenda manipulation where preferences are structured multidimensionally is well known. Equilibria of preference are dependent on the workings of institutions, including the structure of committees and the order of proposal presentation. So preference aggregation, and hence majority rule, is dependent on institutional structure. Now we may see a second, critical source of instability: shifts in attentiveness to issue dimensions. Attentiveness itself can be organized through political institutions, and H. Simon (1977: 159) has studied what he calls "attention directing structures" in business organizations. These parts of organizations serve to focus attention on one part of the environment and monitor it for the decision-maker. In a similar vein, McCubbins and Schwartz (1984) note that oversight that relies on interest groups to raise the importance of issues, a mode they term "fire alarm oversight," can be "rational" for Congress.

At base, the key question is how often the attentiveness shift occurs and, when it occurs, whether it changes outcomes. In the case of the supercollider, the shift can account for the change in outcomes between the two votes, but the structure of the institution allowed legislative leaders to use their control of the agenda at conference committee time to overcome the shift. After the favorable Senate vote, House leaders appointed conferees supportive of the project. The funding was buried in the comprehensive budget for energy and water projects, and the House could vote only on the package. Because of the complexities, one can never rule out strategic voting on the original bill, with supporters voting to oppose in order to gain "political cover" on the deficit bill, strongly suspecting that funding would be restored later in the process. Nevertheless, one can infer that the structure of the political situation changed between the two collider funding votes if political cover were needed on the second vote but not on the first. Even this was not enough to save the project. In 1993, opponents used the rules to bind the conference committee, eliminating the project.

There was also strategic action on the bill that ultimately passed in 1992. Senate Democrats added a provision banning nuclear testing starting in 1996. President Bush and his national security advisers strongly opposed the ban. Rather than veto the bill, however, the president accepted the ban with only minor modifications. His reasoning centered on the supercollider funding: a veto would have given opponents the opportunity to attack the project anew (see Rosenthal 1992). So while the shift in this instance was locally destabilizing, it was not globally disruptive in 1992. But opponents overcame all of these defensive maneuvers by leadership in 1993.

At any rate, the interaction of shifting foci of attention and institutional constraints is fundamentally an empirical question, not an analytical one. There seems to be no mechanism that can push legislatures toward equilibrium in the face of the shift.

Conclusions

This chapter has examined a relatively rare situation: the one in which decision-makers choose differently on the same set of alternatives at two points in time. But this is only a device to illuminate far more important processes in politics: situations in which the decisional context changes even as institutional choice procedures continue as they have in the past. It is easy to see that whether the choices available are the same or different is trivial.

The chapter has unified certain known characteristics of human decision-making, and in particular the necessity of attending to issues serially, with the well-developed formal spatial approach to voting. First, following a suggestion by Riker, I have introduced a distinction between the choice space and the outcome or policy space, and have considered the choice space to be embedded in the outcome space. The choice space is thus imperfectly related to the outcome space even under conditions of certainty. One may view the outcome space as *goals;* the choice space then often forces trade-offs among goals. In many cases, the choice space will be one-dimensional, because it involves more or less of a policy. The policy itself, however, is structured by multidimensional goals (the outcome space). Decision-makers must infer how a policy dimension is relevant to their goals; this problem has been studied formally by social choice theorists Melvin Hinich, Walker Pollard, and James Enelow in their theory of predictive mappings.

Second, I have allowed the salience of dimensions to vary temporally for a single decision-maker and have modeled this by changes in the shape of the indifference curves of the decision-maker. Using differences in the shape of indifference curves among decision-makers to model variations in dimensional salience is common practice. What is different here is conceiving the possibility of changes in salience across time. In effect, then, I have taken the standard social choice preference structure consisting of preferences, represented by axes in geometric space, and preference-saliences, represented by utility curves that depict the trade-offs among the preferences, and allowed them to vary separately in time. I treat preferences as relatively fixed, at least in the short-run, but salience as subject to variable shifts. The advantages include the relative ease with which the approach models choice reversals, and the ease with which the modified social choice model can incorporate findings from empirical decision-making and information-processing studies. This means that utility functions can be "broken" temporally; that is, they are reordered by the shift in focus. This happens because evaluative dimensions are differently weighted in the judgment process at the two points in time, even though the ideal point remains fixed.

In general, an individual-level shift in attentiveness to preferences must be communicated in order to affect a collective choice. Hence the communication of structure occurs when new dimensions of evaluation are inserted into a political debate. This communication of structure is substitutive and noncompensatory, and as a consequence is not well described by a marginalist information model. But communication among decision-makers does not mean that all decision-makers will be captivated by the contagion of the communication of attention to the new dimension. There will often remain powerful interindividual differences in attention shifts, as was the case in the supercollider vote.

Peter Ordeshook, after comparing preferences for angel food cake and a Bach prelude, notes that the comparison seems rather silly and is problematic not because of any failure of rational assumptions about preferences but because "the example fails to specify a decision context" (Ordeshook 1986: 12). What kind of political theories can be built if the theorist always has to specify decisional contexts in an ad hoc manner? Context, after all, is always changing. Moreover, if we really do believe in overarching utility functions, such comparisons should be handled with ease. That we feel uncomfortable with Ordeshook's example speaks to the powerful influence of context on decision-making.

Incorporating attention into models of political choice is certainly more consonant with empirical findings. First, because attention tends to shift episodically rather than gradually, this model of decision-making fits the findings from studies of policy agendas better than a model that requires changing policy preferences. Second, it captures a central tenet of the issue-definition literature, that the distribution of winners and losers in a conflict situation often changes when new issue-definitions are proposed. Now we can see how this might work at the level of the individual decision-maker. Finally, this approach suggests a change in our understanding of the concept of policy mood (or perhaps how we might explain policy moods). Moods can be a function of changing preferences, or they might be a function of attention shifts from one dimension of conflict to another. Such an approach could aid in understanding changes in electoral behavior and speak to the debate concerning the rationality of the voter.

5 Raising and Focusing Attention in the Mass Public

> "Do you know Haggarty?"
> "No."
> "Have you heard of him?"
> "No."
> "Ben never mentioned him to you?"
> "No. I told you. I've never heard of him."
> "Forgive me. Sometimes an answer can vary with a context, if you follow me."
> I didn't. — JOHN LeCARRE, The Secret Pilgrim

In research on mass publics, the notion of contradictory attitudes toward public policies is well established. Political scientists have puzzled over the apparent contradiction between the majority of Americans' adopting generally tolerant perspectives on civil liberties and rejecting support for free speech and assembly for specific groups; between their adopting a conservative ideological position and wanting increased spending for all sorts of public programs; and between their wanting low taxes and wanting increased public spending (Bennett and Bennett 1990; Free and Cantril 1967). In perhaps the most influential line of research in mass political behavior, Philip Converse noted that considerable response instability existed in responses to fixed public opinion questions and that this instability was due to the lack of structure in mass belief systems. He backed up his assertion with detailed analysis of open-ended questions, finding few conceptual referents. Hence he argued that most Americans had few meaningful beliefs and that what beliefs they had were ill structured (1964).

In large part because of these findings, public opinion polling led to a cynical view of the mass public and its commitment to preserving democracy. Public opinion polling suggests that the mass public is untutored in the constitutional bases for government, is not knowledgeable about current political events, and sometimes seems prone to adopting undemocratic policy positions. In the minds of some political theorists, democracy is protected more by political elites who participate at high rates and understand the basic framework of democracy than to the mass public to which it was entrusted. To many, modern opinion findings give support to the suspicions of the authors of the Constitution that public participation would be a useful counterpoise to autocracy but would not be a viable mechanism of governance. Data never speak with complete clarity on any subject, and the position that modern public opinion research supported a pessimistic view of the average voter as not particularly capable of political reasoning has been questioned by such scholars as V. O. Key. Nevertheless, only recently has a more benign view of the mass public begun to prevail in empirical studies (Popkin 1991; Page and Shapiro 1992; Sniderman, Brody, and Tetlock 1991).

Bypassed in this debate was a major quandary: if in fact the typical American held contradictory attitudes about politics and public policies, how were these contradictions resolved? Perhaps they need not be. Zaller and Feldman (1992: 609) write that "for most people, for most of the time, there is no need to reconcile or even recognize their contradictory reactions to events and issues." In effect, Zaller and Feldman accept the existence of what they term a "fundamentally ambivalent public" (p. 611). They argue that this ambivalence toward most political objects accounts for the response instability that is observed in public opinion research. The typical public opinion questionnaire frames issues in ways that structure the ambivalence, calling forth particular aspects of the attitudes people hold on political objects.[1]

It is unlikely that the mass public differs in any meaningful way from elites in holding contradictory preferences. As Margolis (1987: 221) notes, "Every reasonably sophisticated person realizes that he holds inconsistent beliefs." It may be that elites are more willing to acknowledge the constraints on choice, but it is unlikely that underlying political preferences differ so drastically as some students of public opinion suggest. Indeed, having contradictory preferences across policy domains is fundamental to the decisional model explicated in this book, and chapter 4 illustrated how even sophisticated decision-makers can look inconsistent when they move from one evaluative dimension to another in making choices. While the politically active may well have superior knowledge about politics in comparison to the less involved, both groups of citizens are subject to changes in evaluative frames and the seeming inconsistencies in decision-making that follow.

1. Perhaps because the study of mass political behavior has been framed by the issue of belief system structure, the issue of response instability has been a core concern of researchers. Yet instability can be overstated. Zaller and Feldman (1992: 581) present data from the 1980 National Election Studies Panel Study conducted in January and June of 1980 that, of the individuals who wanted cuts in health and education in January, only 53 percent kept the same position. But most of the "inconsistents" moved to a "middle" position or were unsure. Only 11 percent had moved to a "keep spending same" position. Parenthetically, Zaller and Feldman's use of all categories and percentagizing on the corner inflates the impression of disarray in attitude reporting.

Issue Frames

Shanto Iyengar (1991: 11) has written that "people are exquisitely sensitive to contextual cues when they make decisions, formulate judgments, or express opinions. The manner in which a problem of choice is 'framed' is a contextual cue that may profoundly influence decision outcomes." Framing deals with the salience of certain aspects of the decision-making situation. Psychologists Kahneman and Tversky (1985) have shown that choices between outcomes involving risk can be altered by changing the language in which equivalent choices are described. Framing is an important concept but, employed alone, suggests that outcomes can be altered willy-nilly by shifting the frame of the issue. That is, without specifying exactly how frames affect outcomes, we are left with an infinitely malleable public.

One avenue of attack is the accessibility bias, discussed in chapter 3. This suggests that human judgment is strongly affected by the accessibility of information on the topic, because people only retrieve small portions of information. This is kind of an "off the top of their heads" approach to making decisions. Easily accessible "frames" are more likely to be used to understand issues than those that require more thought to recover. Iyengar (1991: 131) argues that the mass media supplies such accessible information, and that accounts for the power of the media in influencing opinion. This approach also may account for response instability in opinion questionnaires (Zaller and Feldman 1992) and would seem to imply a great deal of instability in preferences in the mass public, both individually and collectively (the latter because of the pervasiveness of the mass media in modern society).

In the case of mass publics, it may be fruitful to focus on the role of varying attention to preferences as a mechanism that human decision-makers use to integrate contradictory preferences or attitudes toward political objects. That is, it is quite possible that public attitudes are consistent within domains (a point that Iyengar 1991: 127 argues; see also Iyengar 1990) but are contradictory between them. Integration may occur through variations in attention or salience among domains (or, more correctly, variability in attentiveness may allow them to exist in logical contradiction without much felt dissonance). This would not deny the power of framing; it would simply suggest that much framing in politics occurs through episodic shifts in attentiveness to reasonably well understood political predilections. This approach also would lead one to hold considerable reservations about accessibility biases. Contradictory preferences and shifting attention would imply choice instability without adding the accessibility notion; *any* incoming information could potentially cause a shift to a new evaluative dimension that would subsequently dominate decision-making.

This tactic for understanding decision-making in the mass public is consistent with the direction of work of Sniderman and his colleagues at Stanford University (Sniderman, Brody, and Tetlock 1991). Basing their work on the decision-making theories of Simon and Kahneman and Tversky, these scholars see decision-making by voters as being dominated by several heuristic devices that substitute for the lack of information about politics and that work to integrate political belief systems. The Stanford scholars do not deal with attention shifts, but I will suggest in this chapter that the tendency to make episodic shifts in attentiveness to political objects is a major heuristic in mass publics and that these shifts in attentiveness have policy-relevant implications.

General shifts in attentiveness imply changes in the *salience* of issues (Rabinowitz, Prothro, and Jacoby 1982). There are many reasons that issue salience can change over time. One reason is that the underlying facts of a situation can change. People may become attentive to the issue of crime because the probability of being victimized has, in fact, increased. In other cases, the "facts" have not changed but the meaning of the fact has changed for the voter. Edwards and his colleagues point to the unemployment rate as an economic variable whose meaning for voters has changed over time because of unemployment insurance and increases in the percentage of women and children in the rate (Edwards, Mitchell, and Welch 1992). In many cases, voters react to events that are played out by elected officials and other political elites. That is, election campaigns or policy activities of policymakers serve to focus attention on issues or values that previously were not emphasized. In situations where issue salience has changed, we may have a change in voter choice with little or no change in underlying preferences.

President Bush and Drugs

The phenomenon of changing issue salience in the absence of changes in preferences can be most easily seen in the case of so-called *valence* issues. These are issues on which the overwhelming number of voters have a single position. Prevailing opinion is so strong that no opposing position seems possible. For a politician in an election to decry crime does not lead an opponent to defend it. Valence issues are important because politicians often link the raising of an issue to a policy solution; a crime wave demands harsher penalties. Should voters respond and become attentive to crime, we would not normally say that they have changed their preferences on crime policies. At one level, we recognize this. At another, however, journalists and even some political scientists talk about "mood swings" and "shifts in public opinion" as if something very definitive has occurred. In reality, a shift in salience may have occurred, with no changes in preferences about politics and policies. As we have seen in earlier chapters, this distinction is important, because attentiveness shifts more rapidly than do preferences, yet outcomes can be changed by attention shifts alone.

Shifts in salience do occur and can be measured through public opinion polling. For more than half a century, the Gallup polling organization has queried the American public on its conception of the "most important problem" facing the nation.[2] In recent years, the problem of illicit drugs has occupied a major place in this measure of voter attentiveness. Drug abuse is a classic valence issue; while there are individuals who defend the unregulated use of mind-altering drugs, most of the American public opposes their use. (That alcohol is not similarly treated indicates the cultural basis of valence issues.) Figure 5.1 depicts changes in the salience of the issue of drug abuse during the period 1987–92. Note the increase in attentiveness after the election of George Bush in 1988. In his campaign, President Bush initially gave high profile to the drug problem, and he moved aggressively on that front after his election. In his first major television address on September 5, 1989, he announced his "war on drugs."

After the speech, television coverage of the problem increased eightfold (Barrett 1990) and polls indicated that drugs were rated as the most important problem facing the nation by almost two-thirds of Americans. Then the salience of the issue began to slip and was at 10 percent by early 1991—approximately where it had been during the 1988 election campaign. A peak in awareness of the drug problem was caused primarily by presidential attention to it.

It is likely that the rise in awareness of the problem did not correspond to changes in the facts of abuse. Studies of reported drug use pointed not to a rising problem but to a declining one. Drug use in the general population and among high school students had been declining since the late 1970s (National Institute on Drug Abuse 1989; Treaster 1991). In 1989, a greatly publicized cocaine scare occurred, particularly around the use of "crack" cocaine. Yet reported cocaine use had been declining since 1985. However, arrests for drug-related crimes and cocaine-based emergency room admissions were increasing, and the latter indicator had increased dramatically. It is likely that these indicators

2. The wording of the question presumes that there is a "major problem," although "none" is treated as an acceptable answer by Gallup coders.

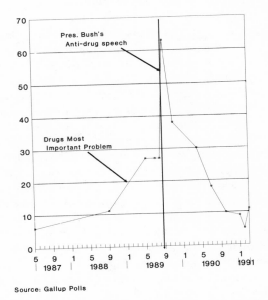

Source: Gallup Polls

Fig. 5.1. Drugs as the "most important problem facing the United States."

were affected by the national focus on the drug problem, which included funding for police activities and for monitoring systems. The divergence in the data led William Bennett, President Bush's "drug czar," to declare that two drug problems existed: a general "casual user" one, which was improving, and a "heavy user," or addict, problem, which was worsening. At any rate, the evidence solidly pointed to a generally improving drug abuse situation, not a worsening one.

Neither is it likely that public preferences for policy action had changed very much during this brief period. Mayer (1992: 132, 392) shows that attitudes toward drug usage changed solidly between the early 1970s and the mid-1980s, first in a liberal then a conservative direction after the mid-1970s. In 1973, the National Opinion Research Center (NORC) at the University of Chicago reported that 80 percent of the public opposed legalization of marijuana. That fell to a low of 67 percent in 1978; by 1986 those opposing had reached 80 percent again, with little change in the late 1980s. Compare these changes with the shifts in attentiveness documented in figure 5.1. Changes in attentiveness toward the drug problem, then, shifted dramatically during the early Bush years, a change that was far more abrupt than changes either in policy preferences or in the severity of the problem. (Indeed, the percentage favoring legalization of marijuana was not changing during the period.)

Public Attentiveness in Parallel Publics

The drug policy example may be an extreme case, because of the attention that the Bush administration directed at it. So we need a more comprehensive look at changes in attentiveness to problems over time, and a comparison with changes in preferences. The task is complicated because we don't have studies that compare attention and preferences for *individuals;* hence we must rely on comparisons within the aggregate of citizens. This is an important limitation, because it is possible that any stability in preferences (or attentiveness) is underlain by considerable offsetting shifting on the part of voters. We do have evidence of considerable preference instability in panel studies conducted by the National Election Studies (NES), but it is possible that response instability may be overstated and in any case will be strongly affected by the wording of questions, which have the unfortunate effect of stressing context.[3]

Given this caveat, it is nevertheless well worthwhile to study collective attentiveness and collective preferences as they move through time. At any point in time, a considerable variety of politically relevant topics may be on the minds of voters collectively, even if any single voter is troubled by only a very circumscribed set of concerns. When asked which of these are most important, different individuals often give different answers. So people do not always view problems similarly, even when critical events serve to focus policymaking attention. A poll taken during the 1991 Persian Gulf War registered only 41 percent of the American public as rating the war, international trade, or any other aspect of foreign affairs as most important. Over 30 percent were concerned with the economy and 10 percent remained concerned about drugs and crime.

What accounts for differences among individuals in attentiveness to politically relevant topics? At least three possibilities exist. In the first place, citizens more attuned to politics may be more sensitive to changes in the prevailing political winds. That is, political information may account for variations in attentiveness. Second, social location may account for differential attentiveness to political objects. Working-class individu-

---

3. Modern question wording by the NES thus inflates the impression of inconsistency. In order to be "realistic," researchers ask such questions as: "Some people think the government should provide fewer services, even in areas such as health and education, in order to reduce spending. Others feel it is important for the government to continue services it now provides even if it means no reduction in spending. Where would you place yourself on this scale, or haven't you thought about this?" This asks for the use of two fundamental evaluative dimensions that are firmly rooted in the culture: government spending for worthy causes versus limiting government. In such situations, attentiveness to the underlying dimension can easily shift answers.

als or women or blacks may perceive different problems than do the middle class or men or whites. Third, partisan commitment may color the perception of public problems. Republicans may be more sensitive to problems of social control than are Democrats, for example.

While these three reasons for differential perceptions of problems seem distinct, they are not so distinct empirically. That is, the less educated tend to occupy lower-class occupations and are more likely to identify with the Democratic party. Nevertheless, we can examine differences in perceptions of policy-relevant problems among these parallel publics (Page and Shapiro 1992), as they have left their traces through time in the public opinion polls.[4]

We first examine differences in attentiveness to problems by levels of education, the "great differentiator" in public opinion studies (Sniderman, Brody, and Tetlock 1991). Education generally differentiates among individuals both because it fixes a class location in the modern, information-based economy and because studies show educational level to be the variable most closely associated with political knowledge and participation. Because our major interest is shifts in attentiveness, we plot the breakdowns across time for all Gallup polls asking the "most important problem" question from mid-1989 through late 1993.[5] Examining figure 5.2, we see that the percentage of Americans rating the economy as the most important problem moved from around 20 percent in mid-1990 to 60 percent in mid-1992. Two aspects of this graph are noteworthy. First, differences in attentiveness by educational level are trivial. That is, educational level does not discriminate among individuals in their attentiveness to the economy as a major problem. Second, educational classes move in tandem in response to shifting saliences of problems. That is, there are generic shifts toward and away from attentiveness to policy-relevant problems.

4. In the tabulations below, I have combined categories used by the Gallup polling organization in order to group items consistently and to allow general comparisons across extended periods of time. I combined comments on the economy, recession, poverty, and inflation into a general category on the economy. Drugs, crime, and social unrest were combined into a category labeled "social control." All references to war, foreign aid, and foreign trade were placed in the category "foreign affairs."

In the figures, "grade school" means individuals with a grade school education or less, usually only between 5 and 6 percent of the sample. "High school" means individuals with more than a grade school education, but with no college or higher educational attainment. This category is usually about 52 percent of the sample. "College" means at least some college and runs about 42 percent of the respondents. The rest refused to answer or didn't know.

5. The studies were conducted with the support of the Center for Presidential Studies at Texas A&M University.

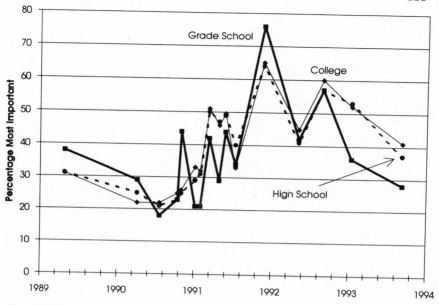

Fig. 5.2. Most important problem: the economy (all mentions).

Similarly, variability in the perception of foreign affairs as a major problem varies greatly (due to the Persian Gulf War) but education does not differentiate attentiveness to the problem. Citizens of all educational levels, on average, moved in tandem. Issues of social control (drugs, crime, social unrest) were only slightly more complex: there were some differences among educational levels, but this variability was less pronounced than temporal variability. Here concern with issues of social control seem to have been pushed off the public agenda first by the Persian Gulf War, then by economic performance.

If we examine figure 5.3, which tabulates the proportions of people most concerned with the federal deficit, we do find differences among educational levels. In mid-1990, the deficit was primarily an issue of college-educated individuals. A quarter of them saw the deficit as most important, but only 6 percent of grade-school-educated citizens did. By late 1991, as the deficit was expanding at an increasing pace in a deteriorating economy, more educated Americans joined the less educated in dismissing the deficit as the major issue. So we see that, in general, educational groups move in tandem as particular problems wax and wane in policy salience. Even though it is unlikely that economic changes affect citizens of different educational levels equally, the groups become attentive to economic problems simultaneously, or at least they have during the early

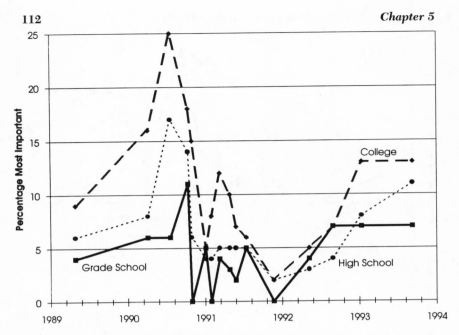

Fig. 5.3. Most important problem: the federal deficit (by education).

1990s. Furthermore, attentiveness to economic problems does not vary much among educational classes for any one year.

Other aspects of social location may differentiate individuals in their attentiveness to national problems. If we classify citizens by race, by sex, or by party affiliation, we see that in no case does social location affect attention to the economy as a national problem. In each case, shifting concerns over the economy from mid-1990 through mid-1992 vastly overwhelm any differences in social location or partisan affiliation.

For other issues, social location does matter. Women and blacks are marginally more attentive to foreign affairs and to issues of social control (crime and drugs). These differences among groups are considerably less pronounced than shifts across time, however. Women and blacks are significantly less attentive to the federal deficit as a national problem, as are Democrats generally. These differences are strong and persistent; as figure 5.4 shows, blacks were almost completely indifferent to the deficit during the early 1990s.

Finally, women and blacks are attentive to different aspects of the economy. If we divide economic problems into variable or business-cycle mentions, on one hand, and structural aspects of economic distress, on the other, we find that women and blacks are far more sensitive to the latter. As figure 5.5 indicates, changes in attentiveness to poverty (and

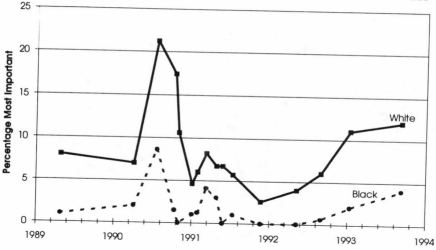

Fig. 5.4. Most important problem: the federal deficit (by race).

hunger) as national problems shift over time for all social groups, but the difference between men and women is persistent. Note, however, that attentiveness to poverty among women and blacks does not change in the same manner as does attentiveness to general economic problems. It seems that attentiveness to business-cycle economic problems pushes concerns for structural aspects of poverty off the agenda, even for those groups most sensitive to them.

Issues do differentiate social groups; blacks and women are more attentive to problems of drugs and crime and are less cognizant of the federal deficit as a national problem, whereas the college-educated find the deficit more troublesome. Moreover, women and blacks tend to focus more on structural economic issues than do men and whites. Generally, however, these differences among social groups are overwhelmed by shifts in attentiveness to problems over time. Party affiliation fails to distinguish substantially on almost all issues, and education does not distinguish attentiveness for most issues.

For almost all issues, changes in perceptions of national problems temporally are far more pronounced than are cross-sectional differences among social groupings. For the economy, foreign affairs, and social control, social groups move in tandem. Attention shifts tend to be generic. Iyengar and Kinder (1987: chap. 5) offer experimental evidence that helps explain these findings. They write: "When problems flare up and capture the attention of the media, agenda-setting effects show up most immediately among those directly affected by the problem . . . But if cov-

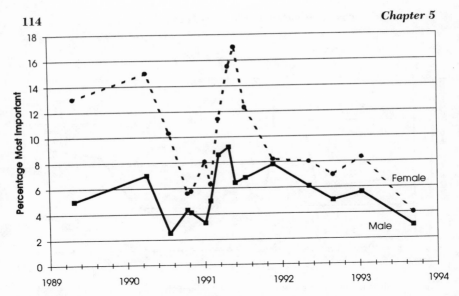

Fig. 5.5. Most important problem: poverty (by sex).

erage continues, and the problem stays at the top of the media's agenda, . . . agenda-setting effects will begin to register as deeply among those viewers whose personal lives are untroubled by the problem given national attention" (pp. 52–53).

Generic shifts in attentiveness to policy-relevant problems may help account for findings in the voting behavior literature that indicate that citizens tend to vote more on the basis of their perceptions of the state of the economy than their own situation or prospects—the *sociotropic voting* phenomenon. It may be that the preferences for government action remain constant (and differentiated by educational classes) but that attentiveness to economic matters is subject to a generic shift. As we have noted earlier, such shifts in attentiveness can alter voting outcomes.

General Shifts in Attentiveness: A Half Century of Data

In the above section, I showed that groups tend to move in tandem when new (or recurrent) problems face the political system. We may examine generic shifts in attentiveness to problems in the mass public over the period 1939 to the present, thanks to the persistence of the Gallup polling organization in asking the same question in the same format over that period of time (Smith 1985).[6]

6. The marginals for the half-century study of attentiveness were supplied by the Roper Center for Public Opinion Research at the University of Connecticut. The Roper

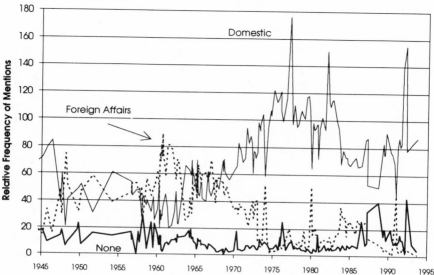

Fig. 5.6. Most important problem: domestic versus foreign affairs.

As a first measure of shifts in attentiveness, figure 5.6 presents the "most important problem" data with all domestic policy categories combined, compared to responses related to foreign affairs. In addition, the final category of "no answer, unclassifiable, or none" is graphed for completeness. Because people sometimes cite more than one problem even when asked for *the* "most important problem," the totals for this graph often sum to more than 100 for any particular poll. It is clear from the figure that foreign affairs has declined as a concern of Americans even as the world, it is said, becomes more interdependent. Americans were concerned primarily with military involvement (Korea, Vietnam) and the Soviet nuclear threat rather than trade or other international problems.

In the late 1960s, domestic policy concerns eclipsed foreign policy concerns for good (or at least for the duration of the series). I have developed broad categories that allow the examination of the long-run trends in the domestic policy concerns of American citizens. Figure 5.7 plots whether citizens are focusing on the economy or on other domestic pol-

---

Center is able to provide marginals from the actual polls themselves for the period 1954 to the present but must rely on releases from Gallup for earlier polls. As Mayer (1992: appendix A) has shown, releases from polling organizations can be inaccurate, although he has the most confidence in Gallup. I have combined categories from the marginals provided by the Roper Center to study the long-term trends in the data.

icy issues. Most domestic policy issues are either social policies, such as social security, health care, or welfare, or issues of social control, which include urban disorder, labor strife, drugs, and crime. The category also includes civil rights and liberties, because scaling studies conducted during the late 1960s and early 1970s suggest that citizens tend to think of these issues as falling in a relatively coherent domain (Weisberg and Rusk 1970; Rusk and Weisberg 1972). Responses relating to foreign affairs have been eliminated from the total, so that figure 5.7 may be interpreted as plotting the most important *domestic* problem of the country.

Examining the gross patterns in the data, one could conclude that concerns with economic problems tend to correspond with the general health of the economy. This is particularly true after 1960. The 1960s were generally a period of declining concern with the economy, with other domestic issues dominating. After 1970, a growing trend toward concern with the state of the economy occurred, peaking in 1982. Then a general decline in the salience to economic problems occurred through the 1980s, with the upturn depicted in figure 5.2 taking place in the early 1990s.

Economic problems may involve either recession and stagnation, or inflation (and, occasionally, both, as in the 1970s). Figure 5.8 separately depicts the three major economic problems of inflation, economic de-

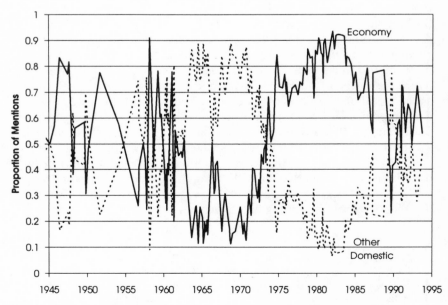

Fig. 5.7. Most important problem: economic versus other (domestic only).

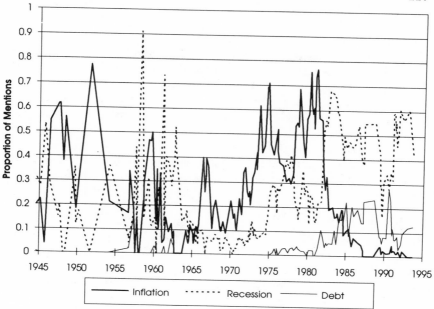

Fig. 5.8. Most important problem: economic (domestic only).

cline[7], and the federal deficit. The rise and decline of inflation as a concern during the 1970s and early 1980s is clearly in evidence, and seems to correspond to objective indicators of the character of economic problems.

Of the major categories of noneconomic domestic policies—social welfare, social control, government as a problem, and the environment— only the issue of social control commonly reaches a threshold of attentiveness. Except for a couple of brief spikes, social control always eclipses general concern about other noneconomic issues. Americans are more concerned with issues of social disorder and its control than with any other noneconomic domestic issue, at least as assessed by the "most important problem" question. These issues became especially important in politics during the 1960s, when the issue of race divided the parties (Carmines and Stimson 1989) and the "new social issues" offered advantage to the Republican party with its "law and order" campaigns. Underlying the pattern of figure 5.7, then, is basically an alteration between attention to the state of the economy and attention to social control issues. We return to the emergence of these issues in the next chapter.

7. A combination of "recession," "poverty," and "the economy."

Examining figures 5.6, 5.7, and 5.8 suggests rather substantial changes in issue salience in the mass public over a relatively short period of time. For example, between 1970 and 1975, the figure for those who were most concerned with domestic policies other than the economy fell from 80 percent to 20 percent. Between 1983 and 1987 this figure rose from 10 percent to over 75 percent, only to fall rapidly to around 40 percent. These measures of attentiveness are, of course, very gross and may not indicate the attention structures of policy-relevant elites. But temporal variability in problem identification in the mass public is impressive, as is the apparent connection between problem identification and objective economic conditions.

The Stability of Preferences

I have argued that mass attentiveness to policy objects is subject to fairly radical shifts over a short period of time. What about mass preferences? Like attentiveness, preferences differ considerably among individuals, but how they vary over time is what we want to study. There are two related issues here. First, are individuals stable in their preferences? Second, is the mass public stable collectively? There is evidence of considerable variability in responses to survey questions from the panel studies conducted by the National Election Studies program at the University of Michigan (Zaller and Feldman 1992). There are problems with the particular wording of questions, which stress trade-offs of underlying values.[8] The General Social Survey, conducted by NORC, does not use the "trade-off" wording, asking instead about spending levels directly.[9] The questions are probably less valid as indicators of actual choice, but they are better indicators of temporal changes in opinions, because they avoid raising diverse contexts.

Reviewing the responses to these questions over the period 1973 through 1989, Linda and Stephen Bennett write that

8. See note 3 above. In essence, NES tries to get voters to weigh contradictory underlying evaluative dimensions to get closer to the hypothetical choice that a voter might make. So NES researchers ask for a comparison between spending reductions and service cuts. When voters want both, however, context is critical, and decisions are made when evaluative dimensions are evoked. That is, people don't normally make decisions the way NES is asking them to in its hypothetical questions. What NES researchers report as unsophisticated instability may instead be a quite understandable use of the "attentiveness heuristic."

9. The specific wording is: "We are faced with many problems in this country, none of which can be solved easily or inexpensively. I'm going to name some of these problems, and for each one I'd like you to tell me whether you think we're spending too much money on it, too little, or about the right amount."

With but few exceptions—one being spending to protect and improve the environment—the percentages [of responses to NORC
questions about federal spending levels for problems] vary so little
over time that any differences could be due simply to sampling variability. The period from 1973 through 1989 saw major changes in
the political fortunes of the two major political parties, of individual
personalities, and even trends in opinions on economic and social
issues. But when it comes to public opinion about the national government's spending on these key domestic and foreign problems,
very little movement occurred (1990: 89–93).

In a similar vein, the exhaustive examination of archived public opinion
polling studies by Page and Shapiro (1992) finds scant evidence of episodic, abrupt shifts in collective American opinions. On the other hand,
using a similar approach to that of Page and Shapiro, William Mayer
(1992) finds an amalgam of substantial changes and remarkable stability
in American public opinion. In dividing the years 1960–88 into four periods, Mayer reports that 1960–65 was a period of generally stable attitudes; 1966–73, of increasing liberalism; 1974–80, of predominantly conservative movement; and 1981–88, of moderate liberal shifts in opinion.
But Mayer argues that opinion shifts in the general public were far less
pronounced than among political elites, pointing especially to the rise of
the liberal movement in the Democratic party (1992:315–40).
    It is clear that, in the aggregate, policy preferences can change. In
some cases, cumulative preference change in the mass public can be remarkable, as in the case of race relations since 1960 (Mayer 1992). But
over most issues, preferences for policy action, as well as attitudes on
many social issues, are stable. Of course, we do not know how particular
individuals reacted. It may be that individuals do shift quickly among
policy positions, as suggested by the NES panel studies. It may also be
that the panel studies overestimate instability in policy preferences by
raising particular issue frames.
    A final indication of the relative stability of mass preferences in com-
parison to attentiveness can be gleaned from a comparison of the "most
important problem" data with a generic measure of policy liberalism
from an analysis of the policy-relevant preferences of Americans developed by James Stimson (1991). We may compare relative variability on
the attentiveness measures plotted in figure 5.7 with the Stimson generic
liberalism measure. Stability on the liberalism measure is quite impressive in comparison to attentiveness, which cycles more or less in correspondence with the health of the economy. If we calculate a coefficient of
variation, which is a measure of relative variation (the standard deviation
divided by the mean of the series), we find a value of 0.085 for the liberal-

ism preference measure but 0.407 for attentiveness to economic problems. A rough interpretation of these measures is that variability for the liberalism measure, on average, is about 8.5 percent of the mean value of the series. For attentiveness to the economy, however, average variability is 41 percent of the mean.

Tables 5.1 and 5.2 document in more detail the stability of preferences and the volatility of attention. Table 5.1 presents coefficients of variation (along with means and standard deviations) for various components of the "most important problem" series. Table 5.2 presents coefficients of variation for the NORC spending categories.[10] In *no case* does the coefficient of variation for a spending measure exceed the lowest coefficient of variation for an attention measure.[11]

Preferences, whether measured by Stimson's generic liberalism scale or by the NORC desired spending items, are scantly affected by business-cycle variability. Attentiveness to key problems, however, seems to be dramatically affected by the business cycle. It may seem obvious that people pick out the economy as a major problem when it *is* a major problem. However, their general preferences do *not* change in the face of changes in economic circumstance. Put starkly, attentiveness is sensitive to context, while policy preferences are less sensitive. It is, of course, likely that, given a major shift in context (say, a prolonged period of economic decline), policy preferences would shift. Even the pronounced recessions of the early 1980s and early 1990s pale in comparison to the Great Depression, and all pale in comparison to the economic problems of non-Western societies. That is, it is quite unrealistic to expect preferences and attentiveness to be completely unrelated, given enough variability in context. But, given the constrained range of variability in economic performance in the United States, policy preferences have changed very little in the aggregate, at least in comparison to changes in attentiveness to those problems. In the United States, people do not become overnight socialists when confronted with economic difficulties, but they do focus attention on the problem almost overnight. It is a change of focus, not a change of mind, that has occurred.

This evidence is admittedly limited and very dependent on the ques-

10. I have averaged the coefficients of variation across the three categories of spending preferences (too little, too much, about right) because there are differences among the categories, although the differences are not systematic across questions. That is, for some questions the "about right" category is most variable; for others, it is the "too much" or the "two little" category.

11. The NORC spending measures are best viewed as attempts to assess *direct* preferences for policies, rather than the Stigler-Becker preferences for outcomes. This means that they are potentially sensitive to context.

TABLE 5.1 Variability for "Most Important Problem," 1945–92
(annualized data)

Topic	Standard Deviation	Mean	Coefficient of Variation
Totals			
All domestic	26.04	69.84	0.373
Foreign affairs	20.33	31.56	0.644
None	6.35	10.43	0.609
Sum		111.83°	
Domestic			
General economy	22.43	55.07	0.407
Social	22.43	44.93	0.499
Sum		100.00	
Domestic (fine)			
Inflation	20.81	25.67	0.811
Recession	13.16	16.24	0.810
Poverty	4.84	4.16	1.162
The economy	7.93	5.24	1.513
Social control	21.29	32.27	0.660
Social welfare	4.63	5.51	0.840
Government	5.88	6.22	0.946
Deficit	6.23	3.75	1.660
Environment	1.34	0.79	1.696
Sum		99.85	

Source: Gallup polls.

°Sums to more than 100% because of occasional multiple mentions by respondents.

tion wordings used by survey researchers. Nevertheless, the evidence strongly suggests that, if we separate out attentiveness from preferences as best we can, preferences are remarkably stable in comparison to attentiveness.

The Effects of Attention Shifts

We now turn to the issue that will preoccupy us for the remaining chapters in this book: how the individual decision-making model detailed so far affects the policy activities of democratic political systems. First, we ask a large-scale question: what are the effects of attention shifts in the mass public on the policymaking activities of public officials? Political scientists have found this to be a difficult issue, because the interaction between mass publics, on one hand, and elected officials and other policy elites, on the other, is complex and contingent. There is no simple relationship between mass opinion and policy output, because the relation-

TABLE 5.2 Variability of Mass Preferences, 1972–91

Topic	Coefficient of Variation[*]
Foreign aid	0.143
Defense	0.301
Big cities	0.143
Crime	0.105
Drug education	0.137
Education	0.232
Environment	0.225
Welfare	0.166
Health	0.171
Blacks	0.122
Space	0.207
Social security	0.112 (1982–91)
Highways	0.122 (1982–91)

Source: NORC.

[*]Averaged across the three categories of the question "Spending too little, spending too much, or about right?"

ship is mediated by what V. O. Key called the "activist strata": those citizens who form groups to influence government. If the issues that concern the activists are not the same as those preoccupying the mass public, then the correspondence between mass opinion and policy outcomes can be problematic. At the very least, politicians can be pressed in more than one direction.

Second, the direction of causation is not always clear. Mass political attitudes (and probably attentiveness) often *trail* the policy activities of government, responding to the political spectacle offered rather than affecting it (Baumgartner and Jones 1991). Often there is a complex, two-way flow of causation between mass opinions and the activities of policymaking elites. We saw above how President George Bush's "war on drugs" attracted mass attention—even more people focused on drugs as the major issue facing America than on the Persian Gulf War a year and a half later. Here clearly the causation flowed from elite to mass. On the other hand, had there not been some state of readiness in the public to accept the message, the leap in attentiveness to drugs would probably not have occurred. Perhaps this had to do with the generally rosy state of the economy at the time, offering a "window of opportunity" through which the president could turn the nation's attention to drug abuse.

At any rate, shifts in issue salience should affect other aspects of the process of governing. Edwards (1989: 207) writes that "framing issues in ways that favor the president's programs may set the terms of the debate on his proposals and thus the premises on which members of Congress cast their votes." I have tried to show how framing and the salience of evaluative dimensions are directly related, because framing involves evoking new dimensions of evaluation. It is not so clear that such shifts in the evaluative bases of decisions in the mass public will affect public policies, because the mass public is seldom interested in the often-arcane maneuvers of political elites, because organized groups may push in a different direction than the mass public would favor, and because it may be that public policies affect public attention rather than the other way around. So it has not been as easy as it might seem to study the relationship between political attitudes in the mass public and public policy outcomes.

One area where we do have some empirical studies on the relationship between attentiveness of the mass public to particular policy issues and the policy actions of government concerns presidential policy successes. If the president is proposing issues for policy action that are salient to the hopes and fears of the general public, then it seems probable that he will be more successful in getting his program through Congress. Ostrom and Simon (1985) suggest a contingent model of presidential approval in which issue salience determines the relationship between presidential action and public support. The more an issue is on the public's mind, the more efficacious are the actions the president takes to move his program through the legislative branch. These investigators also argue that presidential support itself is contingent, writing that "erosion of public support [for the president] produced by departures from peace and prosperity will depend upon the degree to which public concern is concentrated upon these fundamental expectations" (1985: 355). That is, if the public is concentrating on the domestic economy (prosperity) and things are going sour in foreign policy, then the effects on the president's overall stature are minimal. In a similar vein, Edwards and his colleagues show that presidential approval is a function of issue salience (measured in terms of media coverage). That is, if foreign policy is most salient, then that issue dominates the overall approval rating of the president. If the media is most attentive to the economy, then perceptions of economic policy success dominate general approval ratings (Edwards, Mitchell, and Welch 1992). So evidence exists that generalized presidential approval is contingent on the particular issues that are salient to voters at the moment.

This matters little unless general approval affects the president's capacity to govern. Conventional wisdom suggests that presidential approval affects governing capacity, and some studies have supported this. Ostrom and Simon (1985) show that the president's legislative success is influenced by his public support. If so, then attention shifts in the mass public can affect the course of public policy through its effects on approval ratings of the president and other policymakers.

A Black-Box Estimate of Policy Effects

To illustrate the potential power of incorporating attentiveness in models of policymaking, we may examine the so-called black-box models of the policy process. In these models, political scientists try to estimate the causes of policy outputs without worrying very much about the specifics of how policymakers made decisions. Policymakers are assumed to deliver policy outputs in response to inputs, such as changes in mass preferences or economic conditions. Inputs and outputs are carefully measured in order to overcome the limitations of ignoring the specifics of decision-making. The investigator using the "black-box" approach develops a tentative equation which relates several independent variables (the inputs) to the governmental policy outputs. Then, using statistical techniques, he or she allows the data to indicate the magnitudes of the effects on policies, if any.

We may take an example from defense policy. Spending for defense changes on an annual basis in response to various conditions, such as whether the nation is at war and what kinds of weapons systems have been authorized in the past (since they must be paid for in the present). But defense spending may also be sensitive to changes in the political mood of the country. Thomas Hartley and Bruce Russett (1992) have developed a model of U. S. defense spending that incorporates changes in public opinion, as well as variables such as external military threat and the size of the past military budget. Their model includes as inputs the following: (1) changes in public preferences for increasing or decreasing the defense budget; (2) the magnitude of the external military threat to the country; (3) the past size of the defense budget; and (4) resource crowding, that is, demands that government fund other programs. While the Hartley-Russett model is simpler (and thus perhaps less complete) than some others (such as one developed by Ostrom and Marra 1986), these investigators have been able to measure public opinion with considerable precision, relying on pooled public opinion measures from six different polling organizations. Hartley and Russett find public opinion to be a significant predictor of military spending, along with the size of the budget deficit (a measure of resource crowding), Soviet military spending (an indication of the external military threat), and the size of the previous year's military budget (a measure of "sunk costs" and incremental budget making).

The Hartley-Russett model is based on an approach pioneered by Page and Shapiro (1983), who related general changes in public opinion across time to changes in budgetary outputs in several policy areas. In effect, the Page-Shapiro (and the Hartley-Russett) approach adopts a preference-satisfaction criterion of democratic influences on policymaking: public preferences change, and public policy changes as a consequence. The effect of mass preferences as estimated by Hartley and Russett is indeed impressive, even if the exact nature of the linkage is not really known.[12]

Our distinction between attentiveness and preferences implies a somewhat different standard of democratic policymaking in assessing the linkage between mass publics and defense policy. Democracy may be seen as a mechanism for information processing and problem solving as well as a mechanism for preference satisfaction for collective goods. Open, democratic institutions act to discover and respond to social problems as they cross the threshold of attention of citizens without having to wait for more glacial changes in preferences.

It is not enough simply to measure mass preferences. Attentiveness to situations that activate those preferences is also critical. Shanto Iyengar's (1991) studies show the profound influence of context on political decision-making and imply that preferences must be activated in a decisional context. When citizens become aware of a context, in this case, a particular problem, their preferences become activated. So it may be that democratic governments are more responsive to changes in attentiveness to problems than they are to the particular distribution of opinion on a problem.

We may use the Hartley-Russett model to assess this possibility by simply adding a measure of attentiveness to foreign affairs to their model. In doing so, I have made certain modifications. Instead of the deficit, I use interest paid on the debt to assess resource crowding, under the assumption that the sheer size of the deficit is less important than the reactions of the capital markets to it and that it is the reaction of the capital markets that serves as at least one brake on deficit spending. Instead of a direct measure of external threat, I use a "filter theory" in which external threats are filtered through generalized attention to foreign affairs.[13]

12. The defense preference measure assembled by Hartley and Russett contains substantial variability, probably more than similar series for preferences for domestic spending (Bennett and Bennett 1990: 89–93).

13. So I have dropped the assessments of Soviet defense spending used by Hartley and Russett, assuming that the attentiveness measure will pick up this and many other foreign policy threats that might affect the model. There were other outside threats besides the Soviets—for example, the threat that China would enter the Vietnam War. It seems at least a first approximation to conceive of various threats as being filtered through the attentiveness measure. Moreover, the Hartley-Russett model involves five independent variables and a lag of three years for Soviet spending. The consequence is to lose

The attentiveness measure is constructed from the Gallup poll questions concerning the "most important problem" facing the United States presented earlier in this chapter. Answers were aggregated into a general category of "foreign affairs," although most answers concerned defense threats. Polls were averaged on an annual basis. The measure of preference for defense spending is from Hartley and Russett, and assesses the extent to which current spending is "too little." Attentiveness and preferences were lagged one year, following Hartley and Russett, as was interest on the debt. This is because budget cycles make it impossible for government to react immediately to changes in preferences or attentiveness. The dependent variable defense spending is also lagged in order to capture incremental defense spending; Hartley and Russett use a slightly different approach, differencing.[14] The (t − 1) subscripts for the variables in equation (1) indicate these lags.

Then the initial model to be estimated is

$$D_t = a + b_1 A_{t\text{-}1} + b_2 P_{t\text{-}1} + b_3 I_{t\text{-}1} + b_4 D_{t\text{-}1} + e_t, \tag{1}$$

where

D is defense spending;
A is attentiveness to foreign affairs;
P is aggregate preferences for spending increases;
I is interest on the national debt.

Results of a regression analysis of this model are shown in table 5.3.[15] It can be seen that only attentiveness and interest on the debt are statisti-

---

seven degrees of freedom in a model estimated with only twenty-six degrees of freedom at the outset (the time series is from 1965 to 1990). Adding more variables is not really practical, and the filter approach is plausible theoretically.

14. The two approaches are similar:

$$D_t - D_{t-1} = a + \mathbf{b}\mathbf{X}_t + e_t,$$

where D is defense spending and $\mathbf{X}_t$ is a vector of independent variables equivalent to

$$D_t = a + D_{t-1} + \mathbf{b}\mathbf{X}_t + e_t.$$

If D_{t-1} is included as an explicit regressor, then the effects of the lag can be assessed via the regression coefficient. (If the coefficient is unity, differencing and lagging are exactly equivalent.) Because D may be correlated with other independent variables, the coefficients will assess net effects.

15. Because of the typical autocorrelation problems in measures of governmental spending, I have used an autoregressive model with rho, the autocorrelation coefficient, estimated using a maximum likelihood approach, after differencing.

TABLE 5.3 U.S. Defense Spending in Millions, 1965–90, as a
Function of Attention and Preferences

Variable	Coefficient	Std. Error	*t*-ratio
Constant	1,171.80	188.80	6.21
A_{t-1}	7.87	3.59	2.19
P_{t-1}	2.89	2.19	0.84
I_{t-1}	0.74	0.32	2.32
D_{t-1}	0.04	0.15	0.26

$R^2 = 0.869$; R^2 (adj) = 0.844.

Note: Estimated with an autoregressive model using a maximum likelihood approach to estimating rho.

cally significant; surprisingly, lagged defense expenditures are not. In this, a linear model of influence on policy, mass preferences do not influence defense expenditures.

The discussion above, however, does not really imply a linear (or additive, because the terms of the equation are added together) model for the policy influences of preferences and attentiveness. That would suggest that changes in preferences cause changes in defense spending, and then changes in attentiveness cause some more changes, and that each factor is independent of the other. Rather, the discussion suggests that defense preferences become active when citizens are focused on foreign affairs. That is, preferences become relevant only when a policy area becomes salient. For preferences to become important, citizens must attend to them; so preferences are not likely to influence policies on their own. This *preference activation model* implies an interactive approach; attentiveness and preferences interact to influence policy outcomes. This means that we need to use a multiplicative rather than a simple linear, additive model. If, for example, attention to foreign affairs were hypothetically zero in the mass public, then no matter what preferences for defense spending were, they would not affect spending at all. If attention were very high, then the effect of preferences on spending would be very large. Hence we enter the product of attention and salience into the model, dropping the linear entries. Now we estimate

$$D_t = a + b_3 I_{t-1} + b_4 D_{t-1} + b_5 A_{t-1} \cdot P_{t-1} + e_t. \qquad (2)$$

Note that A and P, attention and preferences, are multiplied together in the equation. Results are presented in table 5.4. This is the preference activation term in the model, and its effects will be assessed by the coefficient b_5. The preference activation model is a better fit than the linear model, with the coefficient of determination moving from .869 to .887

TABLE 5.4 U.S. Defense Spending in Millions, 1965–90, as a
Function of Attention and Preferences: A Salience Model

Variable	Coefficient	Std. Error	*t*-ratio
Constant	1,168.50	174.10	6.71
AP_{t-1}	0.26	0.07	3.66
I_{t-1}	0.72	0.30	2.50
D_{t-1}	0.09	0.11	0.82

$R^2 = 0.887$; R^2 (adj) $= 0.871$.

Note: Estimated with an autoregressive model using a maximum likelihood approach to estimating rho.

and the regression coefficient for the product of attention and preferences statistically significant ($t = 3.23$).[16]

A linear estimate of the role of preferences (for military spending)
and attentiveness (to foreign affairs) resulted in statistical significance for
attention but not for preferences. A model incorporating the interaction
of preferences and attention fit better than the linear model, with the
preference activation term in the equation being statistically significant.
This suggests that preferences are most influential on defense policy
when the topic of foreign affairs is salient to them.

The model I have presented here is obviously a rough approximation
to estimating the determinants of defense spending. It is not my objective to provide a complete model of the process. Rather, I hope to highlight a mechanism involved in policy responsiveness that has thus far
been ignored by those studying the determinants of public expenditures:
preference activation in the mass public. The results seem to suggest that
models of policy responsiveness need to incorporate both preference satisfaction and problem identification. Representation implies not a mechanistic response to citizen preferences, which in any case may well be
contradictory. Rather, some preferences are more important than others.
This exercise suggests an approach for weighting aggregate citizen preferences temporally: through the extent to which a policy arena is salient
to them. Where policies are salient, it is likely that responsiveness is
more forthcoming.

Conclusions

Iyengar (1991: 130) writes that "individuals' attributions of responsibility for political issues show significant short-term flux . . . Therefore,

16. If we include attention, preferences, and their interaction in the model, attention
is significant, the interaction is significant, but preferences are not significant. This result
would imply that situation (as filtered by attentiveness) affects outcomes *directly*, over and

the conventional 'dispositional' explanation of public opinion and political behavior that grants monopoly status to stable personal influences . . . must be revised to allow for contextual influences." Yet his experiments on the influence of the media show that media frames that run contrary to personal predispositions are less influential than when they correspond (1991: chap. 9).

It would seem that any theory of the influence of mass opinion on public policies would have to take into consideration *both* the long-term stability of personal political preferences *and* the "inherently circumstantial nature of human judgment" (Iyengar 1991: 130). There are, of course, many different issue frames that might affect policy-relevant opinions in the mass public. We are interested in this book only in those frames that are relevant for the policymaking process. And in this analysis, it makes a big difference whether we treat the public as infinitely malleable, subject to whatever issue frame is offered by political elites, or whether we view frames as relatively enduring, but as ebbing and flowing in response to political events.

If we view policy preferences as relatively stable across time, and attention to those preferences as both variable and sensitive to incoming information, then we have a model that is capable of linking the relevant aspects of mass opinion with the policy process. This chapter has presented some limited information from mass surveys that suggests considerable stability in mass preferences for federal spending and other political and social attitudes, but highly variable attentiveness to the major problems facing the country.

Conceiving of mass publics as holding relatively fixed preferences but being open to new contexts as issues change reframes the old debate about ideology. Ideology has tended to be valued as a marker of rational voting behavior and has normally been assessed in terms of consistency across time and constraints among idea-elements. The paradox of temporal choice should sensitize us to the fallacy of inferring rational decision-making from consistent decisions. They are not the same. Indeed, consistency in choices in the face of changing circumstances can imply inflexibility. It has been a major mistake of public opinion research to hold consistency among attitudes and within attitudes across time as so fundamental to rational voting in democratic societies. While one would not want continual shifting without firm grounding, one would like to see enough flexibility to incorporate changing context into the structure of preferences.

---

above the interaction of preferences alone. This is theoretically satisfying, since government responds to threat independently of mass preferences.

Finally, to anticipate the second part of this book, raising and focusing attention in the mass public has the potential of destroying or modifying undemocratic aspects of elite decision-making. This idea was first articulated by E. E. Schattschneider as "conflict expansion." When elites differ, they (and especially the losing side) tend to appeal to the mass public, thus activating citizens in a policy debate. In the case of defense spending, many critics have complained that the relationship between the military, congressional committees, and weapons suppliers has been corrupt and undemocratic. This situation worsened as President Reagan built up the defense budget rapidly during the early 1980s. As one can see from figure 5.6, public attentiveness shifted toward foreign affairs and defense in 1979, with a majority of people being supportive of more defense spending (see Wlezien 1993). After a few years of preoccupation with domestic issues, mass attention turned again toward foreign matters in 1984—but this time with a more critical view. Support for defense had fallen dramatically, probably because of the massive defense buildup. The late 1980s brought increased pressure on the defense establishment, and the end of the Cold War brought even more pressure. By that time, military bases were being closed and contracts for weapons canceled. While one would not want to attribute the decline of the defense establishment to the correspondence between mass attention and dropping support for defense, clearly this provided the backdrop to what amounts to a massive policy change.

It may be, as students of the mass media have noted, that public opinion concerning the national political agenda follows news coverage of those problems (Rogers and Dearing 1988). But the data in this chapter show changes in attentiveness to the economy as the economy worsened; to foreign affairs as defense budgets soared, and again as the Persian Gulf War unfolded; to drugs as the Bush administration sought to make that issue a national priority. Clearly, media reporting reflected what was happening; just as clearly, political elites sought to frame these issues in a light favorable to them. Most important, policymaking is different when an issue is discussed in an atmosphere of great attention; yet in even the relatively short run, public and media attention is fickle. How policy changes as attentiveness changes is the subject of the second section of this book.

PART TWO

The Paradox of Issue Evolution

The aim of the game played by political institutions seems considerably more difficult to define than that for other forms of human action.

— LORENZO ORNAGHI

Political decision-making can be best understood by separating preferences for policy outcomes from attention to those preferences. In this approach, preferences are treated as goal-states. That is, political decision-makers generally care about policy goals rather than the particular policy means themselves (so long as a role for "brand loyalty," whether it be for Fords or Democrats, is recognized). It is, of course, granted that means and ends exist in complex causal chains that include a great deal of contingency and uncertainty. But decision-makers really do try to move toward goal-states, not just away from problems.

In the political world, decision-makers can order their preferences within a policy domain fairly reasonably. A policy domain is a set of (direct) preferences relating to a single general goal. But it is the general nature of the political world for goals to be almost always in conflict. This is true of the rest of the world too, but in some parts of the rest of that world, constrained choices are so obvious that they are built into the decisional situation. This is particularly true in the economic sphere, where money forces constrained choices and serves to integrate those choices.

In politics, choice domains are not integrated through

any metric. As a consequence, constraints between policy domains are not so evident. How many politicians have claimed that government spending could be increased with no increase in the size of government due to projected economic growth? Because integration across domains is difficult in politics, *homo politicus* often achieves consistency through shifts in attentiveness to underlying goals. Some people, of course, do integrate, most often by weighting one dimension of evaluation so much higher than others that conflict does not occur. But most of us shift our decisions according to what dimension of evaluation is preoccupying us at the time.

The use of attention as a heuristic to integrate conflicting goals implies that, in politics at least, most people have utility functions that may be severed or "broken" across time. That is, they can (and generally do) order preferred states within a domain but do not generally do so among domains. If we look at a decision made at one point in time, we will see a decision-maker who has a complete ranking of preferences as well as a ranking among domains. But the decision-maker's ranking among domains is subject to attention shifts, implying that the ranking among domains is somewhat superficial. When attentiveness shifts, the underlying evaluative dimension that structures political action shifts and *choice reversals* among the presented alternatives may occur. Using surveys of the mass public, we may separate attentiveness and preferences and examine their paths through time. It seems clear that attentiveness is far more variable than preferences and that both are probably important in the policymaking process.

Part 2 of this book turns to an analysis of the implications of this choice model for the democratic policymaking process. This is a course of action well worth pursuing but fraught with pitfalls. To begin, one must select what aspects of the policy process are worth explaining. A considerable amount of effort in political science has been directed at estimating the correspondence between the policy-relevant attitudes of mass publics, or elites, or some proxy for their political demands, on one hand, and policy outputs, on the other. Chapter 1 noted that such an approach stems from one important function of political democracy: satisfying citizen preferences. Then one must draw connections between relevant aspects of policymaking and the decision-making model. If preferences are contradictory, government, staffed with decision-makers and responsive to external forces, should reflect this. In particular, the policy actions of government could shift as attentiveness to particular dimensions of evaluation shift.

Linkages, however, are not simple or transparent. It is not immediately evident that episodic shifts in individual attentiveness have anything to do with lurches in the policy process. Indeed, even the idea of the existence of major policy shifts is controversial. For example, many political scientists have emphasized the stable structure of conflict organized by a two-party system of impressive staying power. Yet it is abundantly clear that the American political system is capable of processing a vast variety of relevant political issues. Hence we must examine the *paradox of issue evolution*, the paradox that diverse issues reach the agenda abruptly and are processed through a political system dominated by stable institutions and enduring partisan coalitions. Policies are subject to severe and abrupt changes, but the preferences of mass publics are far more enduring, and the institutional structures that articulate and aggregate those preferences are stable. This is a systems-level analogue to the paradox of temporal choice: abrupt policy change occurs within a system of stable preferences and stable institutions.

Just as individual decision-makers are subject to the *serial shift*, so too is government. Many issues are processed in parallel, without the active interest of the macropolitical institutions (Congress and the president). But this can change when the issue becomes salient and policy action is taken; these institutions must process the new issue serially. The shifts must be discrete and discontinuous; hence there is often a policy leap from incremental processing to nonincremental processing as the issue moves from serial to parallel processing.

The next four chapters explore the paradox of issue evolution in the light of serial shifts in policymaking. Because the links between the policymaking process and individual decision-making are not simple, one may fully accept the model of choice detailed in the previous chapters and still be skeptical of the policy implications I draw.

6 Macropolitics: Is Political Conflict Recurrent?

It would seem that the American political system must deal with a panoply of issues at the national, state, and local levels, a confusing array of topics that range from regulating buildings to providing subsidies to farmers, from providing investment tax credits to businesses to financing prekindergarten education. Yet most of these issues can be categorized according to a limited number of broader policy domains. The reason that issues can be categorized into a small number of policy domains is that political conflict tends to activate similar coalitions, both in national, state, and local legislatures and in the mass public. This probably stems from the relative stability of policy preferences that characterizes both elites and mass publics.

If such stable issue-frames characterize political decision-making, then a key issue concerns how political conflict evolves. Stable issue-frames imply stable conflict (if issue dimensions are continually present and if attention shifts do not occur) or recurrent conflict (if attention shifts occur). But the American political system processes different issues now than it did a hundred, fifty, or even ten years ago. Hence we have the *paradox of issue evolution:* how do issues evolve when political conflict is either stable or recurrent? To begin to examine this issue requires that we first try to understand the process of issue-framing and how new issues get defined in terms of old frames of reference.

Policy Domains in the Mass Public

As noted in the previous chapter, a main source of debate in the public opinion literature has centered on the coherence of belief systems in the mass public. The decision-making model developed in the previous chapters allows for a considerable amount of seemingly logical incoherence, because it allows for (indeed, virtually requires) inconsistent goals. But inconsistent goals or preferences do not imply disordered politics. Individual decision-makers are able to organize political stimuli such as candidates, issues, and groups into reasonably stable domains. More specifically, the model implies that *homo politicus* uses a limited number of evaluative dimensions to structure the political world, even if these

dimensions are themselves not well integrated and are downright conflictual.

So *homo politicus* must organize the political world, in which candidates, parties, and issues all are multidimensional in their attributes, in
terms of his goals, which are conflictual themselves. If the citizen shares
with other citizens similar general evaluative dimensions, even if he or
she differs in particular positioning on those dimensions, then the task
will be very simplified. This chapter will survey empirical studies that
suggest that these frames of reference are quite similar among citizens.
Then it shows how differing attention to those dimensions can have
strong consequences for the evolution of public policies.

If frames are widely shared, then new political issues are likely to call
forth the established domains of evaluation. Political conflict would recur
because new issues tend to fit into old frames. Issues, however, are multidimensional, and it is not immediately evident which evaluative dimension will be evoked; this is considerably influenced by context. Hence
political conflict can be recurrent even if superficially similar issues are
defined differently in different eras, because issue domains tend to
be stable. This section will examine some of the evidence that points to
within-domain coherence in political belief systems.

About a decade ago, John Jackson (1983) developed a model of the
structure of policy opinions in the mass public that involves (1) a common orientation, or the tendency for opinions to cohere within general
policy domains; (2) a policy-specific component; and (3) party identification. In following opinions across time (using a panel study from the National Election Studies conducted in the late 1950s), Jackson studied the
degree to which preferences were related to a common orientation (or
underlying evaluative dimension) and explored the extent to which party
served as an organizing cue for the issues. Jackson concludes that "the
most significant result is the observed presence of a large, stable, and
influential common orientation that accounts for a substantial part of
people's preferences on the domestic policy items of government-
provided jobs, education aid, and health care" (p. 857).

Jackson summarizes an electoral system that, in the late 1950s, was
remarkably stable. "With preferences and identifications being simultaneously related and exhibiting high and nearly equal levels of stability we
have the picture of an electoral system in relative equilibrium during the
late 1950's. Were individual preferences *or* the relative party positions to
change, this equilibrium would be upset, and we would observe changes
in party identification and voting choices" (1983: 859).

It is true that changes in preferences could alter the system, but on the issues that Jackson studied preferences probably have not changed all that much (Page and Shapiro 1992; Mayer 1992). Nevertheless, there is little doubt that in the 1960s the system was destabilized as new issues flooded the political system. Mayer (1992) suggests that this destabilization occurred through the intrusion of a new set of values, or dimension of conflict, into electoral competition. This new dimension competed with but did not replace the old economic issues that had held together the Democratic electoral coalition forged by President Franklin Roosevelt (and which were represented in Jackson's analysis). This new domain concerned social liberalism; in the late 1960s and early 1970s the Democratic party was split asunder over the social issues of race, dissent, and civil liberties. Carmines and Stimson (1989) argue that, indeed, American politics were transformed during the 1960s and that racial divisions drove the transformation. That is, race was responsible for the disruption of the old economic-based coalition and became the most important distinguishing feature between the parties. But other issues were intertwined with this shift, particularly environmentalism, consumerism, and antiwar activism. The stable divisions that had ordered American politics since the Great Depression seemed to be under sustained assault, threatening moderate Republicans and conservative Democrats, who were uncomfortable both with the New Left and with the New Right, which was reinvigorated by the fresh challenge.

An old, economics-only (or government intervention versus limited government) conflict dimension was being replaced in electoral politics by a multidimensional structure. There is good evidence that, during this period, a two-dimensional spatial structure was necessary to account for voter evaluations of candidates and issues.[1] In their path-breaking use of nonmetric scaling techniques on mass publics, Herbert Weisberg and Jerrold Rusk studied the National Election Studies' "feeling thermometers," which asked respondents to assess how warmly or coldly they felt toward candidates, issues, and groups. The researchers correlated the

1. The spatial model of electoral choice which underlies dimensioning efforts has itself been vigorously criticized. If voters can't order candidates, issues, etc., then spatial electoral models make little sense (Stokes 1963; Rabinowitz and MacDonald 1989). On the other hand, Brady and Ansolabehere (1989) studied preference orderings for presidential candidates among California voters, finding generally orderly preferences. I would note that disorderly preference orderings would not imply the absence of utility functions, as the authors suggest, but, rather, the existence of more than one dimension of evaluation. Brady and Ansolabehere also report that individuals tend to endorse candidates whose issue positions are congruent to their own. Finally, the authors note that voters may lack knowledge, causing indifference. In general, this study offers considerable support for the spatial approach.

responses to the feeling scales, treating the resulting correlation coefficients as estimates of similarities.[2] Scaling techniques recovered two dimensions of evaluation in election studies conducted in 1968 and 1970. In 1970 the two dimensions were related, while in 1968 they were not (Weisberg and Rusk 1970; Rusk and Weisberg 1972).[3] Other studies support the two-dimensional political conflict structure. A study of Detroit-area party activists using direct estimates of similarities yielded an almost identical two-dimensional structure, with the dimensions related (Jones 1973b). Rabinowitz (1978) scaled candidates, groups, and issues in 1968 and 1972, again finding a satisfactory fit in two dimensions. Poole and Rosenthal (1984) report one major and one minor dimension in 1968–80 elections, but they do not scale groups or issues with the candidates.

Rusk and Weisberg (1972) identify the vertical dimension in their scaling study as a traditional political party dimension, with Republicans at one end and Democrats at the other. The second dimension divides black militants, rock festivals, and marijuana users from the military, the police, and whites. It distinguishes Nixon, Reagan, and Wallace from McGovern and Kennedy, but does not distinguish Republicans (as a group) from Democrats. Later research by Arthur Miller (cited by Mayer 1992) suggests that by the late 1980s liberal groups were seen as closer to the Democratic party. Mayer (1992) sees the emergence of a two-dimensional conflict structure as the major cause of problems for the Democratic party after 1968. While economic liberalism was alive and well and positively viewed by the public, social liberalism was alive and well and not so well received. Republican successes in the 1970s and 1980s could be seen, at least in part, as a result of a successful capture of the "right" end of the social issue dimension.

The emergence of that bundle of issues termed the *social issues* during the late 1960s and the early 1970s in electoral politics is probably a

2. Nonmetric scaling treats any measure of similarity between candidates in terms of rankings of distances. In a three-candidate election, if candidate A is rated more similar to candidate B than to candidate C, and if candidate C is rated more similar to A than to B, and candidate B is more similar to candidate C than to A, the technique uses as input just the pairings AB < AC; AC < BC; BC < AB. Then the technique searches for the lowest dimensional structure that will account for these pairings. Note that the candidates cannot be placed along a single dimension, so that a two-dimensional structure must be employed. Any measure of similarity may be used; as noted, Rusk and Weisberg essentially used correlations of preference estimates for their similarity measures. Metric techniques such as factor analysis treat the similarities as direct estimates of distances and use these distances as input.

3. In their 1970 study, Rusk and Weisberg (1972) used a three-dimensional structure in ordering groups and candidates simultaneously. The third dimension was less important and seems to have distinguished a separate racial factor.

general phenomenon. The introduction of new dimensions of conflict into electoral politics reflects changes in national policy agendas (Riker 1982). Of course, we do not have the detailed public opinion studies of earlier eras of policy agenda shift, but these shifts have left traces in the historical record—in particular, in election results and in voting divisions in Congress. Students of parties and elections have conceptualized periods of major issue emergence as "realignments" and "critical elections." The reason is that electorally the emergence of new dimensions of conflict is often associated with the movement of groups of voters from one party to another or with the movement of a relatively fluid voting block firmly toward one of the parties.

The emergence of new dimensions of conflict reaches the electoral arena when one party decides to try to capitalize on it and makes an appeal to voters activated by the new dimension. Students of the historical electoral record point to the 1896 election and the 1928–32 period as critical or realigning elections. In 1896 the Democratic party moved to try to capture the "populist," anti-Eastern sentiment in the West and South with its nominee, William Jennings Bryan, while the Republican party continued to appeal to the industrial North and the well-off farmers of that region (continuing to play on regional sentiment). The result was a movement from a relatively competitive party system to one of Republican dominance. In 1928 the Democrats nominated Al Smith for president, a New York Catholic "wet" (anti-Prohibitionist), effectively ending its association with Western populist discontent and initiating an appeal to the Northern proletariat. The vaunted "Rooseveltian coalition" emerged out of the Great Depression and unified poor farmers, Southerners, and Northern workers around an image of a more activist national state.

The problem with realignments is that when they ought to happen, they sometimes don't. The period after the middle 1960s has frustrated many students of electoral behavior because the coming realignment never came. Instead, conservative Democrats, who might have been expected to move into the Republican party, became more of a swing element in elections, tending to vote for Republicans at the presidential level but for Democrats at the congressional, state, and local levels. This should not trouble us particularly, because realignments have sometimes solidified voters in one party (as in 1896, when Northern urban voters opted strongly for the Republicans and stayed there). So a breaking off toward a more fluid alignment seems to be quite consistent with a general theory of the emergence of new dimensions of conflict in the electoral arena.

Perhaps more important, realignments were never quite as "national" as implied by some electoral analysts. Peter Nardulli of the University of Illinois has shown in the most detailed analysis of state-by-state electoral statistics to date that at no time in the history of the country has a unified, sweeping electoral realignment ever occurred (the 1928–32 period was the closest). But several regional realignments have occurred, in which major party switches occurred within states in a region but which did not sweep the nation (Nardulli 1993). It seems sensible that the decentralized American party structure would be subject to regional struggles between the parties as they face new issues within these regions. These regional shifts can, of course, have major policy impacts nationally when they cause congressmen to be replaced and a different candidate for president to be supported. A handful of state shifts can change national political outcomes.

Social Issues and the Attention Shift

So the emergence of new dimensions of conflict probably has been a periodic characteristic of national politics at least since 1828, when elections became democratic enough to reflect mass sentiments. While the social issues of the late 1960s and early 1970s did not result in a national majority for the Republicans, they were real electoral divisions and have endured into the 1990s. Social issue politics in the 1990s center on drug use, abortion rights, the role of women in the workplace and in politics, homosexual rights, and ethnic exclusivity. It is fruitful to analyze the emergence and persistence of these social issues in politics using the framework of choice developed in chapters 2, 3, and 4. It will be recalled that the serial shift in politics is possible only when more than one dimension of evaluation is present and when a constrained choice dimension cuts across the dimensions of evaluation. The parties organize the constrained choice dimension so that it is interpreted as a partisan dimension (rather than a specific policy dimension as in chap. 2).

The partisan dimension can be viewed as cutting across the underlying dimensions of liberalism and conservatism, because parties (and candidates) are the alternatives that citizens choose among. The partisan dimension organizes the broad party images (separating the "Republican party" from the "Democratic party"), but it also may distinguish candidates. For example, Ted Kennedy or George Mitchell may be viewed as "more Democratic" than Richard Shelby or Ernest Hollings in addition to being conceived as more liberal on either the economic or the social dimension. Now let us examine figure 6.1, which is redrawn from Rusk and Weisberg (1972), with the addition of the lines PQ and TS. We may interpret the vertical axis as an economic policy axis, in line with Mayer,

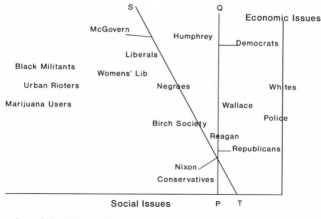

Source: Rusk and Weisberg, 1972.

Fig. 6.1. Candidates and groups in 1970.

with the upper end reflecting more government intervention in the economy. The horizontal axis represents the social issue dimension.

Now, PQ may be interpreted as the axis of partisan conflict, distinguishing Democrats from Republicans. Note that this axis is parallel to the economic policy axis.[4] This result implies that only the economic dimension would distinguish the party positions in the minds of voters and the social dimension would not come into play in deciding between them. But note that while President Nixon is very near to Republicans generally in the two-dimensional space, Senator George McGovern, the 1972 Democratic presidential candidate, is a considerable distance from Democrats generally. One might infer that the axis of electoral conflict in 1972 was displaced from PQ to TS. Both dimensions of conflict are relevant to the voting choice, because the dimension of electoral conflict cuts both axes.[5]

The candidate of the Democratic party moved to capture new issues and revealed a second dimension to politics. The Republicans, in their appeals to voters, stayed pat. In our spatial preference metaphor, we may

4. As in any multidimensional scaling exercise, the location of the axes is arbitrary; that is, it is not determined by the scaling algorithm. Rusk and Weisberg placed axes on the basis of a theoretical interpretation of the data.

5. It may be noted that, unlike the constrained choice dimension discussed in chapters 2 and 4, the partisan dimension, which serves as the constrained choice axis, does not force a trade-off between the two dimensions. In elections, direct trade-offs are not as relevant as in legislatures. Moreover, the two dimensions under consideration may not be as subject to the trade-off model—one can have both social liberalism and economic liberalism; indeed, this was the very point of the new Democrats of the period.

treat the candidates as actually moving, implying a change in preferences. What really happened, of course, is that new Democratic candidates willing to exploit the social issue emerged, making themselves visible through the process of campaigning.

This allowed the Republicans to try to shift the attention of voters to
the second dimension, through the infamous and successful "law and order" campaigns. There is no reason to expect that voters changed their
preferences concerning these issues. The structure of electoral conflict
is analogous to that of the supercollider vote we analyzed in chapter 4,
in which no representative changed preferences but many shifted their
focus of evaluation. In the 1968–72 period, the Democrats made the mistake of offering a new conflict dimension that was subject to becoming
highly salient to voters. In the language developed in chapter 4, we may
hypothesize that many voters had indifference contours (the points in
electoral space where candidates could locate and the voter wouldn't distinguish between them) that were elliptical with minor axes oriented toward the social issue dimension. That means that a slight change along
the social issue dimension will have a strong effect on the evaluation of
the candidate by the voter. In effect, the Democrats assumed a typical
voter indifference contour with a minor ellipse oriented toward the economic dimension. If this had been true, Democrats would have been
able to appendage the newly emerging social liberals to their standard
economic liberal base. But when the introduction of the new social issues
allowed voters to focus on that dimension, many having unfavorable
views of social liberalism did so. The Democrats did not broaden their
New Deal coalition; they wrecked it (Mayer 1992).

In figure 6.2 the "typical" voter's ideal point is depicted in two dimensions, along with two hypothesized indifference contours. To make
things a little more concrete, we may assume that the voter is Catholic,
Northern, urban, and a union member. Both indifference contours center on the same ideal point, but they differ in the orientations of the
ellipses that constitute the indifference contours. Democrats shift the
partisan dimension of conflict toward the social issues, assuming that
their core constituencies will be insensitive to the change. If the typical
Democratic voter in 1972 was insensitive, then the voter would have projected his or her ideal point onto the partisan dimension (dividing Nixon
and McGovern) at a point closer to McGovern, as shown in figure 6.2.
The Republicans assumed that this theory was incorrect and tried to
heighten the sensitivity of our hypothetical urban Democratic voter to
the second dimension. The result, in terms of figure 6.2, was a projection
on the partisan dimension closer to Nixon than McGovern, and hence a
vote for Nixon. Of course, we cannot really reconstruct exactly how vo-

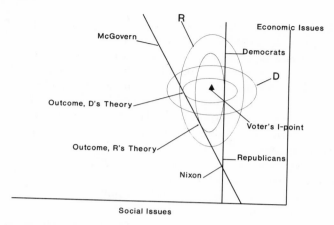

Fig. 6.2. Hypothetical judgments of voters in 1972.

ting decisions were made in 1972 and the "space" in figure 6.2 is an analytical fiction. But the diagram is certainly consistent with current accounts and empirical research in political science.

The Role of Intensity

The spatial model, based as it is on proximities between candidates and voters, leaves no room for intensity as a separate component of electoral choice (Rabinowitz 1978; Rabinowitz and MacDonald 1989). That is, if voters feel negatively about candidates that are distant from them in the issue space, and positively about those close to them, then proximities and intensity correspond. Moreover, such intensity would be a good proxy for a political utility function. It is possible, however, that directionality and intensity don't correspond so simply and that emotion plays an independent role in affecting voting choice. Rabinowitz and MacDonald (1989) develop a directional model in which general policy directions of candidates matter, and these directions are communicated through symbols, which arouse intensity. So intensity and proximity interact to affect choice.

Rabinowitz and MacDonald are right about general directions. If preferences in the mass public are relatively stable within domains, then the general direction of policies is probably more important than specific issue-positions. This conclusion is consistent with the findings of Jackson concerning common components of belief systems. They are also right about the role of emotion. But emotion is often aroused in choice situations where attentiveness shifts. For example, it is common for political candidates to use symbolic appeals to attract attention away from one dimension of evaluation, where they are not favored, to a second dimension of evaluation, where they are. That is why Republicans used highly symbolic appeals in their "law and order" campaigns beginning in 1968. They hoped to turn attention from the standard economic dimension of conflict that had separated the parties since the Great Depression to a new set of issues having to do with changes in the moral fiber of the country, the decline of traditional values, and the rise of a disorderly society emphasizing not traditional freedoms but license.

It is these attention shifts that are most critical to appreciating the strengths and limitations of the spatial model. When they occur, the simple relationship between intensity and proximity is broken and a reshuffling of priorities can occur. If the Democratic party is perceived as the party of economic fairness, that is one thing. The primary dimension of economic liberalism orders choice. If it is perceived as the party of disorder, then that is something else. The second dimension is activated. Often the shift is fraught with emotion for the voter.

In many cases, voters are likely to shift back and forth between the two evaluative dimensions rather than to try to compare the total value they get from the perceived location of the Democratic party on the two dimensions. These shifts in attentiveness can well account for the contradictory remarks that individuals often make in discussing political affairs (Hochschild 1981). A particular voter might want more of the old-fashioned brand of economic liberalism but less of the new social liberalism. These are contradictory preferences given the structure of the situation, because there exist only two parties and neither (at least in the 1970s and 1980s at the presidential level, although within parties these combinations were available) chose this mix of policies. Hence the vote direction depends on which dimension of choice the voter activates. In any case, great political changes can be wrought by the opening up of a second dimension of conflict; many policy issues may be subsumed under the two-dimensional structure. In the early 1970s, issues from antiwar protest to civil rights to women's issues to environmentalism were captured by the new social issues electoral dimension—because citizens with these various orientations were willing to treat them as a more or less coherent cluster.

Legislative Roll-Call Analyses

This chapter has thus far examined the emergence of new dimensions of conflict in electoral politics within a stable institutional frame; that is, these new issues emerged in politics while partisan competition remained limited primarily to the two parties. We now turn to an examination of legislative decision-making and the emergence of new issues. Much of the evidence for stability in policy domains comes from studies of legislative voting, where it has been typical for empirical researchers to report that spaces of few dimensions can account for variability among many roll-call decisions. Like the electoral spaces discussed above, these legislative spaces are analytical; they are useful in isolating the dimensions of evaluation that divide legislators.

In studying legislative roll calls, it is important to note that the stability of legislative voting behavior says nothing about the causes of voting. A model of stable policy dimensions does not mean that legislators vote according to their ideologies, because if their constituents' preferences are reasonably constant (or, really, if legislators' perceptions of constituency preferences are consistent) and they vote according to those preferences, then the issue-space will be similarly constrained for legislative votes. Hence any mixture of the two possible causes can be stable. That is, the existence of stable policy dimensions cannot speak to the causes of that stability (Jackson and Kingdon 1992).

Successfully fitting legislative decision-making on roll-call votes to a low-dimensional spatial structure requires that three things occur. The first is stability: legislators voting together on one vote tend to vote together on others. Otherwise a separate "dimension" would have to be fit to each roll call; that is, a fresh voting coalition would be generated on each roll-call vote. Votes are used to indicate similarities; legislators are most similar when they vote together. As a consequence, votes are most similar when they evoke the same coalition. Similarities among votes (which also implies similarities among legislators) are then interpreted as distances through one of several computing algorithms.

The second condition concerns dimensionality. Given that some stability exists, what is the dimensionality of the space that must be used to account for the patterns of similarities and differences among legislators? In a parliamentary system where defection is tantamount to overturning the government, parties tend to cohere strongly, and any dimensional analysis of legislative voting would completely reflect the party positions on legislation offered by the government, which itself is generally a coalition of parties. In the United States, however, defections from party positions regularly occur. In any situation where there is not perfect agreement within and between coalitions of legislators, many dimensions may be fit (actually as many as there are roll calls with "defections"). Hence standard criteria of fit have been developed. These criteria treat less important dimensions as "errors" or variabilities simply left unexplained.

The third condition relates to generality: how are the spatial configurations of votes and legislators to be interpreted? Given that a space of
small dimensionality is fit to a legislature, how are the dimensions to be
interpreted? Some researchers have preferred a partisan/regional explanation: major dimensions reflect partisanship, with less important dimensions (according to the scaling criteria) indicating defections, usually on
a regional basis, such as Southerners demurring from the Democratic
party position.

The overwhelming body of evidence from scaling exercises of legislative roll-call votes indicates that voting is stable and occurs within a low-
dimensional spatial framework. Clausen's early analyses of Congressional
voting isolated stable dimensions of conflict across Congresses (1967,
1973). By far the most ambitious analysis of congressional voting, however, is the brute force empiricism of Poole and Rosenthal. These investigators have analyzed the entire roll-call record from 1789 to 1985, reporting that "'1.5' dimensions can account for essentially all the behavior
. . . with a simple spatial model that allows for probabilistic voting. We
say '1.5' because, while a second dimension adds significantly in some
Congresses, the second dimension is clearly less important than the first"
(Poole and Rosenthal 1991: 232).

Poole and Rosenthal's interpretation of the low-dimensional structure focuses on the role of political parties: "A party dimension is present
throughout nearly all of U.S. history, while the orthogonal [second] dimension captures internal party divisions" (1991: 235). Party and ideology, in their approach, act to structure political conflict along a basic
liberal-to-conservative dimension. However, Poole and Rosenthal accept
a hypothesis put forward by MacDonald and Rabinowitz (1987) that the
basic dimension of conflict evolves over time. That is, in terms of issue
content, the basic dimension of conflict revolves to capture new issues
brought to the political system for action. Hence "Issues have largely
been dealt with in terms of being *mapped* onto a generalized liberal-
conservative dimension" (Poole and Rosenthal 1991: 258). Poole and Rosenthal write that "there is no question that the Congressional agenda
radically changed during the 1930's . . . [But] did the change in content
bring with it a change in the spatial structure of voting? The answer is
no" (1993: 27). Even the major realignments do not cause the emergence
of new dimensions in congressional voting. So a major task is to explain
how new issues get defined in terms of past voting coalitions and frames
of reference. Note the discussion above concerning Nardulli's "rolling"
regional realignments, which could cause a more incremental movement
of the basic conflict dimension toward the new issues represented by
the realignment.

One needs to be cautious in interpreting the causative factors leading to low-dimensional conflict spaces in congressional voting.[6] First, a low-dimensional conflict structure has been found in at least one state legislature, Texas (Jones 1973a), with the primary factor centering on governmental involvement in the economy. While it is possible that the state's factional structure within the Democratic party accounted for this result, it is unlikely. V. O. Key (1949) noted that factional divisions could not generally substitute for political parties, because they were too unstable and did not allow for accountability. Hence stable, low-dimensional conflict can occur in the absence of party organization.

Second, what gets to the floor of Congress for a vote is a function of feasibility. New dimensions of evaluation may lie seemingly dormant in the voting stage, while all sorts of legislative hearings and other formal and informal actions are occurring. Committees and party leaders serve as agenda-setters, and James Snyder (1992a; but see Rosenthal 1992) has argued that unidimensionality of floor voting is caused by the gatekeeping function of congressional committees. When a coalition of support is assembled, perhaps because of logrolling or vote trading, a formal vote occurs. If such logrolling does occur, all sorts of dimensions of conflict may be present but not be activated in formal voting. This implies that the voting stage in legislatures is not the proper place to look for the emergence of new dimensions of evaluation in the political process.

Generally, the institutional structure of a legislature may force unidimensionality on voting choice. That is, legislators may themselves harbor contradictory goals, perhaps wanting both limited government and increased spending, but the choices offered may force a trade-off between the desired ends. Indeed, any real choice *must* force such a trade-off, because goals are contradictory. If legislators employ these two evaluative dimensions and if the choice is structured by agenda-setters, then even a shift in attention from one evaluative dimension to another will look unidimensional in the voting record. We have already illustrated this

6. Some of the objections to the low-dimensional structure reported by Poole and Rosenthal are technical. For example, Koford (1991) shows that Poole and Rosenthal have assumed constant salience across legislators and that varying salience can cause problems. Similarly, if salience to evaluative dimensions varies across congresses, a low-dimensional structure may be fit to what is really a multidimensional conflict structure (see appendix). Hence Poole and Rosenthal have incorporated an unstated assumption in their work: issue salience varies neither across individuals nor across time.

Poole and Rosenthal's (1991: 232) best response is that this is a function of issue definition, that issue definition can change over time, and that they are not concerned with how issues get defined on the dimensions. But this response avoids the most important question for agenda theorists: how do the panoply of issues competing for attention get defined in terms of the basic conflict structure, rooted as it is in partisanship?

phenomenon with the supercollider vote in chapter 4; the appendix provides an explicit analysis of how salience shifts in multidimensional space can appear unidimensional in the voting record.

At any rate, congressional voting behavior consistent with a low-dimensional, stable conflict structure seems well established. Disagreement among lawmakers is stable and, in spatial terms, orderly. New issues somehow get defined in terms of established frames of reference, at least at the voting stage. Voting conflict in Congress would seem to be both recurrent and evolutionary—recurrent because old voting fault lines continually reappear on vote after vote within and between sessions, evolutionary because the issues change.

The Incorporation of New Issues in an Old Structure

How do new issues get incorporated into old political conflict structures? One favored answer concerns partisan realignment, the process by which parties shift positions to appeal to new groups by raising new issues in order to achieve partisan advantage. Most studies of realignment have focused on shifts in partisan allegiances among groups in the mass public. Realignment theory, however, has suffered because of the failure of many Americans to shift allegiances after 1968, a period demonstrably ripe for realignment. Rather, the number of independents increased, as did split-ticket voting, often leading to the election of a Republican president and a Democratic Congress. We noted above that such movements of groups is probably not inconsistent with a broader theory of electoral change and even realignment, properly understood (Nardulli 1993).

The real problem is that realignment has typically been studied by an examination of shifts in voting groups between parties—in the electorate and in Congress. This has the effect of ignoring the driving force of issues in the process. MacDonald and Rabinowitz (1987) have provided an analysis of structural change, or realignment, that is based in the content of the issues that the political system faces. These scholars start with the fundamental fact that the American political system has dealt with a multiplicity of issues over time and that these issues may cause the structure of conflict ("realignment") to evolve: "Structural change requires change in the political agenda" (MacDonald and Rabinowitz 1987: 778). They conceive of three distinct aspects of political conflict: congressional behavior, mass voting in presidential elections, and partisanship, and they argue that "change in the ideological cleavage among elites [in Congress] becomes manifest first in presidential dialogue and subsequently in the structure of support for the two major parties" (p. 779). Congressional behavior is measured through an analysis of roll-call votes on state delegations, and partisanship and presidential voting is measured at the state level. A factor analysis of these measures by year (1920–84) and across states yielded a stable two-dimensional solution for all three aspects of conflict.[7]

Most interestingly, the structure of conflict has evolved from one factor (or dimension of conflict) to the other across years. That is, the first dimension is primarily responsible for structuring conflict before the mid-1960s, whereas after that period the second dimension is dominant. Because they do not examine issue content in their analysis, MacDonald and Rabinowitz can only speculate about what has driven the shift. They make it clear, however, that they believe it to be the intrusion of social issues, beginning with civil rights, into the political sphere. I noted above that Poole and Rosenthal accept this interpretation of a shift in the issue-basis of the central dimension of legislative conflict.

How do these new issues get incorporated into the two-dimensional frame of reference that MacDonald and Rabinowitz report? If we focus on legislative conflict, it seems clear that both the preferences of members and the structure of the institution are important. Bringing in new members to Congress brings in fresh preferences, but it also brings in members who are attentive to issues different from the traditional issues of the "old guard." But it seems that new members themselves come into Congress in "clumps," with some elections (1948, 1964, 1974, 1992) bringing in more new members by far than other elections. The structure of the institution is also important: how new issues are raised and processed by the system. In Congress, committees perform that function (Krehbiel 1991).

An Analysis of Congressional Hearings

Since all issues voted on in Congress must first pass through the gate of committees, it seems that an analysis of the issues processed by those committees could illuminate how issues get defined in terms of basic dimensions of evaluation. The way to proceed is to examine the topics scrutinized in committees, ideally relating these topics to the roll-call voting dimensions unearthed by the dimensioning studies. In collaboration with Frank Baumgartner, I have taken a "first cut" at the first of these objectives.

7. Factor analysis is a metric scaling technique that is used to put roll calls (or other choices) on underlying dimensions. It treats the correlations between roll calls (choices) as indicative of metric distances between the votes; the higher the correlation, the shorter the distance. The technique fits a spatial solution to the observed distances.

Any single hearing may contain discussions of numerous issues, so that a decision must be made concerning how to treat this problem of multiple issues per hearing. Baumgartner and I chose to examine the keywords used by the Congressional Information Service (CIS) to characterize hearings. CIS uses several keywords for every hearing, much in the way that a thesaurus may list several connotations for a single word. Through a straightforward sampling scheme, we isolated 108 keywords out of all those used by CIS.[8] We followed the keyword throughout the period 1925 to 1990, counting the number of hearings associated with each keyword. Then we factor-analyzed the resulting data, obtaining not the neat low-dimensional structure observed by analysts of roll-call voting but a considerably more complex structure.[9] There were two primary factors, however, accounting for 40 percent (24 percent and 14 percent, respectively) of the variance (compare this to the 74 percent accounted for in the MacDonald-Rabinowitz analysis).

While the more complex, but nevertheless structured, dimensional pattern in the hearings data may reflect differences in data, these differences are more likely a reflection of the more open nature of the process of scheduling hearings before congressional committees. Hearings on bills are referred to particular committees, and only those committees may hold hearings on those bills. The referral process is governed by an elaborate set of rules, but these rules are never conclusive, because the nature of issues changes over time. Hence a "common law" develops among committees vying for control over emergent issues (King 1991, 1994). In recent years, multiple referrals have made the process more

8. Since we wished to isolate about 100 keywords, we first summed the total number of pages in the CIS volumes and divided by 100. This is the number of pages that must be skipped to end up with 100 issues. We actually selected 108 keywords in order to avoid "fractional pages." Then we selected a starting page at random and chose the keyword at the upper left-hand corner of the page. (If the keyword was a person's name, we moved to the next entry.) Skipping the proper number of pages, we worked through all CIS volumes until the 108 keywords were selected.

Then we moved to the computerized CIS data base and traced each of the keywords over time by counting the number of hearings containing the keyword each year. This procedure yielded the 108 time series of counts of the number of hearings that contained the keywords that were used in the analysis.

9. To perform the factor analysis, we created keyword variables, which were the ratio of times a keyworded hearing appeared to the total number of keyworded hearings on an annual basis. So the keyword variable can be (roughly) interpreted as the percentage of the hearing agenda occupied by hearings associated with the keyword during the year. We interpret associated keyworded hearings as indicating an underlying issue. Percentages were used because the number of hearings conducted increases in time, particularly after the early 1970s; hence we guard against the emergence of a pure "temporal factor." Thirteen factors accounted for 82.1 percent of the variance.

open (Davidson 1989; Davidson et al. 1988). More important for the study of policy agendas, chamber rules grant committee or subcommittee chairs great discretion in scheduling of nonreferral hearings, and no rules govern the relevance of the topic to the committee's regular business (Talbert, Jones, and Baumgartner 1994). Hence the scheduling of hearings is far less demanding than arranging a roll-call vote, and always has been. The committee process, then, is the proper place to examine the emergence of issues on the national legislative agenda.

Key word analysis proved somewhat difficult to interpret, because of the wide range of topics keyed. Numerous key words are associated with each factor, some key words are associated with more than one factor, and some keywords are virtually irrelevant to interpretations. Nevertheless, it seems reasonably clear that the second factor involves the standard economic conflict dimension, whereas the first factor includes issues focusing on the environmental and on health consequences of economic growth. Figure 6.3 graphs key word indicators of the two factors across the period of study.[10] The graph makes clear that the second factor, which I suggest is economic conflict, was most important for most of the period of study, with major increases in the late 1930s and a peak in the late 1970s. The first factor emerges as important in 1970, and increases in importance throughout the 1970s and early 1980s, peaking in 1986. This dimension seems to center on issues of environmentalism, health threats posed by industrialization, and safety. It is probably no accident that it emerged at around the same time as the "social issue" emerged electorally. The legislative dimension is mostly concerned with measures that attack the "spillover effects" of industrialism, and the electoral social issue centers on threats to an orderly society. However, the environmental and consumer movements that form the basis for the new legislative dimension were initially seen as threatening to the post–World War II socioeconomic order. At any rate, the times were certainly ripe for change, perhaps providing a "window of opportunity" to challenge the entrenched interests lodged in the industrial regulatory subsystems that had proved to be so beneficial to business interests.

Since the indicators are raw numbers of hearings, the total number of hearings conducted expands as time proceeds. This expansion of congressional capacity to hold hearings seems to have been used to examine the new issues. While the keywords make interpretation somewhat difficult, the manner in which health issues fall on the two dimensions is

---

10. The indices were the four keywords for each factor loading highest on those factors. For factor 1, the keywords were nuclear waste, terrorism, radiology, and insurgency; for factor 2, they were NAACP, allied health, cooperatives, and public housing.

Number of hearings

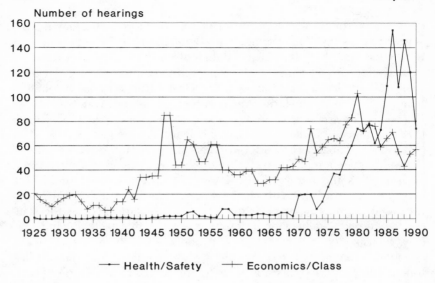

Source:CIS

Fig. 6.3. Congressional hearings: two major keyword factors.

suggestive of the nature of the two dimensions. Health care seems solidly in the old economics-government involvement sphere, whereas health issues of radiation and chemical toxicity evoke the new dimension. Interestingly, racial issues seem mostly to fall on the old dimension rather than on the new one, suggesting a division between electoral politics and legislative politics. Perhaps the social issue was played out somewhat more covertly in Congress than in the mass public.

Even given the problem of interpretation, the keyword approach to the issue content of hearings yields striking conflict patterns across time. It is clear that after the early 1970s, committee business was structured by at least two issue-dimensions and that the new issues competed for salience with the old economic issues dominant during most of the twentieth century. By moving back a step from voting in the process of lawmaking, we can observe the emergence of issues in a pattern considerably different from the more structured voting patterns studied by roll-call vote analysts.

The rise of issues in congressional committees can be analyzed in a manner similar to the electoral analysis presented above. When new issues emerge or when new definitions of old issues become popular, the existing committee jurisdictional structure may not be able to contain the resulting conflict. For example, when nuclear power is thought of as a major contributor to economic progress, hearings on the topic occur in a very limited committee venue. But when the issue comes to be defined as a threat to health and safety, new committees may claim jurisdiction. Now the issue is defined by a two-dimensional frame and politics centers on which dimension is salient. This conflict dynamic emerged frequently in a study of agenda dynamics during the twentieth century conducted by Frank Baumgartner and myself (Baumgartner and Jones 1993; Jones, Baumgartner, and Talbert 1993).

The more complex conflict structure means that more dimensions of evaluation may be present, but it may also mean that a cluster of topics preoccupies the legislative agenda during a limited period of time. Indeed, the factor structure contained several such "temporally specific" issue-factors. For example, a cluster of hearings centering on revenue sharing and housing emerged in the 1960s, expanded in 1971, and petered out during the late 1980s. This cluster was clearly associated with the rise and decline of a national urban policy during the period. The factor accounted for 6.6 percent of the variance in the keywords. A more enduring factor emerged in the 1950s, expanded in the 1960s, and continued into the 1990s. It is difficult to interpret solely from keywords, but it centers on debt financing, insurance, and certain urban issues. Figure 6.4 graphs the factor indicators for the first four factors (accounting for

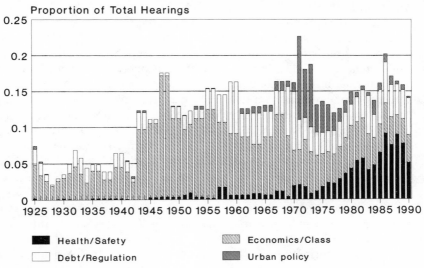

Fig. 6.4. Congressional hearings: four major keyword factors.

Source: CIS

about 53 percent of the variance) as percentages of committee business through time. The specific percentages are not particularly important, because of the use of a limited number of issues to indicate the factors, but the relative emphasis is suggestive. In particular, more issue-dimensions are in evidence later in the period.[11]

Issue Definitions and the Emergence of Conflict

Both mass political attitudes and congressional voting behavior seem to be ordered by an issue structure of low dimensionality. That means that most issues seem to evoke preexisting frames of reference rather than to move independently of the general political discourse. The recurrence of conflict does not mean that conflict is static. New issues do emerge in politics and are transformed in some manner into past frames of reference. So one question is how issue evolution is commensurate with recurrent conflict.

A key to the process is the role of political parties, traditionally the vessels through which conflict is carried. The "umbrella" parties in the United States have motive to incorporate new issues into their programs, hence tending to bring forth similar legislative voting coalitions to the new issues. As the example of the electoral behavior of the Democratic party in the early 1970s illustrates, parties may move to capture the allegiances of newly activated groups of voters, but these moves may or may not be successful electorally.

Emerging issue-dimensions are critical to political change because they open up political issues to more than one interpretation. Where there is one dimension of conflict, any issue is capable of but one interpretation: where it falls on that underlying dimension. Where there are two or more dimensions, the issue is capable of multiple interpretations, *depending on the relative salience of the underlying dimensions.* So rapid political change is more likely when (1) two or more underlying dimensions of evaluation are present in the general political debate and (2) the activities of political actors, or the (random?) occurrence of events, act to shift collective attention from one dimension to another.

By the time issues show up in congressional voting or in mass voting behavior, and even in congressional hearings, it is very late in the issue-definition process. Actors have time to assemble coalitions and define new issues in terms of past frames of reference. The work of scaling theo-

---

11. The fifth factor accounted for only 4.9 percent of the variance but included a keyword (petroleum) that occupied a considerable amount of committee time during the period.

rists shows that this cannot always be done, and when it is not done then new conflict dimensions emerge in the macropolitical institutions and within the mass public. These seemingly new conflict dimensions, however, tend to represent recurrent underlying human political goals—productivity, security, fairness. These underlying goals explain why new issues can emerge within a stable or recurrent conflict structure. At an earlier point in the process, such as when hearings in congressional committees are scheduled, we may observe a panoply of issues struggling for attention. A key question for political scientists is just how these issues come to be defined in terms of prevailing conflict dimensions.

Conclusions

It is possible for political decision-makers to use more than one evaluative dimension to understand any given issue. Any political issue is capable of being judged on more than one evaluative dimension; all political issues are fundamentally multidimensional. Hence much of the political dialogue concerns the relevance of one evaluative dimension over others. Moreover, the tendency of political decision-makers, from voters to legislators, to shift episodically from one evaluative dimension to another causes a fundamental instability in the processing of issues in open political systems.

The prominence of evaluative dimensions in political discourse is directly related to the recurrence of political conflict. The prominence of one evaluative dimension in one political era does not mean that goals are simply ordered on one dimension. It may simply mean that other dimensions are not salient at the time. If economic growth is emphasized in one era, it does not mean that people do not care about health and safety. They may simply not be attending to these concerns—or they may feel that government cannot achieve these aims. If an era of prosperity ushers in great concerns about the health and safety of people, or about the just distribution of goods and services, it does not mean that people are unconcerned about economic well-being. It just may not be so relevant at the time. But the potential always exists for the reintroduction of a preexisting evaluative dimension, thus shifting the political dialogue.

This issue-based approach to political change suggests a somewhat different perspective on partisan realignment. Students of realignment processes tend to focus on dramatic shifts in partisan attachments and the consequences for mass voting patterns. It can be, however, that attentiveness to basic dimensions of conflict within the policy process changes without shifts in partisan allegiances. The study of issue processing in congressional committees suggests that during the 1970s and 1980s new issues emerged in the legislative arena within the electoral framework of an "incomplete realignment" (or perhaps "dealignment"). The system was not dependent on the realignment of voters to initiate shifts in the issue-dimensions that structure political conflict in the policymaking process. What seems to be fundamental is a shift in the understanding of issues (that is, a change in the dimensions that frame issues). This shift may be associated with changes in mass voting patterns, but it does not imply any particular alteration in partisan voting patterns. This would be especially true if one party (the Democrats) is favored on one dimension (economics) and the other party (Republicans) is favored on the other (social issues). Then election campaigns would tend to be fought on the salience of the dimensions.

Periodically renewed attentiveness to preexisting frames of evaluation suggests the possibility of issue cycling or recurrent political conflict. But issues change. Political conflict both recurs and evolves. Much of issue evolution has to do with the politics of making policy, where interest groups are important and electoral politics is less critical. We shall see that issues are processed by Congress somewhat independently of the macropolitical processes discussed in this chapter but that these processes always have the potential of intervening.

7

Policy Subsystems and the Processing of Issues

We begin this chapter by recalling the *paradox of issue evolution:* the paradox that the issues handled by the American political system today are vastly different from the issues handled by the system fifty or even twenty-five years ago, yet the dimensional structure of conflict seems fixed. So conflict recurs, but issues evolve. The ability of the political system to process new issues yet to resist a thoroughgoing partisan realignment is one of the most puzzling, and the most discussed, manifestations of this paradox. To understand issue evolution we must understand more than the overall dimensional structure of conflict, a structure that was laid out in chapter 6. We must also understand how the myriad of individual issues that occupy most of the time and energy of policymakers at all levels of government are processed. It turns out that the overarching dimensions of conflict that are reflected in elections and in the final roll-call decisions of elected representatives are not often relevant to the evolution of issues. But when they do intrude, they play a large role in policy development.

This chapter and chapter 8 discuss the concepts of the *parallel* and *serial* processing of issues, and show how the formation of policy subsystems and the rise of issues to the political agenda are related to the two different modes of issue processing. When an issue becomes of general interest to a policymaking body, political scientists speak of *agenda access*. Most policymaking is conducted within policy subsystems, generally out of the limelight and off the agenda. At the national level, subsystems operate for policies as diverse as agricultural subsidies, urban housing, and the regulation of financial securities. Congress and the president allow administrative agencies overseeing these policies considerable discretion in the conduct of policy, with contact between Congress and the agencies being mostly sporadic and basically friendly. Numerous policy subsystems are proceeding this way all at once; that is, they are making policy in parallel. Agenda access happens when a shift in the processing of issues occurs from a parallel, within-subsystems approach to serial, macropolitical processing (Baumgartner and Jones 1993).

Because of the nature of the relationship between policymaking bodies and policy subsystems, policymaking within subsystems is generally stable and incremental. It is conservative in the sense of changing gradually rather than radically. Subsystem-based policymaking remains so stable because subsystems tend to incorporate those interested in the policy area and to adjust continually to the wishes of the interested. In an open, democratic system, it is not possible to exclude from the process those wishing to make entreaties to government agencies, so even when an agency is not oriented toward the accommodation of interests, it ends up being nudged toward that pattern. Ironically, the very openness that allows interested parties to affect policymaking within subsystems can lead to undemocratic policy decisions, in the sense that the sum total of the decisions made within policy subsystems can be far afield from what the general public might desire.

In this chapter, we examine the role of negative feedback processes, which are self-limiting and conservative, in policy subsystems. Negative feedback implies an adjustment process; if a policy subsystem veers too far in one direction, forces act to bring it back toward a more balanced policy perspective. Policy subsystems operating under negative feedback tend to approximate equilibrium, because affected interests are left alone to work out policy arrangements that suit them. But this equilibrium can be quite different from the equilibrium that would result if, hypothetically, every citizen weighed in on the decisions of the subsystem. Hence the subsystem can drift further and further from the wishes of electoral majorities. This state of affairs is termed *path dependence*, a situation in which the local equilibrium forged by affected interests can be dramatically different from the overall *populist policy equilibrium*, in which mass preferences balance policy outputs.

Because of the powerful forces that buttress policy subsystems, it takes a fairly strong and general mobilization to disrupt them once they are established. Disruption is normally achieved through the intrusion of new dimensions of evaluation into the political debate. Because new issue-frames must be communicated to be effective in the policy process, the role of the media is critical in the formation and disruption of policy subsystems. At some point, the so-called macropolitical institutions—Congress, the president, and the political parties—often become involved in the new dimension as conflict is expanded to the electoral arena. Hence the overall dimensional structure of conflict is both affected by and affects the normal parallel processing of issues in a political system.

The Role of Institutions

We are moving toward a view of democratic politics that stresses the ability of political entrepreneurs and the groups they are able to mobilize to interject new dimensions of evaluation into a staid governmental process dominated by the conservative parallel processing of issues. To do that, it is important that we understand how policymaking in policy subsystems is characterized by "standing decisions" that focus the attention of participants on a limited number of evaluative dimensions. This occurs because in many situations the structure of a decision-making problem is already determined by the institutional context. Institutions often "solve" what Simon termed the design problem (see chap. 3). That is, they structure situations so as to limit choice to a relatively small number of alternatives, usually doing so by causing participants in the institution to focus on a limited number of evaluative dimensions. This does not mean that the rules that are the basis of human institutions completely circumscribe human choice. Any system of rules is complex, subject to varying interpretation, and inconsistent in the application of sanctions. Competing norms can emerge within any formal structure. Moreover, decision-makers are capable of discovering that the rules are not working for one reason or another, and may begin a design search for more workable rules. But for most people most of the time, the simple decision rules that characterize institutions focus attention on a limited range of alternatives structured by a limited number of underlying dimensions of evaluation.

In politics, this happens in policymaking branches as well as in the bureaucracies that implement policy. Policymaking institutions generally factor decisions according to policy means, and implementing structures follow this division of labor. Legislative committees and government bureaus alike are organized along task lines. In Congress, appropriations committees are separate from authorizing committees; and committees themselves are organized according to substantive tasks. Attempts to organize across tasks and according to goals, such as goal-based budgeting, tend not to be very successful.

Political scientists see institutions as rules that are generally accepted as legitimate constraints on behavior by participants. Many times these rules are explicit and are written down, as in the case of constitutions, charters, and enabling statutes for administrative agencies. Sometimes they emerge out of the interactions among participants; they are part of the informal system of norms. For our purposes, institutions in whatever form are important because they dictate what aspects of the situation are relevant. Many organizational rules in service delivery agencies are explicitly designed to cause personnel to attend to some aspects of the environment and to ignore others. For example, as reported in studies of urban service delivery, the city of Detroit, a thoroughly reformed municipality, used standard bureaucratic decision rules to dictate how traditional services were delivered. Such rules as routine search, response on demand, and a "severity rule" in which more severe problems were treated with more coercive options dominated the city's service bureaus. Many other scholars have reported similar findings for a number of other cities (Jones 1980). In Chicago, however, a study of the building regulatory process found that both the standard bureaucratic decision rules *and* a set of "attention rules" based on political influence were operative. That is, the situation was simply structured differently in the two cities—ignoring the political situation could bring problems for the service bureaucrat. Hence service personnel attended to different aspects of the environment in Chicago (Jones 1985).

At any level of government, the institutional context is important in determining just what pattern of adjustment occurs, because political institutions generally operate to direct participants to only limited parts of a complex environment. The process of political adjustment can, of course, occur only with those aspects of the environment that are selected for attention by the institutional structure.

In solving the design problem, do institutions liberate or blind? That is, do they expand the capacity of decision-makers to monitor and react to relevant parts of a complex environment, providing a ready response to changes in the environment through preprogrammed decision rules, or do institutions provide rigid designs, by their nature immediately maladaptive in a rapidly changing world? Bendor and Hammond (1992) posit this dilemma, noting that Simon's position is that organizational life aids in overcoming the limited capacities of individual decision-making through various subroutines (essentially allowing serially processing beings to handle the environment in parallel). On the other hand, Graham Allison, in his path-breaking study of the Cuban missile crisis, points to the "negative, constraining effects of organizational routines" (Bendor and Hammond 1992: 313).

Why do we have to choose? Organizational routines quite clearly do both. Most critically, organizational routines, which after all are conscious designs to solve problems, may well be adaptive for one set of problems or for one time period. Indeed, organizing resources to bring them to bear on a problem requires rules in order to ensure that the activities of participants mesh and are directed at the existing problem. But the use of these procedures in inappropriate circumstances (or where circumstances have changed but the organization continues to use the routines) may lead to problems. One important problem is that the routines can direct organizational attention, and thus allocate resources, to the wrong aspects of the environment. The problem is compounded by the tendency of decision-makers to search for solutions through reasoning by analogy. That is, they may apply organizational technologies to circumstances that are superficially similar but in reality differ in important respects. This tendency to import policy solutions that worked in the past to superficially similar situations has been described as a reliance on *solution sets*—set in both the sense of a collection of elements (that are therefore exportable) and in the sense of a readiness to respond (Jones and Bachelor 1993). Solution sets package solutions and problems together—that is, they both define the problem facing the policymaking organization and steer the organization toward a standard repertoire of policy options. So long as policymakers continue to conceive of the problem in the standard way, they will be led to adopt solutions *in the region* of the existing solutions.

Factoring in Legislative Decision-Making

It may be objected that the best way to achieve goals is to adopt a general strategy that includes a variety of means. In some cases the inclusive strategy is possible, but in many it is precluded by the structure of the institution. This happens not only in bureaucratic agencies but also in the policymaking branches of government. In legislatures, the institutions of committees (in the United States) and parties (in parliamentary democracies) generally structure the choice situation for legislators, leaving them decisions along the relevant choice dimensions but little flexibility in deciding what means are appropriate for the ends they desire. Complex decisions involving trade-offs among underlying goals are factored, and different committees are assigned different parts of the problem. Individual legislators often become experts in particular policy areas, establishing local "fiefdoms" of influence. Such an arrangement, in which institutional structures factor complex decisions, ensures legislative attentiveness to pieces of means and parts of goals. But nobody speaks for the trade-offs.

Students of legislative politics have noted that such arrangements create policy equilibria, known as *structure-induced equilibria* because they are caused by the structure of the institution rather than by a balancing of policy preferences with policy outputs (Shepsle 1979; Riker 1982). The committee structure is organized around means, so that legislators generally decide on a level of a policy and seldom compare the relevance of other policies for collective goals. Moreover, factoring decisions in committees leads to interest-group politics centering on the committees and the administrative agencies that have been created to implement and administer the policies developed and overseen by committees.

Factoring of legislative decisions into single-dimensional structures and parceling out the parts to committees ensures noncyclical majorities within the committee. In chapter 2, we noted that if an issue under consideration incorporates two or more underlying evaluative dimensions, then the preference functions of legislators are not single-peaked; that is, they cannot be ordered along a single dimension. In such a circumstance, there will normally be no equilibrium of choice (Ordeshook 1986; Riker 1980). Hence agenda-setters can theoretically manipulate issues virtually anywhere in issue-space, by offering particular policy packages that appeal to coalitions of decision-makers. This theoretically gives agenda-setters great control over outcomes in decision-making bodies.

But committees don't consider issues that way; rather, they break them up dimension by dimension. So the agriculture committee may consider the agricultural productivity of pesticides but will not incorporate in its considerations the cross-cutting dimension of environmental damage. Environmental committees may consider environmental damage by pesticides but, in the normal course of events, will not be distracted by considerations of agricultural productivity. This forces issues into a single-dimensional frame and reintroduces the existence of a unique equilibrium (which occurs at the preference of the median legislator serving on the committee).

This complex and decentralized policymaking structure raises the question of aggregation. If every committee tends to consider issues dimension by dimension, then how is the issue to be reconstituted for decision-making by the entire legislative body? The most important mechanism for the aggregation of diverse policies is *deference*. There is a tendency for legislators uninterested in a policy area to defer to the interested and the policies they have developed when aspects of the policy come to the floor. Deference is a natural outcome of the processes of selective attention discussed earlier in this book. So the policy is made by committee (actually, by the whole policy subsystem centering on the congressional committee) and is often just ratified by the legislative body.

There is, however, a second source of deference. In any political system, there may be a *core* of alternatives on a policy that are undominated. In effect, the core is the set of alternatives that cannot be beaten by any coalition, given the rules of the game and the preferences of the members (Hammond and Miller 1987). This core might comprise just one alternative, but it could also comprise quite a number of possibilities. The institutional structure of a political system can disempower some coalitions by, in effect, expanding the core. "If institutional features such as bicameralism and the committee system disempower enough coalitions, some policy alternatives may remain undominated. That is, the majority coalitions that prefer some other points to the undominated points become powerless to enforce that preference because they lack the required chamber or committee composition" (Miller and Hammond 1990: 203). If the preferences of legislators change, then the policy may not change, because it remains within the core enforced by the institutional structure. The 1992 supercollider vote discussed in chapter 4 is illustrative. In effect, the large majority of representatives against the project were thwarted by a small majority of supporters in the Senate, allowing leaders to aggregate the measure within a broader budget bill in conference committee. Institutional arrangements allowed supercollider funding to remain within the core of alternatives. American institutions, by protecting a large core of policy possibilities, build considerable stability into the policymaking process.

Now we see two sources of decentralized, subsystem-based policymaking in the United States. The first is disinterest; the second is the denial of many majoritarian positions through institutional arrangements designed to promote stability. The two sources of decentralization are not independent, because the institutional arrangements make necessary a strong mobilization (the construction of a "supermajority" within government) in order to overcome the decentralization implied by a large core. Hence deference can be quite a rational response to the difficulties inherent in the American institutional structure in addition to being the result of the processes of selective attention discussed in this book.

Of course, not all issues can be handled through such decentralized methods. Aggregation does occur across policy domains through a process of negotiation and compromise on budget bills or when legislation will affect most or all policy areas.[1] The mechanisms of deference, bargaining, and cores protected by the institutional structure all preclude any overarching evaluation of the joint determination of multiple goals through policy action, as well as any overall comparison between citizen wishes and government policies.

We might generally note that aggregation is critically influenced by the structure of attention and the salience of issues. Where issues are not salient, legislative leaders and the body of voting members tend to defer to committee proposals. Where issues have attracted attention, committee recommendations are more likely to be overturned and committees must be much more sensitive to the concerns of the general body. Negotiation, compromise, and coalition building generally replace deference on highly salient issues.

By solving the design problem and always presenting decision-

---

1. Congressional budget reforms in the 1970s were implemented to force explicit considerations of trade-offs among policies. Deficits accumulated in the 1980s imply that the aggregation process did not work as intended.

makers with constrained choices, political institutions serve to sustain attention to particular goals over extended periods of time. In essence, they fix attention to a limited number of aspects of a situation, thereby defining and structuring issues. They do so both by factoring complex decisions and by disempowering coalitions, such as the anti-supercollider coalition, that would like to change the status quo. By defining and structuring issues, political institutions provide a conservative influence on politics, allowing for a complex system of mutual deference to sustain itself.

Negative Feedback and Policy Subsystems

The stability imposed by legislative factoring, deference, and the expanded core implies that a major mobilization is necessary to shift policymaking from parallel to serial processing. In order to appreciate the role of a shift from parallel to serial processing in policymaking, we first need to examine how policy subsystems operate in normal times. To begin, we ought to note that there has been some disagreement among political scientists about the exact nature of subsystems. These differences have centered on such aspects of subsystems as who participates in them, whether they are conflictual or consensual, and how large they might be. Here, we will simply treat policy subsystems as those policy arrangements in which only some part of the government is involved; no claim is made that any particular conflict pattern or coalition of actors must be present to warrant the term *subsystem*. A subsystem is just a part of the whole political system that interacts more intensely with its participants than with other parts of the political system.

We now turn to how policies are made within these subparts of the whole political system. Prevailing models of policymaking in the United States have stressed three fundamental characteristics: (1) mutual adjustment among competing groups; (2) incremental change; and (3) negative feedback processes. Policymaking models incorporating these three facets are generally termed *pluralist* systems. Incremental change in such systems can result from the deliberate marginal adjustments of boundedly rational decision-makers, or from mutual adjustment and negative feedback processes. These make the system conservative.[2] Major policy changes would seem to be very difficult under these circumstances, a

2. Physicists call such systems *Hamiltonian;* they are conservative linear dynamical systems. Political scientists might call such systems *Madisonian,* in the sense that the constitutional framework sets up incentives for mutual adjustment rather than domination by a single interest. Actually, the political science models are more like the physicist's dissipative dynamical systems (such as the damped pendulum). This causes the system to move

characteristic that has been both lauded as necessary to stymie excesses and excoriated as blunting the demands of popular majorities.

Feedback is essential in pluralist models of policymaking. The concept of feedback has its origins in the work of Norbert Weiner, who recognized that the control of any process depends on the deviations between the predicted and the actual motion of a time series, which can then be "fed back" as input in order to correct the direction of the process. If the information is ignored, deviations will increase; if the system controller overcorrects, wild oscillations will result (Langton 1989: 16–17). A controller in Weiner's system adjusts deviations in a *negative* fashion: the larger the deviation, the greater the correction in an opposite direction. Thus is the system kept within bounds. Weiner's work was directed at the control of antiaircraft guns, but it also applies to driving a car or correcting one's golf swing, as well as adjusting the supply of a product produced by a company to the demand for it.

Negative feedback can occur in pluralist policymaking systems through two mechanisms: deliberate adjustment and countermobilization. In deliberate adjustment, a policymaker moves incrementally to adjust to the environment, which itself is complex (Lindblom 1959). The policymaker acts much like Weiner's controller. Incrementalism in decision-making results in fewer overcorrections, which can be more problematic than undercorrections. The second policymaking pathway leading to negative feedback, countermobilization, occurs when a push by a group for more action in a policy domain is countered with mobilization from an opposed group. This countermobilization is fundamental to *group theory*, a theory of politics emphasizing the role of groups in an open policymaking process (Truman 1951); it works without a central controller. If countermobilization and deliberate incremental decision-making characterize numerous policy subsystems operating in parallel, then it would seem at first blush that a healthy system of balancing among interests will result.

The rosy results implied by the group theorists have been challenged on a variety of grounds. The most important of these challenges claim that countermobilization is rare because (a) active groups possess disproportionate resources, so that it is not possible for weaker elements to challenge the prevailing distribution of power (Schattschneider 1960); and (b) policymaking is decentralized into numerous structured venues, which insulate affected groups from interference (Lowi 1979). The former objection relates to the distribution of political resources in society.

---

to a restricted region of *phase space* called an *attractor*. This is the kind of equilibrium implied by most pluralist models of policymaking.

It takes resources to achieve sufficient organization; organized groups tend to have more resources and thus are overrepresented. The latter objection focuses on the role of the institutional structure in protecting policy subsystems, which tend to make themselves invulnerable through statute and negotiations with other affected interests. Nevertheless, countermobilization does occur within policy subsystems, leading Paul Sabatier (1988) to characterize many subsystems as dominated by competing *advocacy coalitions,* a state of more or less continual mobilization and countermobilization.

Jonathan Bendor and Terry Moe (1985, 1986) have developed a model of U.S. policymaking within an arbitrary subsystem which highlights the processes of mobilization and countermobilization. To illustrate the abstract model, which should apply to many subsystems, Bendor and Moe ask us to think of a regulatory agency that affects businesses and consumers. The model treats actors as boundedly rational adapters, so that decision-makers adjust to one another dynamically. Specifically, Bendor and Moe postulate three agents in their model: a government bureau interested in increasing budgets and its own discretion; a legislature, interested in votes (which it infers by looking at the actions of the interest groups); and two interest groups, one harmed (business) and one benefited (consumers) by agency action. The model's dynamic is in the "circular flow of influence" among the three agents in the model.

The model is premised on a negative feedback loop: resources flow into the political process in direct proportion to losses imposed by the agency. So if too many costs are imposed on businesses, they become active in trying to influence the legislature, which oversees the agency. If the agency becomes too pro-business, then consumers will become active. Legislators will get involved when they see one group becoming active, thus intervening on the side of the concerned group. This process causes the model to settle down at a "pluralist equilibrium," some compromise position between what business wants and what consumers want.

Figure 7.1 diagrams the "deviation-counteracting" core of a model of subsystem policymaking in a pluralist environment. The regulatory agency may take action that benefits group A; that mobilizes group B, which contacts Congress. The congressional oversight or budget committees move to punish the agency, which causes the agency to reduce the harm it has imposed on the group. In the diagram, the group that is benefited fails to contact Congress; more realistically it just has less influence (or is simply less mobilized) than the aggrieved group. Hence any large policy change is quickly counteracted by the unhappy group, and deviations are always controlled and in bounds.

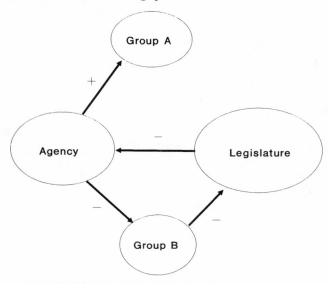

Fig. 7.1. Negative feedback in a policy subsystem.

All change in the model, then, must be exogenous; that is, it must come from outside the system. This is because the affected interests so quickly adjust themselves into a position of equilibrium. If the system is subject to external shocks, then it will tend to return to the pluralist equilibrium or move incrementally to a new equilibrium point. The model is dominated by the politics of pluralist adjustment and the operation of the negative feedback loop. Table 7.1 presents the model in more detail.

Exogenous Shocks and Dynamic Equilibrium: The NLRB

Regulatory and other subsystems are always under exogenous pressure; they are never completely left alone. The major issues, therefore, are, first, how strong are the shocks and, second, how resilient is the subsystem? In some cases, a regulatory subsystem can be enormously resilient, as Terry Moe's study of the National Labor Relations Board indicates (Moe 1985). The NLRB was created during the New Deal as a mechanism to stabilize labor-management relations, which had been plagued by strikes, lockouts, and violence during the early part of the twentieth century. During its early existence the NLRB was vigorously pro-labor, but in 1947 a Republican-dominated Congress enacted the Taft-Hartley Act. Among other things, the act defined a series of "unfair

TABLE 7.1 The Bendor-Moe Model

enforcement $= c$(efficiency) $\cdot$ (budget)	(1)
benefits $= k_1$ (enforcement) $- k_2$ (enforcement)^2	(2)
costs $= k_3$ (enforcement)^2	(3)
consumers' political resources $= k_4 + k_5$ (benefits)	(4)
business's political resources $= k_6 + k_7$ (costs)	(5)
$k_7 > k_5$ [businesses are more effective organizationally]	(6)

Note: Efficiency is the proportion of the budget spent on enforcement; c denotes the units of enforcement purchased by a dollar of spending. Note the negative feedback loop through equations (4) and (5), which dictate that the interest groups direct resources into politics at a rate inversely proportional to their loss functions [eqs. (2) and (3)]. This feedback loop causes the model to stabilize at a "pluralistic equilibrium." This result is not completely intuitive, because significant business advantages are built into the model. Businesses are more sensitive to their loss functions in directing resources into politics [eq. (6)]. Moreover, the loss functions of business are convex (upwardly curving) whereas consumers are concave (downwardly sloping). As enforcement increases, consumers face declining marginal utilities; that is, they are more concerned about the first efforts at enforcement than they are about later efforts. Businesses, however, are more concerned about later efforts at enforcement. These differing loss functions, however, allow for compromise and equilibrium; they in effect weight *intensity*. Consumers care most about initial enforcement, businesses about later enforcement; compromise at a "pluralistic equilibrium" seems natural.

labor practices" that the NLRB was supposed to prosecute and adjudicate. Since then, the NLRB has continually been forced to choose, on a case-by-case basis, between labor and management. Since the early 1950s, the bureau has also operated mostly out of the national limelight.

Moe asks us to consider an NLRB at equilibrium. Then it is subject to an exogenous shock—say, a change of presidential administrations from a pro-business Republican administration to a pro-labor Democratic one. Then labor will become more aggressive and file more complaints, which the NLRB will tend to support. As labor becomes more aggressive, cases with less and less "merit" (that is, cases with less support in the facts) will be filed. This will offer business the opportunity to counterattack, perhaps by engaging regulatory oversight committees in Congress or by appealing to the courts. This is the classic negative feedback pattern that tends to dominate stable subsystems and would lead to a dynamic equilibrium across time. Indeed, in his analysis of case data (a total of twelve thousand cases) for the NLRB from 1948 to 1979, Moe reports a time series that seems to be in long-run equilibrium. It displays no long-term bias toward labor or management (and, indeed, remarkably has an average of 0.5, where 0 is totally pro-business and 1 is completely pro-labor). The exogenous shocks cause only short-term deviations from the long-run average of no bias.

Moe proposes that the bipolar nature of the NLRB's constituency may have something to do with the equilibrium patterns he observes, but suggests that the key variable in equilibrium is not the nature of the constituency but the relative lack of interest on the part of policymakers in the NLRB. So changing administrations may bring in new appointees to the body, but no sustained examination of the modus operandi of the agency occurred between the late 1940s and the mid-1980s (Moe 1985: 1114). Then, however, the Reagan administration began appointing strong ideological conservatives to the board, which destroyed the pluralist balance that had characterized it for almost forty years (Moe 1987; Heinz et al. 1993).

The Rice Wars

If Moe is right, we should be able to find great stability in the face of exogenous shocks even when a subsystem is not bipolar. The so-called rice wars of the 1980s are instructive. The example also shows how subsystems are enmeshed in complex relationships with other government policymaking bodies and how a change in one subsystem may affect another. If these systems interact in complex ways and are all dominated by negative feedback processes, then dynamic equilibrium will be maintained as a pattern of mutual adjustment among parts.

In 1980, the South Korean rice harvest failed and the South Korean government contracted to buy all available California rice.[3] This was not sufficient, so the Seoul government approached Japan to buy more. Under a bilateral agreement between the United States and Japan, however, Japan had promised not to "dump" its heavily subsidized rice on world markets without the acquiescence of the U.S. government. Now policymakers in the Agriculture Department faced a dilemma: approval would anger American rice farmers, but denial could destabilize South Korea, a critical ally. The department tried a compromise: the Koreans could buy the Japanese rice if they would agree to buy more American rice. This compromise did not placate the two most important California rice cooperatives, which retained as their lawyer Joseph Alioto, an influential Democratic politician from San Francisco. The California cooperatives appealed to their allies in Congress, while Alioto attacked State Department officials who had tried to broker the deal.

Once the Japanese purchase was consummated, the fight was on to make sure the Koreans bought the American rice. Members of Congress from the rice-growing areas of Louisiana and Texas joined the fray, engineering a letter to the Korean government signed by more than one hundred members suggesting that the Korean delay in buying American rice involved corruption. Potential suppliers began vying for the Koreans' business, and every deal arranged by the Koreans now generated a con-

---

3. The discussion of the "rice wars" is drawn from Henriques (1993).

gressional uproar as the California cooperatives held out for their exclusive trading agent. Finally, the cooperatives capitulated and agreed to
supply the rice through any intermediary.

The cooperatives by no means "lost" the rice wars, however. The
lesson that most policymakers learned was just how much trouble agricultural corporations could cause when an exogenous shock, even one
from across the sea, destabilized existing subsystem relationships. The
countermobilization by the rice interests, which activated support from
other crop interests, which also wanted to defend protection for their
crops, was strong enough to establish the power of the "rice belt" in the
crop protection game.

This pattern of mutual adjustment and quick moves back to equilibrium is the prevailing approach that underlies most policy studies in political science. Indeed, Bendor and Moe succinctly model the prevailing
approaches to the "balance wheel of pluralism." There is more to policymaking than balance, however. The rest of this chapter begins to explore an alternative, based in a less predictable dynamic that is more
commensurate with the aspects of attentional behavior of decision-
makers and voters that have been detailed in the preceding chapters.

Lock-in and Path Dependency in Policy Systems

One major difference between the outlooks of political science and
economics resides in the disciplines' respective treatments of institutions. Economists have tended to see capitalist economic systems as fluid
and adjusting to changing circumstances, driven by competition to maximize. Political scientists have tended to focus on the institutional limits
to adjustment in democratic systems.

So it is perhaps not surprising that political scientists are rediscovering the adjustment properties of democracies, whereas economists
are finding institutional limits to the adjustment abilities of capitalist systems. In economics, Brian Arthur (1989) has developed the ideas of *lock-
in* and *path dependency* to describe the facets of the economy that prevent smooth adjustment and easy maximization. An inferior technology
may, because of market quirks or unforeseen events, gain ascendancy
over a better-performing technology. Because an industry's start-up costs
are high, because extensive learning is necessary to participate in the industry, and because the coordination necessary to manufacture the good
is difficult to achieve, lock-in can occur. The economy will have problems
in leaving this "local maximum." It becomes historically dependent, or
path dependent, on earlier decisions.

In political science, the ability of affected interests to construct institutional arrangements that protect them from either the competition of the marketplace or the demands of the electorate is standard fare. Indeed, Theodore Lowi (1979) has constructed a complete theory of government based on the protection of such institutional arrangements. In Lowi's approach, the political parties are strongly linked to interest groups, and thus the parties support a system of "mutual noninterference" among the various policy subsystems that constitute the federal government.

The connection between the parties and group interests means that parties often have little incentive to interfere in ongoing policy subsystems. Interest associations form the basis for national party life, infusing funds to parties and their candidates and offering analyses of issues, workers in campaigns, and endorsements. As a consequence, group associations with parties as much as ideologies divide the parties. In congressional races, large amounts of funds are necessary to conduct campaigns, which have become increasingly dependent on the mass media for contacting voters. In 1993, a special election in Texas to replace Lloyd Bentsen as senator illustrates how important groups differ in their orientations toward the parties. Business groups gave almost exclusively to Republican candidates; the plaintiffs' bar gave three-quarters of a million dollars to Democrat Robert Krueger. This particular campaign differed only in that the incumbent was not well entrenched; normally, groups tend to give the most money to incumbents.

Rewards to groups come as policies are awarded to subsystems. Because of the existence of multiple noninterfering subsystems in which the major instruments of democratic linkage, the political parties, are collaborators, any idea of a maximization of mass democratic demands in policy outputs is naive.

So while the terms *lock-in* and *path dependency* might not be familiar to political scientists, the underlying ideas would. Maximization of mass preferences in public policy is impossible; and even an approximation may not be realistic. The system of affected interests has become *locked-in* and *path dependent* in the sense that protected interests yesterday tend to be protected today. But protected interests are only part of the story. The tendency of policymakers within subsystems to seek solutions to emerging problems in the region "near to" the prevailing pluralist equilibrium also implies path dependency in policy actions within subsystems. Solution sets are locked-in both by the prevailing configurations of power and by the tendency of subsystems to shy away from policy proposals that represent a long-jump from the existing local equilibrium.

Parallel Processing in Government

The vast bulk of government action in the United States (or anywhere else) is conducted routinely. Social security checks are sent; welfare applicants are screened; tax returns are audited; teachers conduct
classes; police move out on routine patrol. Moreover, all of this activity
happens simultaneously, and generally without explicit coordination
from central policymakers. It occurs within agencies at all levels of government in the federal system. At each agency, policymaking is conducted mostly by the interested, those who, for one reason or another,
have a stake in policy outcomes. The result is a vast network of policymaking *venues* within which participants share common assumptions
and knowledge, although they may not always agree on policy options.

Thus most public policy is conducted in *parallel:* simultaneously and
without central control. Of course, any single policymaking unit must
process issues serially, that is, one at a time. The local building inspector
can make one call at a time; the city council focuses its attention on one
item at a time; the state legislature votes on one issue at a time. But all
building inspectors are at work at the same time; many city councils may
consider the same issue within a limited time frame; state legislative
committees can all work on different issues simultaneously. So the sum
of policymaking arrangements in the United States amounts to parallel
processing of diverse issues.

This parallel processing system is why students of public policy point
to subsystem arrangements at the national level, with policies within a
particular area made mostly by those interested in the area. It has been
noted that such policy subsystems allow affected interests to seek an
equilibrium without having to deal with the turbulence of interests not
so affected by the operation of the subsystem (Redford 1969). Such subsystems tend to be dominated by negative feedback, because participants
tend to view the issues facing the subsystem similarly, focusing on a single
dimension of evaluation.[4]

The complex network of parallel policy processing units does not
stop with policy subsystems at the national level. Indeed, most direct
policy activity in the United States takes place in the states and localities.
Moreover, the parallel processing system is highly interdependent, with
local units affecting each other and with units at different levels of government that are focusing on the same policy problem influencing each

---

4. The Bendor-Moe model discussed above operates in such a one-dimensional
space.

other; with administrative agencies and courts influencing legislatures; and with legislatures influencing administrative agencies.

Self-Similarity in Policy Venues

The entire system of policy venues, the federal system of numerous policy venues at all levels of government, allows for massive parallel processing of issues. Of course, the states and localities have their own challenges in shifting from parallel to serial processing. Indeed, with respect to policymaking, all agencies process issues in a roughly similar manner. They are all subject to the so-called policy cycle. Students of public policy use this term to refer to the flow of policy activity from the existence of a problem, through the definition of the issue to be addressed, through agenda access by the issue, through enactment of a solution to the perceived problem, to the implementation of the solution. The implemented solution has some impact, which may affect the policymaking system by feedback. Because all agencies proceed according to this kind of a policy cycle, the total of these interlocking policy cycles within venues of policy activity may be thought of as "wheels within wheels" (Jones 1983).

The federal system is in major respects *self-similar* in its policymaking processes, as is the entire network of policy venues. That is, whatever level of policymaking we observe, there are very strong comparabilities in procedures and activities. In particular, the flow of policy, treated abstractly via the policy cycle, looks reasonably similar within every venue of activity. In other ways there are differences, especially with regard to the content of policy. For example, local governments are far more prone to try to bolster the tax base through investment policies than is the national government, which seems more sensitive to pressures for consumption spending (Baumgartner and Jones 1993: chap. 11).

Nevertheless, policymaking systems in the United States tend to have roughly analogous organization and processes, differing more in degree than kind. This is because they are all organized within fairly limited parameters, specified by written constitutions (themselves self-similar) and rules of practice developed within a framework of pluralistic democracy. There seems to be a self-similar organization of governments in a federal system, all operating within local rules that are themselves roughly the same. Moreover, government agencies at the national level are quite similar in procedure while being quite different in the policies they were constructed to address.

The Populist Policy Equilibrium and the Pluralist Policy Equilibrium

The massively parallel processing of issues in a diverse and decentralized political system implies that local equilibria will be reached within most policy venues. This raises the question of whether such local equilibria are consonant with the generalized preferences of the mass public. It is possible, in principle at least, to compare aggregated mass preferences with the decentralized local equilibria implied in the system of parallel processing.

The point at which mass preferences and policy outputs are in total balance with one another may be termed the *populist policy equilibrium*. If we could add up all the preferences for government action across all policy domains and could compare that to the total output of government, then the hypothetical point at which this occurs would be the populist policy equilibrium. This seems to be what Weissberg (1978) means by collective representation, and Stimson (1991) by longitudinal representation. Theoretically we could trace this point across time as preferences changed in the mass public.

Because most path dependency in policy subsystems is buttressed by a prevailing set of ideas about the proper operation of government in the particular policy arena, and because affected interests are allowed to negotiate and compromise until a policy settlement is reached, policy subsystems tend to reach a *local equilibrium*. In many subsystems this is the Bendor-Moe pluralist policy equilibrium, but in some cases policymaking may fall under the exclusive control of a single interest. The equilibrium is dynamic, since subsystem participants react to each other and to changing circumstances in the policy area. But subsystems tend to stability, so long as interference from outside parties is not too dramatic. Bendor and Moe's model of the hypothetical regulatory agency shows why these policy systems are so stable; they are powerful mechanisms for achieving adjustments within prevailing interests—within a legal framework that has been established by the policymaking branches. These local equilibria are structure-induced, because they are a result of the structure of policymaking. Not only are they similar to the structure-induced policymaking systems within Congress discussed above, but they are actually part of these systems, because very commonly congressional committees are the legislative linchpins of policy subsystems.

Hypothetically, at least, we could add up the prevailing local equilibria achieved within policy subsystems. The sum of the local, path-dependent equilibria within subsystems, which are basically structure-induced subsystem equilibria, can be termed the *pluralist policy equilibrium.* Again, this is a hypothetical point; we actually have no way of summing up the various local equilibria to get an overall picture of the operation of the pluralist system. Because of the operation of path dependency, this point is almost certainly quite distant from the populist policy equilibrium.

To anticipate the coming argument, we can note a connection between the limited policy outlooks within policy subsystems and the focus of participants interacting within them on a very limited number of evaluative dimensions. When the more general policymaking institutions become interested in policymaking within a subsystem, the issue has shifted its locus from within the parallel processing apparatus to the policymaking branch, which is capable only of serial processing. This happens rarely, generally when new dimensions of conflict intrude. The new focus is often not favorable to subsystem participants (Baumgartner and Jones 1993). It would be comforting if we could assume that this shift from parallel to serial processing would restore the populist policy equilibrium. Alas, we cannot assume any such thing, as we shall see shortly.

The Hollow Core

In the early 1980s, Heinz and his colleagues initiated a large-scale empirical study of interest representation in Washington. They interviewed lobbyists, the clients of the lobbyists, and governmental officials in four broad policy domains: agriculture, energy, health, and labor (Heinz et al. 1993; see also Laumann and Knoke 1987). They mapped acquaintance networks among the policy elites in each domain using smallest space analysis, a technique for the recovery of underlying dimensions from data that indicate how "close" two individuals are—in this case, whether they were acquaintances. In all four policy domains these researchers found "a roughly spherical structure with a hollow core" that was probably "a consequence of the substantive specialization of the representatives . . . This suggests that autonomous brokers who have the capacity to bridge the four areas . . . do not exist" (Heinz et al. 1993: 300–301). The same pattern emerged *within* the policy communities; again, no brokers existed. Heinz and his colleagues conclude that communication among elites within and among policy communities occurs mostly between allies, and not with enemies or with brokers.

To Heinz and his colleagues, this conclusion implies that policy subsystems are fragile: "The policy-making structure is held together not by the magnetism of a dense core but by surface tension, like a soap bubble. If this analogy implies instability, that is probably appropriate" (Heinz et al. 1993: 302). The implication is that significant events have the power

to disrupt these fragile subsystems held together more by surface alli-
ances than by deep agreement on the fundamentals. This careful empirical analysis suggests that the introduction of new dimensions of conflict,
often carried on a stream of events that allow the definition of the new
conflict structure, can quickly destabilize subsystem arrangements characterized by "surface tension" rather than the "magnetism of a dense
core."

Overhead Democracy and Parallel Processing

During the 1930s a debate emerged in political science concerning
the normative basis for democratic government and its relationship to
the national state that was being put into place. On the one hand, some
scholars lauded the inherent pluralism that was emerging in many of the
New Deal's regulatory agencies with their considerable rule-making discretion. They liked the idea of setting a framework through legislation,
and then letting agency personnel and affected interests work out the
specifics.

On the other hand, some saw the system of delegating power to bureaucrats as undemocratic and as replacing national majorities with
special-interest pleading. They called for hewing to the *overhead democracy model* (Redford 1969). Congress and the president were seen as
making national policy, and the federal bureaucracy (and the states and
localities in many areas of domestic policymaking) were the implementers. Viewed in the perspective of this model, national majorities are created in support of the policies enacted by the "political" (in the sense of
elected) branches of government. Any deviation from their policies by
federal bureaucrats or by state and local officials would seem to undermine democratic majoritarianism.

The debate over overhead democracy continues today. A modern
variant is the *congressional dominance* model. The model was developed
as part of a line of research in *principal-agent relations,* in which legislatures are seen as principals and administrative agencies are seen as
agents of the principals, much in the way that citizens would hire lawyers
or accountants to pursue their interests. Legislatures are not knowledgeable about the specifics of policy areas, but expect the agencies to hold
true to their interests and intentions. The congressional dominance
model simply stresses that agencies defer to the collective preferences of
members of Congress as indicated by statute (Weingast 1984; Weingast
and Moran 1983).

The congressional dominance model has been criticized on both empirical and theoretical grounds. Wooley (1993) notes that presidential ap-

pointees to regulatory agencies have considerable latitude under certain circumstances to support policies that do not correspond to the preferences of the members of the congressional oversight committees. He offers a study of the regulation of banks in which the Comptroller of the Currency (who is responsible for regulating banks) acted independently of each oversight committee. Wood and Anderson (1993) have shown that agency outputs change when presidential appointments to regulatory agencies change. This implies that the president has independent power over the agency's activities and that the oversight committees are not the whole story. The possibility of divergence between supposed agent and principal is heightened when Congress is divided (Wooley 1993). More generally, when the core of alternatives relating to the regulatory area (that is, the number of proposals that cannot be defeated) is large, as it would be with divided party control, then divergence is to be expected (Hammond and Knott 1992). Indeed, congressional dominance may be a special case, occurring when Congress is inordinately unified on the issue—and stays unified over a long period of time. If unity is lacking or if strong interest is lacking, then local forces, including the oversight committees, the affected interests, and the agency leadership, will have more influence. We are back to path-dependent policy subsystems.

The use of the overhead democracy standard has also led to treating the network of partially independent parallel processing units as a problem of control in the process of implementing national laws. The preferred model of policymaking has been one of central control: there is a stage of policymaking in which policies are enacted; then they are implemented. Chubb (1985) views the national government as a policy "principal" and the states and localities as implementing "agents." The problem is that implementation generally goes awry in one way or another. Implementers often have their own agendas, perverting the original "intention" of the law (which, of course, was itself a result of legislative coalition building). Wood (1991) shows quantitatively that a control model works well for national bureaucrats, but breaks down when participants from the states and localities are brought in. New problems emerge, and implementers invent new ways of dealing with the problems that are not consistent with the original statute. This seems to be inherent in the logic of deconcentrated policymaking. It is perhaps better to view policymaking and implementing bodies as having different interests, and then to explore the conditions under which they will cooperate (Stoker 1992).

In modern America, the overhead democracy model seems wildly unrealistic. The attention of the policymaking branches is easily distracted, and when that happens, local forces will move to find their own equilibrium. When general interest in a policy is low, it is certainly in the interest of most members of Congress to leave well enough alone. Nevertheless, central control models do remind us that everything is not decided independently of the central policymaking branches. However, given the very decentralized nature of policymaking in the United States, the best approach to federal policymaking is to see it as affecting (but not controlling) the course of policymaking in a vast network of quasi-independent policy units. Control is impossible; as frustrating as it may seem, influence is the only viable option.

Conclusions: Breaking Path Dependency?

Policymaking in the United States by its very nature defies central control. Organizational theorists have traditionally pointed to span-of-control problems in bureaucratic agencies. Similarly, oversight by Congress is limited by the processing capacity of the legislative body. As a consequence, national policymaking occurs mostly in numerous relatively autonomous subsystems. Perhaps even more important, states and localities play a key and independent role in policymaking because of the legal status of states in the federal system. Hence, for the most part, the national government must use indirect means (such as the grant-in-aid) to achieve national policy ends. Even where national goals are imposed, such as in many regulatory agencies, there exists a complex interaction between federal standards and local demands for specific deviations from uniform policies (Wood 1991).

Given those limitations, policymaking in the United States devolves to a vast number of policymaking units operating simultaneously in parallel, with only minimal and inconsistent oversight by the national political institutions. The result is a tendency to capture by "local" interests. This does not mean that, for example, businessmen always win when confronted by environmental regulations forged by national majorities but administered by local bureaucrats. Organized environmentalists have proved to be powerful local interests in many parts of the country and in the nation's capital. It just means that those motivated to organize and try to influence politics are going to have disproportionate influence and that the apathetic will be left out.

While it might be hoped that such a complex, decentralized system of policymaking would reach overall equilibrium, it does not. Most subsystems in normal times are able to forge local equilibria, but the sum of these local equilibria does not approximate the populist policy equilibrium, that is, the balance of the aggregation of citizen preferences with the policy outputs of government. The reason is path dependency. Local policy subsystem equilibria are contingent on the past policy settlements within the subsystem; as the participants work out new responses to changing circumstances (usually incrementally), they can drift further from the populist policy equilibrium.

The key to the problem of path dependency is not better oversight. Nor is it central control, or a principal-agent relationship between legislature and administrative agency. The joint-processing limitations of decision-makers and of institutions make these things impossible. A better approach is to think about how path dependency might be broken on a reasonably regular basis. In the next chapter, we turn to an analysis of how this can happen.

8 The Serial Policy Shift

The Sea of Faith
Was once, too, at the full. — MATTHEW ARNOLD, *Dover Beach*

Most models and studies of modern political science display a strong faith in certitude. Models of policymaking are rooted in incrementalism, countermobilization, and more or less regular cycles. Statistical analyses tend to rely on linear assumptions, hence on incremental change. Intervention models imply that a straightforward response will be observable after the application of a well-defined policy instrument. Models of public choice are steeped in the rational maximization assumption and the faith that equilibria in politics exist and that they matter more than the interequilibria dynamics. Even as the great Communist systems collapse elsewhere, Western democracies, with their firm foundations in liberal democracy and capitalist economics, seem remarkably stable. Analysts are led by their training and the stability of democratic institutions to impute considerable stability and marginalist adjustment to disruptions in all realms of political life.

I have argued thus far that it is necessary to examine shifts in the processing of information at the level of the individual decision-maker and that shifts from one set of preferences to another can cause disjointed, episodic shifts in choices. We now examine the same phenomenon at the level of the political system (or subsystems). If boundedly rational decision-makers shift from one set of preferences to another as the political debate evokes new frames of reference and if political institutions are themselves path dependent, opening up the possibility of shifts toward a different path of action, then it seems likely that serial shifts in policy outputs will occur.

Chapter 7 dealt with conservative political subsystems, characterized by the actions and reactions of participants in a multitude of policy venues. Decentralization allows for the conduct of most policy activity in a parallel, all-at-once style. Occasionally, however, policymaking shifts into a *serial* mode, in which central policymakers explicitly consider modifications of the parallel processing arrangement which characterizes day-to-day policymaking. Serial processing also occurs when central policymakers decide to create policy where none has existed before. We may say that the policy being serially processed is "on the policymaking agenda"; *agenda access* is the term used by political scientists to indicate a serial shift in policymaking on an issue.

Serial policy processing is subject to the same bottlenecks as serial decision-making at the individual level. Only a very limited number of items can be considered by a single policymaking body such as Congress or some other national, state, or local legislature. Herbert Simon (1983: 79) linked the serial processing of issues to the setting of agendas in democratic legislative institutions: "When questions are important and controversial (and when they are important, they are usually also controversial), they have to be settled by democratic procedures that require the formation of majorities in legislative bodies or in the electorate as a whole. Consequently, the voters or the legislators must for periods of time attend simultaneously to more or less the same thing."

Because serial processing occurs on "important and controversial" issues and because policymakers are simultaneously attending to the same problem, there is generally increased coverage from the news media and other mechanisms of communication. When the shift to explicit policy consideration occurs in central policy organs, we say that the issue has reached the policy agenda. Agenda access, a shift in the interests of central policymakers, is generally accompanied by increases in the attentiveness of classes of participants to the policy problem. Sometimes a major mobilization is stymied; even more often a marginal adjustment to the prevailing policymaking approach occurs. But occasionally a major breakthrough occurs. While not all serial policy shifts are characterized by such policy breakthroughs, policy breakthroughs do not occur in the absence of a serial shift in attentiveness. The shift from parallel to serial processing in a policymaking system is invariably associated with agenda access of a new policy issue (or a fresh definition of an old one), so that the key to serial policy shifts lies in changes in the definition of issues (Baumgartner and Jones 1993).

Issue Definition

It is not easy to predict what issues a political system will treat as important from an examination of the objective social conditions facing it. Indeed, the relationship between objective conditions and policy action is unclear. Even the connection between attentiveness to problems in the mass public and policy action is not clear. The reason is the formidable role that issue definition plays in the policy process (D. Stone 1989; Cobb and Rochefort 1994). The defining of issues so that they are compelling prods to policy action is conducted by a very small number of policy entrepreneurs who seem to derive particular benefits out of leadership activities (Schneider and Teske 1992; Chong 1991). Issue definition is critical in the process of attracting attention during the agenda-setting stage of the policy process.

E. E. Schattschneider (1960) argued that this process of attracting attention to an issue, which he termed the "contagiousness of conflict," had the potential of making the decision-making process more democratic. As more and more citizens are drawn to an issue, usually because of conflicts among elites, the process will more and more approximate the preferences of the majority. Schattschneider saw the pressure-group system as an essentially undemocratic mechanism for the control of conflict, whereas the political parties were the primary institutions for the expansion, and thereby the democratization, of policymaking. Conflict, however, rarely expands unless new issue definitions are put forth by policy entrepreneurs. Moreover, as parties have weakened and the interest-group system has expanded to include more diverse interests, conflict expansion has occurred within the interest-group system, as well as through other means not so directly connected to the party system. Simply put, the process of conflict expansion is more complex than Schattschneider suggested, and it is not so simply connected to democratization as he believed. The key issue is *who is mobilized* to enter the fray. It is safe to say that, with issue expansion, politics will become less easily controlled and less predictable, as Schattschneider noted. But it may not become more "democratic" in the sense of policies matching majority preferences.

Perhaps the most important aspect of the process of issue definition is a shift in attentiveness in the public debate from one underlying evaluative dimension to another. "Policymakers often challenge the accuracy of their opponents' facts; however, it is generally more effective in a debate simply to shift the focus" (Baumgartner and Jones 1993: 107). This issue-reframing process in the public debate over policy directions may be termed *noncontradictory argumentation* (Baumgartner and Jones 1993: 107). Neither side in the debate is really interested in changing preferences, but each is interested is shifting the focus of the debate to previously ignored dimensions of evaluation. The purpose of this activity by policy entrepreneurs is to bring into the debate previously disinterested individuals who are activated by the new focus of the debate.

The environmental movement has followed closely the dynamics described above. Argumentation about regulations affecting the environment has been strongly noncontradictory and has centered on two basic dimensions. The first concerns economic progress and the creation of jobs and wealth; the second centers on the environmental and health harms that are caused by unbridled capitalism. Business executives have argued that environmental regulations detract from growth and jobs. Environmentalists have argued that their proposals don't really cost in terms of growth; that is, they have challenged the growth rhetoric of business groups. But this has not been their primary tactic. Rather, they have tended to ignore the growth arguments, stressing instead the harm done by unregulated businesses to the environment. The argument between business and environmentalists, which seems to have replaced labor conflict as the most important political concern of businesses (Vogel 1989), is almost completely noncontradictory. Neither side spends much effort in refuting the claims of the other; each side tries to raise the salience of the dimension of conflict that is most favorable to it.

The Role of Communications Links

Because issue definition is so critical in the agenda process, communication is fundamental in shifts from parallel to serial issue processing. In a large society, communication even among elite groups occurs through the mass media. Hence the media plays a critical role in policymaking, far beyond its role in the electoral process. There is considerable debate among students of the mass media concerning whether the media "influences" policy outcomes or whether it "sets the agenda" for policy action. Rogers and Deering (1988) argue for a model which, in effect, links media agendas with policy agendas; hence the media influences policy outcomes via the path of influencing the agendas of policymakers.

The most important role for the media, however, is to communicate new dimensions of evaluation into the policy process. Introducing a new dimension of evaluation into a policy process dominated by a single dimension destabilizes (Riker 1982, 1986). But if attentiveness to the new dimension is not reasonably widespread, then the introjection of new concerns will fail. The mass media, as major communications links in modern society, offers the opportunity to issue entrepreneurs to attempt to get relevant actors to focus on the newly introduced conflict dimension, thereby shifting the attention from one dimension to another. Hence issue entrepreneurs have motive to try to capture the attention of the media to introduce a new, destabilizing element into a previously stable situation (Baumgartner and Jones 1993). The modern mass media has a corresponding interest in raising issues, because doing so will attract readers and viewers, which is good for business. Modern reporters, likewise, are interested in raising their own profiles by raising issues. This role has been highlighted in recent political science scholarship on the mass media, moving from a model of "influence" or "agenda-*setting*" to one of communicating images of new issues (or reinforcing old ones) (Iyengar 1991; Iyengar and Kinder 1987).

The Serial Shift

Some years ago, Emmette Redford (1969) distinguished between subsystem politics, which he said provided for an equilibrium among affected interests, and macropolitics, which involved the central policymaking bodies (Congress and the president). In Redford's scheme, losing interests in a subsystem arrangement could appeal to the macropolitical institutions for redress. This "appeals procedure" is one major way in which the macropolitical institutions are drawn into the politics of subsystems. It should be clear that Redford's macropolitical intrusion into subsystem politics and Schattschneider's notions of conflict expansion are closely related.

This shift from parallel, subsystems-based policymaking to serial, one-at-a-time policy consideration is often destructive of existing policy subsystem equilibria. Such movement from parallel to serial is accomplished by bringing in new dimensions of evaluation to the policy process. These new dimensions force a redefinition of an issue, thereby attracting new participants to the policy process. These previously disinterested individuals have different ideas about how to run the policy, and they interfere with the existing subsystem arrangement. Sometimes after a while the new participants lose interest and drop out, but more often the policy subsystem is forever altered by the intrusion (Baumgartner and Jones 1993).

We can see that the serial processing of issues is facilitated by the tendency of central policymakers to group issues along ideological dimensions, as noted in chapter 6. This communicates simply the nature of the conflict, makes it understandable, and allows processing according to past frames of reference. But when the policy shifts back to parallel processing, the policy evolves according to the limited attentional dynamics of subsystems. Actually, it may be seen that policies in subsystems *coevolve* with the collection of participants and their definitions of policy issues within the subsystem. In many subsystems, participants share issue definitions but they don't necessarily share policy prescriptions. So they are continually adjusting to one another, developing policy and its implementation in the process.

Hence there exists a *double dynamic* in policymaking. First, policies evolve within policy subsystems and that evolution tends very much to be incremental. The reasons are obvious: participants tend to share issue-definitions. Countermobilization can occur within well-established policy subsystems, but the process of negative feedback ensures that a new dynamic pluralist equilibrium is found. Hence there is a dynamical process within policy subsystems and it consists of incremental adjustment among interested parties. The second dynamic responsible for policy change is serial processing. When a policy shifts to the macropolitical institutions for serial processing, it generally does so in an environment of changing issue definitions and heightened attentiveness by the media and broader publics. Policy stalemate can occur, or a minor modification of existing ways of doing business can be made. But it is also possible that a major, episodic change can be made in policies, with disruption of existing policy networks and creation of new agencies for implementing policies. Serial processing can result in nonincremental policy changes.

Fundamental to the policy process is what might be called the *temporal allocation of attention*. Attention is a scarce good, and how it is allocated in a political system is related to how policies change. In particular, the degree to which collective attentiveness to public problems is allocated centrally to the serial processing mechanisms or distributed to parallel processing "outlets" determines whether policy proceeds incrementally or episodically.

The movement back and forth between parallel and serial processing can help to resolve the paradox of issue evolution. Most issue evolution does not occur at the level of serial processing; it occurs in parallel. But when issues are transformed by attentiveness to the system of serial processing, old dimensions of conflict are used to understand the issue and to communicate positions. Those more or less stable dimensions of conflict may not be present in the current debate, because nobody is really paying attention to them. New issues often serve to raise old concerns that have been latent in the current public debate. Trade-offs between equity and growth, between freedom and security, between consumption and investment seem to recur in democratic politics; but whole eras seem to be dominated by a limited focus. Hence the job of policy entrepreneurs pushing new issues is to get people to understand those new issues in terms of familiar but currently underused frames of reference. Defenders of the current regime fight back by emphasizing the importance of the prevailing dimension of evaluation; noncontradictory argumentation emerges. Perhaps the underlying dimensions of evaluation are well understood, an understanding that has been honed during two centuries of (more or less) democratic politics. Or it may be that the issue-dimensions are fundamental conflicts that all societies endure. The important lesson is the manner in which shifting back and forth from serial to parallel processing of issues facilitates the evolution of old issues and the incorporation of new ones.

Destabilization in the Policymaking Process

At the national level, the intrusion of new dimensions of conflict into a previously cozy subsystem (or other seemingly stable policy arrangement) invariably involves Congress. Congressional committees and subcommittees provide the legislative anchors for policy subsystems. They are allowed considerable autonomy by the chamber because of the expertise that the oversight committees have garnered in the policy arena and because of the system of mutual deference that characterizes much policymaking in Congress.

A vigorous debate has emerged among students of Congress on the role of committees. The traditional approach has emphasized the ability of committees to influence final voting decisions taken on the floor. Committees are composed of members who have an interest in the subject matter processed by a particular committee, and the legislative body oftentimes simply defers to policymaking activities in these committees in floor votes. A second approach, most forcefully argued by Krehbiel (1991), sees the whole body far more influential than this would imply. Krehbiel argues that for the most part committees simply serve as information-gathering arms of the general body and must tailor their policy proposals to the preferences of the whole body. If committees operate as Krehbiel suggests, then Congress is indeed the dominant principal in legislative-agency interactions and policy subsystems would exist only at the sufferance of the entire body. Structure-induced equilibria would not exist and would be replaced with a true populist policy equilibrium.

Which version one accepts depends very much on how much weight is assigned to the indifference of legislative members. If indifference in the chamber is seen as relatively extensive, then the traditional model would be more likely to hold. Members who do not care are not likely to intervene. If indifference is low, then there would likely be continual interference and tight control by the body into the business conducted by its committees. As noted in chapter 7, indifference and deference can be associated with a large policy core of undominated alternatives. Given the preferences of members and the institutional structure, it may not be possible to change the direction of the committee, so one may as well turn to other matters.

But what if indifference, or its polar opposite, attention, to a particular policy area varies with time? Then the serial shift could affect the relative autonomy that a committee (and its associated entire policy subsystem) enjoys. That is, the subsystem centered on a congressional committee could operate with great freedom until something happened to shift the subsystem into the limelight. Then the committee could expect far less tolerance for its independent actions by the body. This model would assume that the relationship between the legislative body and its committees is dynamic and evolving over time, and is fundamentally influenced by agenda processes. When issues become visible and controversial, then serial processing is more likely and the committees and their associated policy subsystems, the parallel processing units, lose autonomy.

When issues get redefined and previously apathetic citizens become interested in the policy, more members of Congress will be motivated to act as entrepreneurs on the emerging issue. The system of expertise, disinterest, and deference can fail. In particular, more committees and subcommittees may struggle for jurisdiction and Congress can become a "jurisdictional battleground." When the energy issue emerged as critical in the 1970s, the straightforward jurisdictional divisions collapsed as many committees sought to establish their claims to pieces of the issue. As the policy area leaped to the national policy agenda during the oil embargoes, many previously uninvolved legislators were attracted to the area, old policy subsystem arrangements were disrupted, and new linkages were forged (C. Jones 1975; Jones and Strahan 1985).

In general, as issues expand, the old structure-induced equilibria collapse (Jones, Baumgartner, and Talbert 1993). Recall that structure-induced equilibria exist when congressional committees delimit conflict on an issue to only one dimension of evaluation. But jurisdictional struggles almost always involve the raising of a second dimension of evaluation as another committee attempts to claim jurisdiction. In a case that we examine in more detail later in this chapter, in the 1970s Senator Edward Kennedy, head of the Administrative Practices Subcommittee of the Judiciary Committee, wanted to get involved in deregulation. He claimed jurisdiction because of a "price-fixing" charge against the Department of Transportation; thus he was able to claim that procedures were violated. Jurisdictional struggles mean that bills will now often be multidimensional (incorporating the concerns of more members), that committees and their structure-induced equilibria will lose control of the agenda, and that the politics of building coalitions for a floor debate becomes critical. Everything changes when policymaking moves from parallel to serial.

Baumgartner and I (1991, 1993) show that the construction and later disruption of policy subsystems in nuclear power, pesticides, and other areas is associated with increased interest in the media and in Congress, and all involve the noncontradictory argumentation that one expects when new dimensions of conflict are inserted into a debate. Members of Congress have strong motive to hold hearings in "hot" areas that are in the process of being redefined. Indeed, the dynamics of agenda politics work against the long-run stability of many seemingly secure policy subsystem arrangements, causing a pattern of stable monopoly control by committees punctuated by periods of jurisdictional struggle and rapid change (Jones, Baumgartner, and Talbert 1993).

Elections and Policy Shifts

What about the connection between elections and policymaking shifts? It is not as easy as one might think to unify the punctuations in policymaking that occur in Congress with electoral mobilizations of the type discussed in chapter 6. The dimensions raised in an electoral campaign are not so directly related to policymaking processes for a number of reasons. One important reason is the "attention to dimensions" problem. This stems from the problem that multiple attributes always underlie candidates or parties in an election, and the particular dimension that determines the vote direction for critical groups in the electorate may not correspond to the dimensions that are interjected into the policymaking debate between elections. For example, let us assume that Republicans were in fact elected to the presidency because of the social issue in the 1970s and 1980s. Whether this was a determining factor we can't know for sure, but we can say that it was important. Now the so-called Reagan Democrats critical to the election of Republican presidents probably wanted liberal economic policies and conservative social and foreign policies. But they couldn't get that, because candidates supporting such an array of policies were not in the race. So they got conservative economic and social policies (the latter particularly in judiciary appointments). The conservative economic policies they also got included tax cuts for the wealthy and regulatory policies benefiting business (for example, the disruption of the carefully crafted balance between labor and business on the NLRB). Of course, conservative Democrats were only one component of the coalition that elected Republican presidents between 1968 and 1992, save only the Carter interlude. Nevertheless, the fate of the critical conservative Democrats illustrates graphically how the connection between mass preferences as expressed in an electoral mobilization and policy outcomes is quite tenuous.

Looking back to the study of committee hearings presented in chapter 6, one can note the emergence of the "new" dimension of environmental health and safety in 1970. Consumerism was also associated with the emergence of this factor. These issues destabilized many existing policy subsystems during the 1970s: environmentalists and consumer advocates collaborated to attack nuclear power and electric power monopolies in general; environmentalists and public health officials launched a barrage against pesticides, toxic wastes, and general air and water pollution; consumer advocates pushed deregulation in transportation and banking. Environmental and consumer concerns were raised in the elections of 1968 and 1972, but they were likely not determinative. Those elections centered on the social issues of crime, civil rights, and civil disorders and on Vietnam. This would suggest that electoral mobilizations can add to the destabilizing forces sweeping across policy subsystems and other seemingly secure policy arrangements, but cannot dictate directions. The general principle is that elections motivate parties to expand conflict, as Schattschneider noted. But they do not ensure adherence to the "populist policy equilibrium." Rather, they act to destabilize the tendency for interest groups and policymakers to work out arrangements that include the concerned but ignore the general wishes of the less involved.

"All Politics Is Local"

Although the discussion above has centered on the relations between policy subsystems and the macropolitical institutions, the notion of the institutional shifting of attention is quite general. It applies to any organization comprising subparts that have some independent spheres of action (which will almost always be the case). Different kinds of organizations, of course, maintain different ties between the "higher" and "lower" levels of the organization, so that the character of the problem will vary. But it always occurs. It is particularly severe in the case of the American federal system.

When Speaker of the House of Representatives "Tip" O'Neal said that all politics is local, he was thinking of his home district in Massachusetts, highlighting the role that local electoral considerations play in the activities of national legislators. But his words imply something more: that all policymaking is subject to local rules. That is, Congress operates within a generally recognized set of written and unwritten rules, as does the executive branch and the city of Chicago and the state of Oregon. Although these rules are not integrated within a central system of hierarchical control, they do interact with one another in complex patterns of feedback. In the late 1940s Robert Dahl and Charles Lindblom analyzed mechanisms of control, noting that explicit control through formal hierarchy was but one of several ways of controlling behavior. Others included exchange (through markets) and bargaining. All modes ensured predictable behavior among participants. So the existence of local rules governing behaviors does not negate the possibility of public policy. However, the shift from serial to parallel processing of issues does introduce a source of episodic, nonincremental uncertainty into the process.

It can (and often does) happen that feedback from the system of parallel processing into the serial policymaking apparatus occurs. But as these parallel processing mechanisms move along, they can cause problems or opportunities to emerge for the central (federal) policymaking system. The oft-repeated phrase "the states are the laboratories of democracy" implies exactly this feedback process. States try things out, often because states are subject to specifically local forces, and other states imitate. Then the sum of the local forces spills over into national politics and the federal government becomes involved in the issue.

Everything, of course, is not "bottom up." Many policies are the exclusive purview of the national government, from defense to social security. Groups interested in these policies are organized solely at that level. More important, it is possible for the federal government to affect the states and localities simultaneously through general policy enactments; the reverse is not true. But rather than focusing on the independent policy actions of numerous actors in a multiplicity of venues, some political scientists have seen the national government as a "principal" and the states and localities as implementing "agents" in a hierarchical pattern, as noted in the previous chapter.

If the principal-agent format is not tenable, neither is the "local political economy" approach, which in effect trusts the localities to reach equilibrium on their own. It is argued that smaller units can more efficiently provide services than larger ones, in part because of "transaction costs" imposed by large bureaucracies. A similar line of thought suggests matching the size of the unit of government with the type of policy assigned to the unit. Considerable discussion sporadically occurs on the "sorting out" of federal functions, such that the national government would be responsible for nationally relevant policies, while the states and localities would handle local-only policies. The distinction between local and national has generally centered on "spillovers"—how much of the effect of the policy is confined only to the local jurisdiction and how much "spills over" to other jurisdictions.

The problem is that all policymaking systems evolve in response to changing circumstances, generally reaching a local equilibrium that can be quite far from the ideal. The national "populist policy equilibrium" will not be the same as the sum of the local policy equilibria. Sorting policies to levels of government will not work as intended, either, because local forces will continually undermine national direction, which will tend to be unresponsive to local needs.

In a federal system, neither a hierarchical "principal agent" arrangement nor a "political economy" approach that allows maximum adjustment among policymaking units will work as intended, because neither recognizes the inescapable double dynamic of public policymaking. Policymaking systems adjusting to local forces, as they must, will not reach global equilibrium. A central controller will not be able to prevent movement to local equilibria, because the central controller cannot attend to all things at once. We shall return to the issue of adaptability of policy systems in the next chapter, but first we look at the issue of positive feedback in policymaking.

Positive Feedback Effects

Most models of policymaking emphasize negative feedback, yet the serial policy shift implies the existence of *positive feedback*. Positive feedback occurs when change is amplified rather than damped; effects are self-reinforcing and do not stimulate offsetting or balancing countermobilization. There may exist countermobilization, but it is inadequate to offset the amplifying effects inherent in positive feedback. So there tends to be a rapid cascading of effects in positive feedback systems, as opposed to the self-limiting features of negative feedback systems (Baumgartner and Jones 1993; DeAngelis, Post, and Travis 1986).

The two kinds of effects differ in the nature of the "feedback loop" they create going away from and back to a variable. Let us take a particular public policy as a starting point. In negative feedback, the institution of policy action causes countermobilization, in which opponents move to counteract what they see as the undesirable effects of the policy. These are the standard pluralist models examined in chapter 7. There we noted the role of negative feedback and countermobilization in standard models of policy subsystems. When one group gains advantage, another is stimulated to action. The feedback loop is negative. In Lowi's (1979) model of mutually noninterfering policy subsystems, countermobilization is absent, but nevertheless the policy subsystems are affected only by minor changes. In both situations, there seems to be scant room for major policy changes.

In positive feedback, the feedback loop amplifies rather than counteracts deviations. One example of how this works in politics is illustrated in figure 8.1, which depicts a policy subsystem affected by positive feedback. This diagram is roughly similar to figure 7.1, in which a regulatory agency's activities affected two groups; the harmed group was able to

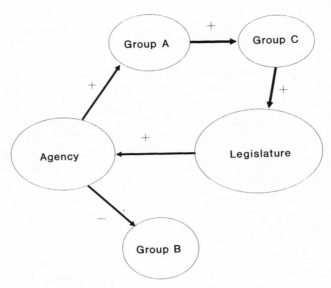

Fig. 8.1. Positive feedback in public policymaking.

gain relief by appealing to Congress. But what if group A, which may have had little influence in Congress, now finds an ally in group C, which does? Group C might be another interest group, or it might be a broad segment of the mass public. In either case, conflict has been expanded. Now all the links in the top of the model are positive; each deviation causes a larger impact. If the agency responds to congressional pressure, groups A and C are benefited, but they put even more pressure on Congress, which responds. As we go around the loop several times, we have not countermobilization but "feeding frenzy." If the positive feedback loop is allowed to operate for a few cycles, the system will explode—here acting to increase the benefits to groups A and C exponentially.

Donald DeAngelis and his colleagues have detailed four general properties associated with positive feedback systems. First, they are characterized by increasing complexity. The more complex the system, the more likely that positive feedback among the complex linkages will occur. Second, they are characterized by accelerating change. Third, they generally display threshold effects: rapid change tends to "kick in" after the system crosses some threshold. Fourth, complex systems are fragile; when positive feedback "kicks in," the system can be destabilized (DeAngelis, Post, and Travis 1986: 10–14). In relatively open systems, positive feedback doesn't last very long, because it is very destabilizing.

But it doesn't have to last very long; great changes happen quite quickly, and when the system settles down, it can have very different characteristics than before.

We noted in chapter 7 that local equilibria, path dependency, and lock-in occur in many, if not most, policy subsystems, which themselves are linked. How does the existence of such conservative systems square with the positive feedback that occurs when policy shifts from serial to parallel? The answer is that brief bursts of positive feedback can alter existing policy subsystems or create new ones. Many policy subsystems are created on the "waves of enthusiasm" that follow what Anthony Downs (1972) called a stage of "alarmed discovery." That is, suddenly there rises a general feeling among many that something is terribly wrong and political mobilization occurs in response to this new discovery. This kind of shift is associated with agenda access, because governments begin to see the problem as needing action. It is true that new issues emerge on such waves of enthusiasm. But as often as not, the supposedly new issues are more like "old wine in new bottles." Such waves are dependent on (1) the intrusion of new dimensions of evaluation into the public debate and (2) communications among political actors. That is, they involve new framings of issues that were previously seen in a different light and they involve the communication of these new framings to others who were previously uninterested in the issue.

Now we can see that the process of attentiveness to evaluative dimensions, so important in individual political decision-making, also plays a fundamental role in the positive feedback processes that exist in strong waves of political mobilization. Noncontradictory argumentation is the fundamental form of dialogue in political mobilizations; the winning side has convinced legislators that their framing of the issue is the proper one. And a type of serial processing shift has occurred: from the private sector, without central government supervision, into public view.

Once created (often after extended conflict and major legislative enactment), many policy subsystems settle into a period characterized by negative feedback, such as that described by the Bendor-Moe model or by "capture," in which the affected interest no longer has to worry much about opposing interest groups. In either case, some demobilization has occurred; in both cases, the mobilization has altered the situation by inserting government into the situation. Now government buttresses the subsystem, and the system settles down into a negative feedback phase such as that so carefully described by Moe in the case of the NLRB. In the future, however, the system may be destabilized once again; this in fact occurred at the NLRB with Reaganism.

Gun Control in New Jersey

Positive feedback in politics occurs far more frequently than is commonly realized. Mobilization and destabilization happen almost continually in American politics, if only we scan not just the Washington scene but the multitude of state and local governments that span the country. If we do so, we observe an incredible amount of change in a supposedly staid and gridlocked governmental structure, mired in a federal system based on the mobilization-limiting notion of checks and balances. A major reason that we miss destabilizing waves of action is that we are conditioned by tradition and education to look for national mass mobilizations on major issues, whereas many times positive feedback systems happen locally.

In 1992 in New Jersey, Republicans won an overwhelming electoral victory. Democratic governor James Florio and his solid Democratic majority in both the Senate and the Assembly (lower house) had passed a major tax increase and restructuring. The initiative equalized educational funding by shifting much of the burden of financing education to the state, thereby reducing the reliance of school boards on local property taxes. The program basically shifted resources from richer districts to poorer ones, thus angering many middle- and upper-income taxpayers concentrated in the suburbs of New York.

The Republicans painted the program as a giant tax increase and an attack on quality education. In November of 1992, they won such large majorities in both the Senate and the Assembly that Florio did not have enough supporters to sustain a veto even if all Democrats voted with him. Republicans moved quickly to reverse the governor's taxation and education programs.

The issue of gun control was somewhat of a sideshow during the early Florio years, but the Democrats did pass a bill in 1990 that banned the sale and possession of semiautomatic weapons. The National Rifle Association objected strongly to the bill and contributed large sums to Republican legislators, who, for the most part, opposed the ban. In 1992, Republicans passed a bill reversing the ban but Florio vetoed it.

Republicans were in no rush to override Florio's veto, because New Jersey law provides great leeway in the timing of an override attempt. The veto-proof Republican majority provided the votes, and the Republican leadership in both houses strongly supported the override. By February 25 of 1993, the leadership was ready and the Assembly easily voted to override on a party-line vote.

Florio did not sit silently by and watch the override, however. He knew that public opinion in the state broadly favored controls on guns, but in New Jersey, as elsewhere, that opinion had never really been mobilized. Florio skillfully depicted the Republicans as pawns of the "out-of-state gun lobbyists" and claimed that the measure would increase crime. In a textbook example of Schattschneider's conflict expansion model, he barnstormed the state, repeating his charge that the NRA was not an association of gun *owners* but a lobby of gun *sellers*. In a state dominated for three years by taxes, by education, and by the economy, with other issues handled quietly in Trenton, suddenly crime and guns were interjected into the political debate.

And Senate Republicans were overwhelmed. Calls from constituents burned out one senator's answering machine. Senate president Donald DiFrancesco, who had never received a single contact on the override issue before the Assembly override vote, had to stack mail all over his chairs. The shift in attention from economics to crime and the gun lobby was epitomized by a letter from a seventy-one-year-old lifelong Republican: "I can no longer support a party who chooses to support a vicious lobby, the National Rifle Association, against the wishes of the people of New Jersey."

By March 1, the first two Republican senators defected, saying they would not vote against the governor. Both had supported the original bill. On March 2, the deputy party leader in the Senate defected. On March 4, Senate president DiFrancesco announced that the override vote would occur on March 15 and that he would vote against the override. The vote was taken at 3:30 on March 15. Twenty-six senators voted against the override, including three of four senators in leadership positions. Fourteen senators abstained, and not a single one voted to override.

Republicans were chagrined that they had completely lost control of the public debate. "Florio had gone from 17 percent in the polls to 40 percent because we were letting him make people stop thinking that this was a man who put a $2.8 billion tax increase on this state," said Senator John Bennett, the deputy majority leader. Democrats reveled in the possibility that they would be able to avoid running in 1994 on the tax and education issues.[1]

Few opinions were changed in the semiautomatic weapon debate in New Jersey. Citizens, or at least enough of them to make a difference, who were generally apathetic on the issue, were in favor of gun control before and after the vote. The Republican majority was just as supportive of the NRA's objectives after the vote, but the uprising had caused a classic "change of focus." "The issue of the gun bill itself was no longer as

1. This discussion is drawn primarily from Peterson (1993).

relevant as the consequences that issue was having on my party," commented Senator Bennett.

Much of politics is about changes of focus. The intrusion of previously neglected dimensions of evaluation can set off positive feedback effects that destroy previously path-dependent processes; in the case of the New Jersey gun control bill, this happened virtually over a weekend. When these processes are unleashed, they can feed on themselves. Each defection by a senator put pressure on the others to defect, until they all did. And no senators seem to have changed their minds about the desirability of freedom of ownership and exchange of weapons.

Finally, new issue definitions in localities can change the nature of the national debate. Florio brilliantly depicted the National Rifle Association not as a citizens' group of responsible gun owners but as the lobbying arm of weapons manufacturers. Hence he could benefit from citizens' general distrust of "the interests." In a preelection poll in the fall of 1993, New Jersey citizens reported that Florio's gun control initiative was "the best thing he did." Enterprising politicians in other states have begun to adopt Florio's tactics. In Virginia, in Massachusetts, and even in the Western states of Utah and Colorado, gun control has become an issue (Rimer 1993). In Colorado, Governor Roy Romer assailed the gun lobby, claiming that "the NRA is a group of Eastern money, Eastern lobbyists, making decisions in a very narrow room" (*New York Times*, September 8, 1993).

The Policy Entrepreneur

Positive feedback occurs when systems are poised to be destabilized. This happens when a policy subsystem (or other policy settlement such as the mutually supportive arrangement between the NRA and New Jersey Republicans) is operating a considerable distance from the optimal. As we have seen, this tends to happen when subsystems reach equilibrium on a constrained issue dimensional structure—that is, the actors within the subsystem (or broader policy venue) are attending to only one or a very few of the possible attributes that underlie a policy. Destabilization can occur with the introduction of a new dimension of conflict—so long as the new framing of the issue can attract adherents.

But destabilization doesn't come free. A subsystem can exist at its suboptimal equilibrium for long periods of time unless *policy entrepreneurs* act to redefine the issue. The problem for these leaders is that they can never be sure a subsystem or other prevailing policy arrangement is poised for destabilization; hence they must take a risk and invest time, energy, and money in trying to change things (Schneider and Teske

1993). Often these entrepreneurs are political leaders—they hold political office and stand to benefit (perhaps by attracting the attention, and thereby the financing, for a run for higher office; or, like Governor Florio, by introducing new issues to stave off disaster on the prevailing dimension of conflict). Occasionally they are not political leaders, but the heads of corporations or citizen groups, and they feel strongly about an issue.

Presidents at the national level (or governors and mayors at the state and local levels) are frequently the primary entrepreneurs seeking to redefine an issue in order to achieve maximum support for it. While political chief executives may act as brokers for the policy ideas of others, in the modern world they must also define a policy agenda themselves in order to be viewed as successful. That agenda must also be "packaged and sold" to Congress, to the media, and to the public. Paul Light notes that, once a program is developed, presidents have some leeway in the aspects of the program that will be emphasized in the public debate. He cites President Carter's hospital cost-containment plan. "The plan could have been viewed as a first step toward national health insurance; it could have been viewed as a plan to control one facet of rampant inflation; or it could have been viewed as a program to reduce federal expenditures for Medicare and Medicaid" (Light 1991: 4). Carter chose the cost-containment rather than the benefit-expansion route, thereby inviting great resistance from liberal Democrats.

Much effort has been directed at trying to understand the motives of these entrepreneurs—why they want to act to provide a "collective good" (by organizing) when they could allow others to do the organizing and still reap the benefit (Schneider and Teske 1993). It is enough to note that people are often motivated by the desire for recognition and that politics often provides an avenue for recognition (Fukuyama 1991). They may also be altruists, but it is not necessary to postulate this.

Searching for Positive Returns: Senator Kennedy and the CAB

One might view policy entrepreneurs as seeking *positive returns to scale*, a point where their marginal or incremental investments in time, money, and organization will yield increasing benefits rather than the decreasing benefits that normally obtain under conditions of countermobilization and negative feedback. They are seeking to stimulate positive feedback in a situation in which negative feedback has traditionally dominated.

In 1969, Senator Edward Kennedy became chairman of the Administrative Practices Subcommittee of the Senate Judiciary Committee. The committee had been created in the congressional reorganization of

1946 to investigate the procedures of executive branch agencies. Under Kennedy, the subcommittee became very aggressive but very eclectic in its targets of inquiry. The investigations were pure oversight and almost never led to hearings on bills. Congressional rules on jurisdiction are far more lenient in the case of oversight hearings, and the more general jurisdiction of the Administrative Practices Committee necessitated little justification for the inquiries.

By 1974, Kennedy was becoming dissatisfied with the subcommittee's "gadfly" approach to the issues and moved to focus the subcommittee's activities. Under the urging of a young antitrust lawyer at Harvard Law School, Stephen Breyer, the subcommittee moved into the arena of economic regulation. For tactical reasons, it zeroed in on the Civil Aeronautics Board, which was responsible for the regulation of rates and routes for the airline industry. The reasons were pure political calculation: no powerful forces save the industry itself were likely to be supportive of the CAB (trucking deregulation would unite the industry and the teamsters union in opposition), and consumers and economists could be forged into a coalition supporting price deregulation and competition. Finally, the mood was right: the Ford administration had begun to talk seriously about deregulation, and significant centers of activity in the administration, particularly the Antitrust Division at the Justice Department, could be counted on to support the effort (D. Simon 1977a: 15–16).

So Senator Kennedy was searching for an issue that would focus his subcommittee and give him publicity as an effective legislator. To do that, he needed both an effective strategy and a target that would allow rapid successful results. In the language of this chapter, Kennedy was seeking for positive returns to scale, a point where, with some effort, he could obtain substantial results. He could not, of course, predict the course of events. He and Breyer only analyzed the probabilities of success. Success in this instance consisted of substantial change in policy and considerable publicity for Kennedy for being responsible.

Fortunately for Kennedy, the CAB, established in 1938 to rationalize the air transport industry, was continuing to play by the old rules. The "stagflationary" economic environment of the early 1970s had led to severe problems in the airline industry, and by 1974 Pan American Airlines was near bankruptcy. The Department of Transportation and the CAB wanted to raise fares on international routes, Pan Am's mainstay, but was having trouble getting the upstart "charter" airlines to agree. The result was a meeting in which airlines were, in effect, invited to fix their own prices. Now Kennedy could hold hearings on the administrative practices of the price fix. Immediately, however, a jurisdictional squabble erupted.

Senator Howard Cannon of Nevada, chairman of the Aviation Subcommittee of the Senate Committee on Commerce, and Senator Warren Magnuson of Washington, the committee chair, objected to Kennedy's hearings, explicitly mentioning in a letter to Kennedy the Pan Am problem. Kennedy postponed, but ultimately held, the hearings.

During the hearings, the Ford administration sided with the Antitrust Division, which had opposed the rate fixing, thus handing Kennedy a victory: not only had he highlighted the problem of price fixing, but also he had received credit for a policy change. The success in these hearings led to two other hearings in January of 1975. Breyer says he learned from the rate hearings "to view the hearings as theatre" by making sure they had a central theme, that they corresponded to changes in administrative policy, and that the press could be activated to publicize the activity (D. Simon 1977b: 16). Again, the hearings empowered the forces of deregulation in the administration: the first witness in the hearings, the Secretary of Transportation, announced that the Ford administration would shortly introduce legislation to deregulate the airlines industry.

The publicity generated by the Administrative Practices hearings, the forces favoring deregulation in the executive branch, and the heightened attention to the issue by President Ford all pressed Senator Cannon, not particularly favorable to deregulation, to hold hearings on the issue in his Aviation Subcommittee. President Carter made deregulation of transportation a centerpiece of his administration, appointing members favorable to deregulation to the CAB. In 1978, Congress passed a bill deregulating the airlines and eliminated the CAB. Senator Kennedy had found his positive returns to scale.

Disarray in Defense and IGR

Subsystems come in all sizes and varieties. Some are relatively small, such as the rice crop protection subsystem discussed in chapter 7. Some are enormous, such as the agriculture "subsystem" consisting of all programs directed at the production and distribution of U.S. agricultural products. And some fit within others, such as the rice crop protection program's position within the larger agricultural support system. This property of policy subsystems can be termed *scale*. Geographers are used to viewing regions of the world similarly, from the smallest scale of human activity (the neighborhood) to the largest (the "world system"). Indeed, all complex systems have the properties of scale and self-similarity (the parts look similar to each other and the whole in many relevant aspects). Here we look briefly at two subsystems at the largest scale: the defense establishment and the intergovernmental relations network.

Each is composed of numerous subparts, which themselves are interdependent, but each is a clearly definable sphere of action and can easily be treated holistically.

Of all the policy subsystems in Washington, the most cozy and the most lucrative was that forged between the defense establishment and the contractors and suppliers of weapons and other services. The network of congressional committees, defense weapons programs, and the industrial companies they sustained spawned Eisenhower's "military-industrial complex" and served as the basis for Douglas Cater's (1964) "iron triangle" metaphor. Defense contracts were infamous for their laxness in enforcing cost-overrun procedures, and ex-procurement officers often went straight to work for contractors upon retirement from the service. While the defense committees and appropriations subcommittees were the mainstays of congressional support for defense spending, most members of Congress were protective of defense installations and defense contractors in their districts. This spawned a vast network of logrolling and mutual noninterference that offset any ideological attacks on military spending by liberals. Indeed, many congressional liberals found themselves attacking defense spending but defending expenditures in their districts. Defense personnel at the Defense Systems Management College learned how to buy weapons and studied Pentagon-congressional relations, reading in their textbook that "defense acquisition is a two-way street. Dependence on each other produces a 'win-win' situation. Work toward it" (Ricks 1993).

Signs everywhere point today to a subsystem under severe stress. With the collapse of the Soviet Union as a major security threat to the country, the defense budget has become the primary target for deficit reduction initiatives. Base closings, once such a controversial prospect that Congress authorized it to be done through a commission whose report could be rejected but not amended, are now accepted as fate. The 1993 weapons procurement budget was less than half of the $96.8 billion authorized in 1985. In 1993, only seven freshman representatives requested assignment to the Armed Services Committee, whereas nineteen wished to be assigned to the Science and Technology Committee, generally thought of as a weak duty station.

One result has been a breakdown of the relations between contractors and military procurement officials as their interests have partially decoupled. Military installations have been allowed to bid on repair and maintenance work once done by contractors, often underbidding them. The defense industry lobbying arm, "which once talked of a government-industry partnership, is bitterly accusing the Pentagon of trying to nationalize the defense industry" (Ricks 1993: A1). A second result has been a severing of the "pork barrel" approach to military bases. As bases are slated for closing, the argument that local economic harm will result is not taken as a serious objection any more—only military needs and budget realities are entertained as serious criteria of evaluation.[2]

Beginning in the mid-1960s with President Johnson's Great Society, the federal government undertook a grand initiative in domestic policy. Much of this initiative used intergovernmental aid to achieve domestic policy aims. President Nixon's New Federalism moved toward decentralizing the categorical grant structure used by Johnson, thereby giving state and local officials considerable discretion in the use of the funds. State and local officials, in concert with sympathetic domestic Cabinet departments and their local members of Congress, constructed what Beer (1976, 1977, 1978) called the "intergovernmental lobby." Working with private interests, such as the developers, contractors, and unions that would benefit from highway, public housing, and capital-intensive central city projects, public officials formed broad "benefits coalitions" (Anton 1989) that stressed the benefits coming to the district rather than the programs used to channel these benefits. To supporters, it was a way to achieve national domestic aims while ensuring the general support of localities. For opponents, it was a vast domestic pork barrel. But supporters and opponents alike saw an almost untouchable network of beneficiaries, many of them powerful local politicians using the benefits of the intergovernmental aid system to construct coalitions of powerful supporters in the business, labor, and public sector communities.

The network collapsed. Under the onslaught of budget cuts in the late Carter and early Reagan years, the once-touted "intergovernmental lobby" fell apart. Intergovernmental aid, especially in the "high pork" categories of housing and community development, declined precipitously, dropping more than 50 percent between 1978 and 1983. The system found few defenders in Congress during these years; the carefully crafted network of support mostly evaporated during a remarkably brief period (Baumgartner and Jones 1993: chap. 7; Levine and Thurber 1986). Now the defense establishment, the vaunted "military-industrial complex," seems to be experiencing a similar trauma.

There are other similarities. Both subsystems were vast—quite different from, say, sugar subsidies (Cater 1964). Both seemed untouchable at full tide. Left alone, their congressional committee supporters would

---

2. Congress had to invent a new institution and procedure, the base closing commission, whose recommendations cannot be rejected either by the president or by Congress piecemeal, in order to control logrolling. But this was done, strong evidence of the ability of democratic institutions to operate according to different rules when the context changes.

not have entertained their dismantling. But both came under pressure from forces beyond the subsystem—from macropolitics. They were swept up in larger issues, in changes in the conceptions of government, changes demanded by presidents, by congressional parties, and by mobilized citizens. At the largest scale, macropolitics had intervened to make less important the carefully crafted support networks in these subsystems. In both cases, the budget was the instrument that was used to change fundamentally how the subsystems worked. For all the writing about the disaggregated nature of the budget process, it can and does act as a mechanism of aggregation, sometimes forcing great changes in policy subsystems. It happened in the case of the intergovernmental lobby, as Carter ratcheted down domestic spending to fund defense and as Reagan pushed through his massive budget reconciliation bill that enforced severe limitations on domestic spending. It happened in the case of defense, as declining international threat, concern with the deficit, and increases in domestic "entitlement" spending caused a less spectacular, but nevertheless powerful, disruption of existing arrangements through spending limitations. In these cases, the budgetary process was the point of entry for the interference of macropolitical forces in the politics of subsystems.

Destabilizing Waves of Mobilization and Punctuations

Characteristic of major change in politics are destabilizing waves in which positive feedback effects replace negative feedback and countermobilization among affected interest groups. A policy issue becomes highly visible in the media; previously inactive individuals become interested; the precise pluralist balance within the multiple venues of parallel policy processing is disrupted; policy is processed in serial fashion; previously independent subsystems spill over into one another. These waves of policymaking may be linked to electoral mobilizations. Numerous new government interventions followed Franklin Roosevelt's election in 1932. New initiatives in environmental law, safety, and deregulation swept through the system almost simultaneously during the early 1970s, issues that were raised in the elections of 1968 and 1972, and which seemed to be a logical consequence of the period of positive governmental activism inaugurated by Presidents Kennedy and Johnson. The connections between elections and policy outcomes can be tenuous, however. Few elections provide a clear mandate, in part because the candidates are evaluated by voters along a number of dimensions and in part because the dimensions that affect the policy process later may not be identical to the dimensions that were determinative in the election. What can be said, however, is that elections can be part of a pattern of destabilization, contributing to positive feedback effects.

These destabilizing waves of action can lock-in new institutional structures, causing policy path dependence in which whatever ideas drove the initial mobilization form the basis of the definition of the issue and how it is treated in the newly created policy subsystems. These institutional frameworks are also subject to the activities of the interested. As the strong force of mobilization declines, the more normal forces of stability and negative feedback take over, protecting the system from being easily destabilized.

The twin forces of issue frames and participation by the interested cause classic political lock-in. This would seem to result in a policy process that is always suboptimal, from the viewpoint of either democratic responsiveness or economic performance. Even if a policy subsystem were perfectly crafted to perform optimally, lock-in and path dependency within a dynamic environment would soon lead to suboptimal performance. And we know that all policies are fraught with political compromises that ensure nonoptimal performance at the outset.

But the way in offers a way out. Mobilizations not only create subsystems and other broadly shared policy arrangements but also disrupt them. It is unusual for a policy, once within the purview of government, to be cut asunder, but it does happen. One example is the deregulation wave that swept transportation subsystems during the late 1970s (Baumgartner and Jones 1993: 210–14). It is much more common for such waves to alter the very way a subsystem does business. The nuclear power regulatory subsystem, for example, was transformed from a "captured" agency bolstered by a booster joint congressional committee to one that strongly interfered in the domestic nuclear power business under the demands of environmentalists and consumers (Baumgartner and Jones 1991). The allegedly powerful "intergovernmental lobby" lost influence rapidly after 1979; major disruptions in housing, transportation, and economic development subsystems occurred (Levine and Thurber 1986; Baumgartner and Jones 1993: chap. 7).

One may think of mobilizations as occurring at all levels of scale, from the minor adjustment to the major disruption. Many processes, including earthquakes and ecological extinctions, follow a skewed distribution such that many small events occur but only a few major ones (Raup 1991; Bak and Chen 1991; Waldrop 1992: 304–6). One issue for democratic governance is whether institutions can be designed to cause more or less continual disruptions of path-dependent policy arrangements so that new issues may enter the public debate without causing disruption of the fundamental institutions themselves.

So long as destabilizing waves operate to create and disrupt policy subsystems, the potential for a disjointed, but adaptive, policy process exists. That is, the punctuations that wrack the policy process in the United States may have adaptive features, making the system more responsive than has been previously recognized. We must be cautious, however, in assuming that these punctuations imply a kind of "voter sovereignty" analogous to the "consumer sovereignty" of economics. Mobilization in democracies is necessarily partial, because of the multiplicity of venues of action that exist and because of the phenomenon of selective attention that we have examined in this book. In a world where most of us want both a clean environment and productive industries, does a mobilization on environmental issues act to enforce "voter sovereignty"? It may be clear that the old ways of doing things, in which business interests had primacy within systems of limited participation (Cobb and Elder 1983), have been altered by the intrusion of environmentalism. It is not so clear that the issue expansion process that environmentalists were able to cause in the early 1970s enforced "voter sovereignty." So the path of policies traced through the combination of incremental adjustments within policy subsystems and serial shifts may be adaptive, in the sense of responsiveness to active forces. But they may not enforce a dynamic, disjunctive populist equilibrium. The next chapter examines these issues in more detail.

9   Governments as Adaptive Systems

> *Most systems of interest to humankind—economies, political organizations, games, ecologies, the central nervous system, biological evolution . . . when they settle down, are either "dead" or uninteresting.* — JOHN HOLLAND

The previous chapter investigated the continual shifting from serial to parallel processing within government. Because of the phenomena of lock-in and path dependency, in which basic issue definitions are shared and participation is primarily by the interested, policy subsystems normally perform suboptimally. This suboptimality would seem to occur whether one used democratic performance or economic performance or some less well defined notion such as adjustment to changing socioeconomic circumstances.

One fundamental question is whether the serial policy shift is adaptive. Given that policy subsystems, characterized as they are by path dependency, perform suboptimally, does the serial shift offer a way of lurching toward optimality? It may be that incremental adjustment is *not* preferable to the episodic lurches associated with movement from parallel to serial processing, because of the inability of incrementalism to disrupt the policy system enough to overcome the suboptimal performance of path dependency. Three possibilities exist: (1) the serial shift is more or less random, reflecting policy "fads"; (2) the shift is cyclical, reflecting the ebb and flow of groups and parties into the policy process; and (3) the shift is (or at least can be) adaptive and hence carries an evolutionary component.

Fitness Functions

Commentators and analysts alike are forever imposing criteria of performance on government. Consider these: governments are inefficient; governments are unresponsive; governments are redistributive in a manner that interferes with capital accumulation; governments are responsive only to special interests; governments are the handmaidens of capitalists. It is easy to see that these baldly stated phrases imply performance standards, or what I have termed *dimensions of evaluation,* and that these criteria are themselves contradictory. It would seem that a government cannot be the "handmaiden of capitalism" and simultaneously destroy the incentive to accumulate—at least until one recognizes that the ability of governments to process issues in parallel can act to reconcile these inconsistencies.

We might view such critiques of government in an *adaptive systems* framework. An adaptive system is one continually adjusting to its environment. It could be a biological organism or a species or a robotics device in manufacturing or a social system. In the case of democratic government, the criteria for adjustment to the environment are multifaceted and the calls for better performance on any of the criteria suggested in the above paragraph can be seen as attempts to call attention to parts of the environment where there exist problems. In the context of the study of adaptation and evolution, biologists and computer scientists modeling adaptive processes would call these performance standards "fitness functions" (Packard 1989). But the term *fitness function* probably underestimates the complexity of the environment facing a species, which consists of both the physical environment (terrain, climate, etc.) and other organisms (prey, predators, and competitors for an environmental niche). Langton (1989: 37) complains that "it is very easy to underestimate the complexity of environmental interactions [in evolutionary models]. Most such models provide overly simple environments within which certain behaviors are preordained as 'fit' and others as 'unfit'."

Generally, a biological fitness function for a given phenotype (the realized organism, as compared to the genotype, its genetic structure) is the number of offspring that survive to reproduce. It is assumed that, on average, an organism evolves to a "fitness peak" of characteristics because of the pressures of natural selection. The problem, according to Packard, is that "the biosphere does not appear to have any *a priori* fitness function defined." The problem is twofold: the environment is dynamic, and the combination of genes and chromosomes is nonlinear under the influence of enzymes—a process known as *epistasis* (Holland 1992: 10). For these two reasons, it is not possible to infer fitness from a linear interpolation of existing phenotypes. Hence it may be futile for an analyst to prespecify a fitness function for an organism (Kauffman 1993). Rather, evolution "occurs as a result of a population of subsystems changing in response to interactions between them" (Packard 1989: 142). Fitness functions are dynamic, changing in a complex pattern of coevolution in which the environment of organisms is composed primarily of other organisms, which respond to evolutionary adaption of each other.

Biologists use a hill-climbing metaphor to describe the adjustment of organisms to their environment (which in the short run consists mostly of other organisms; organisms basically coevolve with one another). "The paradigm is one of local hill climbing via fitter mutants toward some local or global optimum" (Kauffman 1993: 33). Natural selection acts to move organisms up hills toward fitter forms; but the landscape itself is continually deforming in response to climate changes and changes in evolutionary paths of predator and prey. So an organism on a constant landscape is subject to finding a local maximum (a "hill") in its "search" for fitness rather than a global maximum (the tallest "mountain"). As a consequence, natural selection, even natural selection on a constant landscape, doesn't ever guarantee the best form for an organism. One might say the organism satisfices. But the situation is even more problematic if the landscape is continually deforming in response to the evolutionary patterns of other organisms (as well as to climate and other facets that make up the "landscape" that dictates the organism's fitness function). Many biologists thus conclude that natural selection cannot ever ensure maximization.

An evolutionary approach is relevant to policymaking within a complex and open environment such as that provided in liberal democracies. If we unpack critiques of government action, we invariably find an underlying prespecified "fitness function." These fitness functions may be quite appropriate, but they almost always underestimate the complexity of the environment that faces government. And because fitness functions for policy action often are contradictory, maximizing the function can cause more problems than "muddling through."

General Adaptive Systems

Packard's "intrinsic" model of evolution follows work by John Holland (1992) which sees such intrinsic adaptation as a general feature of dynamic systems. Holland (1992: 1) writes that "complexity makes discovery of the optimum a long, perhaps never-to-be-completed task, so the best among *tested* options must be exploited at every step." Holland claims that most systems of action are like this: they are dynamic, shifting, out of equilibrium, and always seeking:

> Most systems of high interest to humankind—economies, political organizations, games, ecologies, the central nervous system, biological evolution, etc.—rarely, if ever, "settle down" to some repetitive or other easily described pattern. Such systems are
> • intrinsically dynamic (When they settle down they are "dead" or uninteresting.)
> • far from global optimum (There is always room for further improvement, though the system may perform quite well in a comparative sense.)
> • continually adapting to new circumstances (The strategies or

structures that determine the system's interaction continually change, often with accompanying improvements in performance.) (Holland 1989: 463).

Is it possible that democratic governments are general adaptive systems? The study of adaptation is grounded in the view that certain systems are information-processing entities in one form or another. That is, business firms process information from the demand and cost signals they receive; organisms adapt by natural selection; computer programs can be written which specify outcomes but not process. "Since a given structure performs differently in different environments—the structure is more or less fit—it is the adaptive plan's task to produce structures which perform 'well' (are fit) in the environment confronting it" (Holland 1992: 4). Then the adoption of any set performance standard would be temporary as the structures and policies adopted change in response to changing circumstances.

Schumpeter's Lament

Viewing governmental systems as adaptive systems in complex environments is very attractive, but we must first ask what are the aspects of the environment that such systems are adapting to. Institutional economist Douglass North (1990) has argued that the differences in growth rates among nations are larger than one would expect given economic theory. North finds, in effect, that political institutions can create incentives that cause participants to maximize behavior that is contrary to the achievement of long-run economic growth. In terms of the arguments developed in this book, we might say that other dimensions of conflict can intrude to cause participants to attend to other incentives than those associated with wealth maximization. At any rate, wealth maximization is clearly one measure of the success of a political system.

It would seem that authoritative governments adapt to different aspects of the environment than democratic systems; but let us focus only on democratic systems. It is easy to caricature democratic governments as, for example, acting to "maximize votes." The fitness function would involve only the counting of votes and nothing more. So a second criterion for democratic governments is the satisfaction of mass preferences for public policies.

It is not so clear that these criteria are compatible. On the one hand, the most successful capitalist systems coexist with liberal democracy. On the other hand, there are good theoretical reasons for worrying about the compatibility between capitalist wealth accumulation and mass democracy. The economist Joseph Schumpeter (1950) fretted that democracy would, at some point, undermine capitalist incentives through its urges to satisfy mass preferences at the expense of institutions developed to accumulate capital. Others have extended Schumpeter's thesis by arguing that democracies act to maximize votes by enacting policies that redistribute income, undermining incentives for wealth accumulation that encourage long-term growth. Mean income is greater than median income, because the income distribution is skewed. Hence politicians can build majorities based on redistributing mean income until it is at the median (and the redistributive politician loses his or her majority) (see Meltzer and Richard 1978).

Certainly in the United States, and (to a lesser extent) in many European democracies, this hasn't happened. I suggest two major reasons. The first is the multiple venues of policy action that allow privileged groups to influence policy within subsystems. Policymaking within these venues can proceed according to different logics. Moreover, much policymaking in democracies is isolated from popular majorities and responds to more local (that is, less general) political forces. The second reason for the failure of democracy to destroy capitalism is the intrusion of multiple dimensions of evaluation into the general political debate. Voters, like other decision-makers in politics, are not locked into one dimension of evaluation in their orientations to politics.

It is not at all clear that mass publics will conspire with vote-maximizing politicians to weaken capitalism seriously. That is where the adaptive systems framework becomes useful. Because government is subject to multiple pressures from the environment (two of which are overall wealth maximization and the fair distribution of income), analysts who focus on only one of those dimensions will miss the potentially adaptive processes inherent in democratic governance.[1]

Resource Suppliers and Resource Demanders

Pressure from the environment ensures that governments are often not subject to a single, simple "fitness function." For governments, sim-

1. When discussing adaptive systems, we must be careful not to idealize such processes. The classic adaptive system is the predator-prey evolutionary "arms race" in which prey and predator each adapts to the other's new technique. This, the so-called Red Queen effect, can lead rapidly to a local equilibrium. Slight changes in the environment or evolutionary pathway can lead to explosive growth and spectacular crashes. If, for example, a prey manages an adaption that stymies the predator pretty completely, the prey would rapidly increase, resulting in overcrowding and a crash in the prey population. So adaption is very much *not* a smooth process.

A major difference in human societies is their ability to design institutions, thinking explicitly about performance criteria. One of the great challenges in the design of human

ple maximization is the route to disaster. While students of national politics have been slow to recognize this, urban politics scholars have directed considerable attention to the problem of contradictory imperatives on government.[2]

Local governments in democratic systems may be seen as struggling with four sets of forces: local electoral coalitions, local economic pressures, external governmental pressures, and external economic pressures. It seems democratic for local politicians to defer to local electoral coalitions, but we know that in pluralist systems most interelection demands are put forward by interest groups. Politicians tend to defer to urban interest groups if possible because of the fear of electoral mobilization against them otherwise (Dahl 1961). In many cities, the most organized groups are public employees; clearly they are resource demanders. Deferring too much to such groups can mean alienating resource suppliers, however, by raising taxes.

Paul Peterson (1980) has claimed that the demands of capital accumulation within the city are primary, because the small size of local governments means that they are more dependent on a limited number of "export industries." That is, they must defer to the wealth producers in the community; otherwise these businesses may leave town. So local politicians are in the situation of performing a balancing act: they must attend to their own electoral coalitions, as well as to the local economic elite, who not only are wealth producers but also have considerable resources that can be directed into influencing local elites (C. Stone 1980).

Local electorates do not always join in with the resource demanders, however. For example, they can be persuaded (usually through the appeal to the production of jobs) to support efforts at wealth maximization in the city (Jones and Bachelor 1993). Indeed, the imperative to attract and retain businesses is itself not subject to simple maximization. Local political leaders cannot just keep tax bases low and wait for industry. Industry needs a public infrastructure; moreover, many industries now also look at the provision of critical services such as education, and even amenities, by a community to help them attract and retain a high-quality work force. So even the attempt by a community to maximize its tax base is a multifaceted task.

---

institutions is to recognize their adaptive capacities and try to design them so that the adjustment process is not subject to such violent punctuations.

2. The major reason is that the small size of local governments makes them highly subject to external influences and highly dependent on wealth creation within their boundaries. Hence the very weakness of local governments led scholars to view them within a contradictory imperatives framework.

Even the tension between electoral coalitions and tax base maximization does not exhaust the problems of local governments. They must also attend to the demands of higher levels of government, particularly the state government. Localities are the legal offspring of the states; as a consequence, they are subject to numerous mandates from state governments on a variety of topics—from the length of the school year (for school districts) to the rules for bargaining with employees. To a lesser extent, localities are affected by mandates from the federal government; they may also be strongly influenced by actions by state or federal courts. Finally, the city is subject to broader capitalist forces because of the manner in which they finance capital improvements. Having to sell bonds in an international market means complying with the dictates of bond-rating firms (Shefter 1985).

As a result of these complex demands, local governments in the United States have spawned both a wide variety of formal structures and a variety of informal arrangements among actors both within government and outside it. The combination of formal and informal arrangements constitutes the city's *regime* (C. Stone 1989, 1993). The regime may incorporate local business leaders and local politicians, but it also may include labor leaders, neighborhood groups, and political leaders at other levels of government (Jones and Bachelor 1983). It also may vary considerably across fairly limited time spans as the city reacts to new challenges and new participants become active in city politics.

This cursory overview of pressures on local governments, where the literature is best developed, indicates the complex adjustment process that must underlie government. Simply put, there is no one underlying dimension of evaluation that local government leaders can use for the purposes of maximization. They are subject to different "imperatives," and each imperative carries with it a different evaluative criterion. Surely adaptive processes in economies or ecologies are complex, but nothing quite matches the contradictory demands put on governments.

A major reason for this is the separation of supply and demand in governments. Economies based on voluntary exchanges imply a balance between the demand for a good or service and the paying for it. But nonvoluntary exchange is a part and parcel of politics; those demanding policies and those supplying the resources are never completely identical. So demands from voters or interest groups for policies never imply a willingness to pay for them. As Senator Russell Long of Louisiana was fond of saying, "Don't tax you; don't tax me; tax that man behind that tree."

As a consequence, the adaptive process for governments must involve shifting back and forth among several basic evaluative standards.

One major shift concerns whether to respond to resource suppliers or resource demanders. Hence democratic governments may be unlike other adaptive systems in one major way: they have contradictory goals. After all, the goal of a firm is to make money for its owners. The "goal" of an organism is survival and propagation. But government has no such simple single goal; in consequence, conflict in politics often involves the very evaluative dimensions that define the "fitness function."

Fitness functions in ecosystems and in economies may not be determinate, but all involve "winning." Fitness functions in democracies also involve "winning" as parties compete for electoral support and groups strive to achieve particular policy outcomes. But in democratic governments complete victory is often self-defeating; a total victory of policy demanders over policy suppliers would wreck the system for both. Moreover, these are not the only dimensions of evaluation that affect governments; we have discussed in a previous chapter the intrusion of the "new social issues" into mass politics in the United States since the late 1960s.

Viewing government as adaptive to both resource suppliers and policy demanders, as the urban political economy literature suggests, can move us from a single-minded reliance on one standard of performance. But the logic is contradictory. That is, it is difficult to conceive of a smooth fitness function that would involve the claims of both demanders and suppliers. It is far more likely that one dimension of performance evaluation (either meeting demands for policies or refraining from extracting so much productive capacity out of the system of voluntary exchange that the productivity of the tax system declines) will dominate. If so, then governments will be very subject to adapting to a local maximum or "false peak." One understanding (wealth maximization) may dominate at one time and become vulnerable to attack by a competing understanding (fairness in distribution of wealth).

Collective Action

Another way to think about the peculiar problems of government as an adaptive system involves the issue of collective action. Government coercion has been justified as necessary to produce collective goods. Collective goods are goods that everyone can consume if they are provided; access cannot be denied. Hence those policies can be viewed as being in the interest of all to consume but in the interest of nobody to supply. Because voluntary exchange will not produce these goods, it is in the interest of every member of a group or political system to "free-ride," that is, to let other members supply the good and then enjoy the results. But everyone thinks this way; hence the good will be undersupplied. So governments use coercive tax policies to make sure that these goods are supplied (Olson 1965). Unfortunately, there seem to be no mechanisms to limit the oversupply of such goods, at least in open systems (Olson 1982). Or at least it has been argued.

Political scientists have studied the collective action problem as a prisoner's dilemma game. In this scenario, two prisoners guilty of a crime and held incommunicado have two choices: to maintain an alibi or to confess. Authorities have structured the situation so that confession will yield a more lenient sentence. Because of uncertainty, the equilibrium "solution" to the problem is to confess, thereby ensuring a suboptimal outcome for both prisoners (but ensuring that neither will serve a maximum sentence).

While the prisoner's dilemma game is illustrated using a specific situation, it is in actuality a very general model for a variety of processes. It mimics behaviors in which cooperation yields a higher payoff to both parties in an interchange than does narrow rationality. Jon Elster (1979) sets up the game in a general fashion to explore its relevance for the collective action problem. He specifies the prisoner's dilemma as a game between "me" and "all others." There are two strategies {x, y}, and /x,y/ means "I" choose x, "all others" choose y; {C,D} means "I" cooperate, "all others" defect. Then Elster (1979: 19–20) specifies the payoff (fitness function) of the game as the following rank order:

1) /D,C/
2) /C,C/
3) /D,D/
4) /C,D/.

That is, the best thing to happen for "me" is that "I" defect and all others cooperate, thereby providing the collective good without my having to work for it. "It is immediately seen that whatever the others do, my best strategy is always D. As the others are in the same position, they will also choose D, the ensuing and fully predictable outcome being /D,D/, which is worse *for everyone* than /C,C/" (Elster 1979: 20). The lesson is that strategic action can lead to suboptimality; that is, collective rationality and individual strategic rationality are in conflict.

The prisoner's dilemma game has been used to model arms races between nations, the use of incentives to lure businesses to cities and states, and a variety of other situations in which individual rationality and collective rationality are in conflict. Use of the prisoner's dilemma concept is not confined to studies of human behavior; biologists have used it to model the coevolutionary strategies of two interacting species (Maynard-Smith 1982).

The Iterated Prisoner's Dilemma

The iterated prisoner's dilemma "game" is used to show how collective goods (in this case, the freedom ensured by neither prisoner confessing) will not be supplied under conditions in which communication is not possible. But communication is often possible. Moreover, the prisoner's dilemma game is static, whereas policymaking is dynamic. Different strategies emerge when the prisoner's dilemma game is iterated. Robert Axelrod's famous "tournament," which asked experts to provide solutions to the iterated prisoner's dilemma game, suggested that players could find ways of "communicating" intentions. In particular, TIT FOR TAT, in which a player would first cooperate, then do whatever the other player did, yielded high total scores in the iterated game in comparison to other strategies (Axelrod 1984).

The fact that players *could* find an adaptive strategy in the iterated prisoner's dilemma game does not mean that they always *will*. Axelrod has examined the emergence of various strategies through computer programs that mimic evolution. That is, there is a selection effect on the strategies used by players such that effective strategies are more likely to be used in future rounds of the game.

Kristian Lindgren (1992) has developed a simulation of the iterated prisoner's dilemma using a genetic algorithm with extended "memory" and with perturbations. That is, "players" remember their past strategies (up to five iterations), but the world facing the players is frequently disrupted by the input of random perturbations. Selection operates on the success patterns of the strategies, producing more strategies that yield successful patterns. In observing the simulation over long periods of time, Lindgren noted that a complex dynamics emerged. In particular, "Almost all simulations have in common that during the evolution of the system a number of long-lived metastable states (periods of stasis) appear in a certain order. These periods are usually interrupted by fast transitions to unstable dynamic behavior to new periods of stasis" (1992: 301). Observing the interaction of strategies in coping with the iterated prisoner's dilemma game, *punctuated equilibria* emerged.

Remember that Lindgren was working with a model that was initially developed to examine human behavior. Hence it is difficult to dismiss these results as applying only to the world of biological evolution. Other scholars using simulation have also uncovered patterns of punctuated equilibria. Kauffman and Johnsen (1992) in a model of evolutionary dynamics also based on game theory report that a general feature of their results "is intermittency and bursts of change" (p. 365). Coevolving species can reach Nash equilibrium, a point in a game in which neither player has any motive to change, because movement will cause a decline in payoffs. Because there can be multiple Nash equilibria at any one time and because an evolving game will produce new equilibrium points, the species will occasionally shift off current Nash equilibrium in a cascading effect. Most interestingly, the most "adaptive" evolutionary strategy exists when "Nash equilibria just tenuously form across the ecosystem. In this poised state, co-evolutionary avalanches appear to propagate on all length scales" (Kauffman and Johnsen 1992: 325–26).

Other computer models of ecology have attempted to construct full-blown evolutionary "worlds" full of coevolving species complete with parasites. One implication from these studies is that the genetic "material" (the computer code underlying the observed strategies of computer organisms) seems to continue to evolve even though the strategies seem to be stable, at equilibrium (Levy 1992: 207; Hillis 1992; Ray 1992). So many iterated models of evolutionary dynamics also yield intermittent patterns of stasis and change, leading one observer to comment that "punctuated equilibrium emerges spontaneously in computational evolution" (Levy 1992: 226–27).

The Assurance Game

The provision of collective goods in the public policymaking process, however, often does not resemble a prisoner's dilemma. The provision of collective goods can resemble rather an *assurance* game in which players all know that they will be better off if the good is produced, but do not want to be the "sucker" who does all of the providing. Hence they must be assured that everyone is contributing a fair share. Change the payoff matrix just a little from that in the prisoner's dilemma and the outcome becomes indeterminate. In the assurance game, the rank orders of preferred outcomes are (in Elster's terminology)

1) /C,C/
2) /D,C/
3) /D,D/
4) /C,D/.

We now have the aforementioned assurance game. The only difference between the two scenarios is that in the prisoner's dilemma actors would rather "free-ride" (defect while others cooperate) than enter into a completely cooperative arrangement with others, whereas in the assurance game actors would rather everyone cooperate than be a free rider. The payoff ranking of strategies means that people basically want to cooperate (/C,C/) but also want to avoid cooperating while others defect (/C,D/).

The assurance game models a "stag hunt," where several prehistoric hunters are in search of a stag. If they all cooperate, they can bring down a stag. But it is always possible for a single hunter to capture a scrawny rabbit, clearly an inferior outcome. So for any individual it is better to cooperate, so long as everyone else is cooperating (Stoker 1992). Elster notes that the provision of collective goods (/C,C/) is dependent on information: "In the Prisoner's Dilemma the requirement of full information is not necessary for the solution to emerge, but in the Assurance Game the slightest uncertainty or suspicion will make an actor choose D rather than C" (1979: 21).[3]

Nothing dictates that one game rather than another structures the provision of collective goods. The conceptions of the actors involved determine which form the collective action game takes. Elster (1979) argues that in a prisoner's dilemma game played in small communities, where players share premises and information, the prisoner's dilemma is likely to become transformed into an assurance game.

Dennis Chong (1991) has used the assurance game to study leadership and followship in collective action situations (particularly the civil rights movement), where Elster's conditions probably hold. Chong shows that "bandwagon" effects occur when large numbers of people begin to be assured that they are not going to be "suckers" and that the collective good indeed will be produced. "Although there are high start-up costs to collective action, the attraction of individual cooperation increases with the total level of contributions" (Chong 1991: 114). Similarly, at some point (perhaps after the good has been produced) the prisoner's dilemma reasserts itself, with rapid drop-off in participation.

All of this suggests that politics can involve a considerable amount of rapid shifting from a prisoner's dilemma scenario to an assurance game and back again. That is, leaders often structure a situation to try to evoke the assurance framework and avoid the prisoner's dilemma conception among followers. In addition, there are other "games" which could structure a system of action. The point at which one game is substituted for another may often correspond to shifts in evaluative focus at the individual level (for example, from a supplier to a demander perspective). New issue-frames are being introduced into a decision-making situation.

3. Elster distinguishes human decision-making, characterized by conscious strategies, with animal strategies, which may evolve in various cooperative and competitive arrangements through natural selection. He argues that animals can play prisoner's dilemma games and can even find cooperative strategies, but that only humans can play assurance games.

Game theory is simply a direct and powerful way of modeling contextual structure. Proper modeling of context is, of course, critical, but context itself can change such that a previously appropriate model no longer describes how participants understand the circumstances. When understandings change, punctuations in decisional outcomes are likely to occur.

The collective action problem also shows the necessity of separating attention to context from preferences for public goods. Everyone prefers the collective good; this is true whether a prisoner's dilemma or an assurance game is being played. Hence failure to produce has nothing to do with preferences and everything to do with attentiveness to context. If an evaluative framework is *not* shared, then the context will be viewed as a prisoner's dilemma and the collective good will not be produced. But if the framework is shared, then an assurance scenario is likely to prevail and the collective good is more likely to be produced, depending on the action of leaders in the issue-definition process. Preferences are relatively fixed, and politics is not at all about changing anyone's mind.

The shift from parallel to serial processing of issues is often associated with the movement from a prisoner's dilemma game ("this doesn't involve me") to an assurance game ("I'm concerned, but I won't be active unless others are") for the disinterested. To the extent that serial processing resembles an assurance game, communication of the assurances becomes very important in assembling a coalition for action. Communication often occurs through rhetorical devices that activate and mobilize; neutral information tends not to work very well. As Marcus and Mac-Kuen (1993) show, raising anxiety tends to promote search. To the extent that information can be colored to raise anxiety, the formation of collective action coalitions is enhanced. The "alarmed discovery" stage of Downs's *issue-attention cycle* looks very much like a shift from a prisoner's dilemma game to an assurance game. One might see the initial situation as condition 3 of a prisoner's dilemma game. Companies pollute and citizens let them; both have defected from providing a collective good. Then, suddenly, the game changes. "We've been taken for suckers" was very much the rallying cry against the polluting companies by the environmentalists that Downs uses as his example. This shifts the game (at least among citizens) from prisoner's dilemma to assurance. We can achieve the collective good if we cooperate. Chong shows that leaders are critical in assurance games and that they are motivated by factors outside the game itself—that is, factors that are different from those activating other players.

In the shift from one game structure to another, communication is critical. Moreover, communication cannot proceed according to an incrementalist, fact-collecting approach, in which one adds fact upon fact, slowly and painstakingly illuminating the decision until one has enough information to decide. Communication when the structure of the game is involved is not additive. Rather, it is substitutive, with one game form is being substituted for another. It is also infused with emotion, because emotion stimulates reevaluation of a situation and search for solutions. Shifts in understandings about the game being played are a major reason for the punctuations that occasionally emerge in the evolution of issues within a political system. It would be a mistake to assume that such shifts in game form all emerge from the exhortations of leaders. Objective conditions may well have changed. Even where objective conditions have offered the possibility of a shift in the structure of a situation, however, leaders will generally have to communicate and mobilize.

When Will Punctuations in Policies Emerge?

We may now return to the issue of adaptive shifts in the dynamics of policy subsystems. A policy subsystem, broadly conceived, consists of (1) interested participants sharing a common frame of reference; (2) "contrasystem" leaders, carrying an alternative frame of reference; and (3) apathetics, sharing the prevailing frame but with little intensity. Because the apathetics are capable of shifting their lightly held frames and because they can simultaneously enter in as significant political factors, the mobilization of the apathetic is a critical component in subsystem change. This mobilization tends to occur with a shift from parallel, within-subsystem processing of the policy to serial, high attention processing of the policy.

Subsystems almost always exist at a path-dependent local maximum. Policymaking generally satisfies the participants, and few others care. If we think of the existing subsystem arrangement in game theoretic terms, then the system is at a Nash equilibrium which none of the existing participants have any motive to desert. Incrementalism "down" the peak from the path-dependent maximum will satisfy no one, since all will be able to see that things are deteriorating in general. Policy lock-in is all the more powerful because there is a local maximum; the position is adaptive, even if a more adaptive position exists. It is possible that the subsystem will be able to move toward a position closer to the hypothetical populist policy equilibrium, perhaps as participants see the handwriting on the wall and move to forestall actions by the policymaking branches that could be disruptive of the prevailing patterns. Often this does not occur, because of the selective attentiveness of subsystem participants to local dynamics. If some participants in effect try to shift to an assurance game to protect the collective good (the survival of the subsystem), they risk being exploited by others who see the situation as a prisoner's dilemma.

So more radical shifts are often the manner in which subsystems are changed. The role of the few policy entrepreneurs with contrary frames of reference can be critical. Moving from a path-dependent local maximum frequently involves a sudden, episodic shift. That shift necessitates the interjection of a new dimension of evaluation, which simultaneously serves to put the policy issue in a new context and to intrigue the previously apathetic. Cascading interest often leads to cascading policy change as the new dimension of conflict captures the attention of central policymakers.

Leaping to an Inferior Equilibrium

The phenomenon of leaping to a new equilibrium may suggest that the episodic shifts that characterize moving from parallel to serial policymaking is adaptive. Actually the claim is weaker: that the major way to move from a path-dependent local maximum is through the serial shift. But the resulting movement may well not settle on a superior point and it will be just as subject to lock-in and consequent path dependency.

In 1988, residents of the East Coast were treated to the spectacle of medical wastes, human excrement, and dead dolphins washing up on their beaches. Residents were irate; news stories consistently covered the disaster. In response, Congress passed, without a single dissenting vote, a ban on the ocean dumping of sewage and garbage. "This is a turning point in human history," crowed one congressman. Representative Thomas Manton of Queens initially opposed the act, arguing that it would only shift the waste from sea to land. But he commented that "nobody wanted to discuss the relative risks or merits. It had been a bad summer, and we all wanted to be able to say that we did something. So we passed a law. I tried to have a debate. And it was like I was trying to destroy the planet." An environmental protection official said, "By 1988, ocean dumping had become taboo, about as politically incorrect as any disposal of waste can be. Maybe it was a good thing that happened. Maybe not. But it was not decided on the merits. Congress acted on emotion, not on data."

The law forced the city of New York, which dumped its sewage at deep sea, to spend over $2 billion for new disposal facilities and landfills. What is most remarkable about this story, however, is that ocean dumping had absolutely nothing to do with the beach pollution of 1988. It was caused by the dual sewage- storm-drainage system that New York, like many other older U.S. cities, uses. Heavy rainfalls cause overflows in the sewage treatment facilities, resulting in releases into the ocean. So the law was completely misdirected, forcing vast expenditures on an alternative disposal method that is not necessarily technically superior (Specter 1993).

This may be a particularly horrific example of the serial shift, but it is instructive. We can see the interjection of new dimensions of evaluation into a policy debate (suddenly the ocean is not viewed as an infinite resource or receptacle); the symbolic appeal of a focusing event (beach pollution); the rapid focusing of attention of central policymakers as the policy shifts from policy subsystem (the EPA and local disposal officials) to serial processing; and the leap to a new policy alternative. As Kingdon (1984) has noted, the solutions and problems may be drawn from different "streams"; that is, they may be connected even though they are unrelated. Environmentalists in effect used the symbolic event of beach pollution, caused by antiquated sewer systems, to solve another problem entirely, ocean dumping.

Was this adaptive behavior? On one dimension, it clearly was not. Enormous expenditures resulted from a problem, and none of those expenditures went to solving the problem. On the other hand, environmentalists achieved heightened sensitivity to disposal methods; perhaps neither the problem of inadequate sewage systems nor that of ocean dumping would have been addressed without the serial shift. What is clear is that a new local maximum was reached; that it was reached rapidly in a cascading, bandwagon pattern; and that normal cost-benefit calculations were suspended during the process. Normal cost-benefit calculations were not sufficient to address the perceived problem, and in that sense they were not adaptive. Whether the serial shift was technically adaptive is less critical than the fact that the shift is necessary to move from the incremental-dominated local maximum to a new point of policy action.

Cooperative Games and Evaluative Ends

It would be reassuring if we could argue that the political world was all about convincing people that they ought to move from a prisoner's dilemma contextual definition to an assurance definition of a situation. Unfortunately, life is more complicated than that. Much of politics has to do with competing conceptions of collective ends rather than exhorting citizens to drop their narrow prisoner's dilemma definitions and to see the world as an assurance scenario.

In a perhaps overly simplistic manner, we may depict the political world as a cross-classification between the structure of the game and the nature of the end. In effect, ends and means both may be affected by definitions of the situation. Suppose we have but two ends, or evaluative dimensions, involved. Then our ends-means cross-classification looks as is depicted in table 9.1. Now the "supergame" involves attempts to structure a situation *both* according to its means (whether we are playing a prisoner's dilemma or an assurance game) *and* according to its ends (whether we are pursuing growth or equity, for example).

Subsystem politics, then, involves playing a prisoner's dilemma game (let's all be selfish and not get involved) along a single dimension of evaluation (whether growth, equity, or some other dimension). The path dependency and lock-in that characterizes subsystems is powerfully protected by prisoner's dilemma scenarios and by the justifications of a particular evaluative structure. Those who would change the prevailing pattern of power must simultaneously activate the disinterested (convince them to play an assurance game) and shift the evaluative focus. The two are, however, linked: only new evaluative dimensions will interest the apathetic to play in the assurance game.

Governments as Contradictory Adaptive Systems

The approach developed here treats policymaking bodies as adaptive systems subject to continual shifting back and forth from parallel to serial processing. Instead of fretting about the failure of central control, it views the consequent indeterminacy and conflict as quite natural outcomes of the dynamics of complex systems. Government, however, is a peculiar kind of complex system, because sporadically the normal parallel processing arrangements within a given issue area are replaced for a time with serial processing, characterized by high interest and rapid diffusion of information via the media.

So, in effect, decentralized, democratic government provides a dual

TABLE 9.1 **Means and Ends in Government**

| | | Ends: | |
		Growth	Equity
Means:	Prisoner's Dilemma		
	Assurance		

adaptive process. Policymaking within a subsystem may adjust to changes in the configuration of forces operating on the subsystem. This process can lead to satisfactory outcomes and actually can lead to quite substantial policy changes (Jacob 1988). But usually this process will settle at a local equilibrium that is structure-induced (enforced by the design of institutions). The intervention of macropolitical forces as processing shifts to a single stream often breaks the path-dependent equilibrium of subsystems, setting the subsystem on a new course.

Seeing episodic disjointed change as potentially adaptive suggests that institutions could be designed to incorporate this facet of political change. First, we must note that, while the parallel-serial metaphor is extremely useful in understanding policy dynamics, it would be more appropriate to see a *distribution* of serial disruptions from the trivial to the monumental. Trivial adjustments tend to be path-dependent. Extreme shifts are highly disruptive, perhaps destructive of democratic institutions themselves. We seem to need a system that is highly responsive to incoming information but provides considerable stability so as to avoid the "false positives" exemplified by the congressional ban on ocean dumping. Interestingly, computer scientists show that the processing of information is optimized when a system is poised at "the edge of chaos," that is, when it is neither too organized nor completely chaotic. Kauffman (1993) believes that "evolution to the edge of chaos" increases an organism's survival capacity: an organism is neither too orderly to resist changes for too long nor too chaotic in structure to react to every perturbation in its environment. He terms this region of evolution as "the complex regime." Basically, organisms in the complex regime have a "ready response" for both major and minor disruptions in the fitness landscape (Kauffman 1993: 280).

Similarly, a stable, open, decentralized government would seem to be superior in adapting to changing circumstances. Too much order would leave government too hidebound to respond to changing circumstances. This would occur in a system of mutual noninterference, in which policy subsystems were allowed to govern unmolested. But it would also occur with principal-agent approaches to government. In both cases, massive mobilizations would be required to cause proper adjustments. In statistical parlance, the system of governance would be too tolerant of Type I errors—too acceptant of the "null" hypothesis that no policy change is needed. Too little order, and the system will be buffeted about, creating all sorts of fresh suboptimal policy positions by overresponding. The result would be numerous "false positives"; the system would too easily reject the hypothesis that no change is needed.

Governments, as complex and often contradictory adaptive systems, must process in parallel. The attention of central policymakers is limited. But parallel processing systems will always fall prey to local forces. Political theorists have long recognized the tension between order and freedom; now the theory of complex, adaptive systems has implications for the design of human governing institutions.

10 Political Choice and Democratic Governance

There is no reason why here rather than there, why now rather than then. — Pascal

In this book I have developed a model of temporal political choice based on the role of shifting attentiveness to preferences, a shift based on varying evaluations of context. Then I have explored the wider policymaking implications of the episodic shifts in attention that are implied by the model. There are, of course, other aspects of temporal choice that affect politics, including the preference for present over future consumption (the discount utility model) and changing evaluations of what is possible (the direct effect of political context). And it is inescapable that preferences change—people's basic values, their wants, and their needs do evolve. But in the short run, shifting attentiveness to basic preferences critically affects decision-making.

The model I propose in this book is quite general, affecting most areas of life. But it is especially relevant for politics, where collective decision-making and the use of coercion to impose constraints on decision-making are prevalent rather than voluntary exchange and private goods. Most important, in politics a simple metric does not exist that allows comparisons among diverse alternatives. In economics, the price system allows such comparisons. In the absence of a standard metric, decisions are much more subject to the serial shift. Of course, in economic decisions attentiveness to a single or a limited number of evaluative dimensions of a product or service allows producers to compete by highlighting new aspects of their products. Advertising strategies often emphasize dimensions of evaluation that have been overlooked by competitors. But the price system always allows a comparison among units in a manner that is only imperfectly available in politics. For a car, one may ask, "How much am I willing to pay for improved safety?" implicitly comparing an attribute (safety) to a standard (price). In politics, one may ask, "How much am I willing to give up in economic liberalism to emphasize social conservatism?" but that is a comparison that is much more difficult to make. People generally end up comparing on the most salient dimension—the preference that they are most attentive to.

The manner in which citizens process political information has impli-

224

cations for the operation of democratic institutions. Indeed, one of the original objectives of this study was to try to forge some links between certain characteristics of human decision-making and the operation of democratic political systems, particularly the tendency of such systems to shift episodically from one issue to another. These shifts seem to be disruptive without being destructive; that is, they disrupt cozy subsystem arrangements and upset existing political settlements, but they do not destabilize the entire system of governance.

Two basic issues are suggested by the analysis presented here. One has to do with democracy, the other with desirable public policies. First, is the serial policy shift, as it is practiced in the United States, democratic? Clearly the shift is related to the activation of new participants and the disruption of oligarchic arrangements and comfortable political settlements. But democracy may imply something other than a form of "creative destruction"—Schumpeter's characterization of capitalism. It may require hewing to the "populist policy equilibrium." If so, then the shifting from parallel to serial processing is not sufficient. Second, is the serial policy shift adaptive, in the sense of providing a good "fit" to the demands of the environment? Even if a political system followed the path of the "populist policy equilibrium," it would not necessarily adopt the policies that best fit the environment. The reason is that the environment of any political system consists of more than the wishes of the voting public. Before we turn to these issues, let us review the argument to this point.

Overview of the Argument

Humans are serial processors of information. That is, they generally have to focus on a single task at a time; we say that they are *attentive* to the single task.

Every stimulus (and therefore all information) is structured by multiple attributes or dimensions. Each object of choice, from a political candidate to an automobile, has several attributes, attributes that are more or less relevant to an actual choice. Cars can be characterized by price, by color, by quality, by comfort, by efficiency, or by prestige value. Candidates can be seen in terms of their partisan affiliation, their political ideologies, their articulateness, or any number of other attributes. Many attributes are not relevant to a choice situation (candidate's shoe color), but many are in the proper context.

When people evaluate these dimensions, they may be termed preferences. Because they are multidimensional, preferences are often in conflict. Preferences are treated two different ways by students of decision-making. Sometimes they refer to the choice itself: would you prefer, for example, candidate A or candidate B? The second use of the term *preference* refers to outcomes of the choice; the choice is the "strategy." I have termed the first use *direct preferences;* I have denoted the second use *Stigler-Becker preferences.*

Now, it is quite true that people can become "brand loyal"—that is, they can prefer one strategy to another, somewhat independently of the outcome. One may vote for the Democratic candidate because of the policies proffered. Or one may vote Democrat because one is "brand loyal"—a "yellow dog" Democrat in the South or a "brass collar" Democrat in the North. Much confusion can be avoided if we stick to the notion that the choice is a strategy for bringing about an outcome. Then "brand loyalty" can be incorporated as one dimension of the outcome space. Of course, we still will need to be appreciative of the complexity of "ends-means chains," whereby one end becomes a means in a changed context. But the distinction between preferences relating to objects of choice (direct preferences) and to more basic goals (Stigler-Becker preferences) is nevertheless a good starting point.

As serial processors, human decision-makers have great difficulties integrating the multidimensional preferences in the absence of a standard metric. It is so onerous, especially in circumstances requiring reasonably quick decisions, that decision-makers normally don't do it. Often they *factor* problems, or break them up into smaller parts for attention. Unfortunately, it may become very difficult for decision-makers to reintegrate the parts into a coherent whole. Rather, they tend to fall prey to cognitive polarization, viewing a stimulus in terms of one dimension of evaluation, then shifting rapidly to a second when cues dictate. The lack of integration of domains may not be so evident at one point in time. But in temporal choice, inconsistencies are glaring.

Shifts in attentiveness to preferences (or evaluative dimensions) are generally how decision-makers in politics integrate diverse dimensions. Attentiveness can refer to selectivity in cognition about the environment. Indeed, the term *context* is used to refer to what aspects of a complex environment are salient to a decision-maker at a particular time. Because preferences (in the Stigler-Becker sense) are evaluated attributes, these attentiveness shifts also affect what preferences a decision-maker will pursue. Hence a change in the focus of attention can change the preference to which a decision-maker attends.

Attentiveness may shift quite rapidly in comparison to preferences, which tend to be more stable. Contexts of decisions almost always change more rapidly than do basic values and preferences. Problems press in, causing a reorientation of attention to preferences.

Shifts in attentiveness to preferences mean that comprehensive utility functions may be severed temporally. Temporal severing of utility functions via the attention mechanism causes the reordering of preference *domains* or *dimensions*. From the vantage point of rational choice, a world in which preferences are reordered whenever a change of context occurs would be an unstable world indeed. There is no provision for such behavior in the rational choice model; indeed, the discounted utility model is the major tool for understanding temporal choice in that model. Understanding preferences as stable and attentiveness (or the *weights* of the preference dimensions) as variable makes sense of a potentially disordered world.

Utility functions that are severed temporally imply the possibility of choice reversals. Identical choices at two different points in time may be decided differently, even though *at each point utility functions may be described by the standard axioms of rational choice (completeness and transitivity).* A model that does not incorporate dynamics is not going to be very useful in understanding politics, where dynamics dominates statics. The rational model is essentially static; as such, it is not capable of dealing with such essential political processes as the emergence of new dimensions of conflict in the political dialogue. Cross-sectionally, decision-makers may approximate the rational model—preferences are completely ordered and transitive. But the orders may be different because of changes in the attentiveness weightings for the preference dimensions. *Hence it is as important to understand attention as preferences in politics.*

Shifts in attentiveness mean that new dimensions of political conflict may emerge quite suddenly (at least in open, democratic systems). If new understandings of political issues are widely communicated, then collective attention may be focused on the emergent dimension of conflict. The *structure* of a decision-making situation is associated with the relevant dimensions of evaluation that are used by participants. Hence communication is fundamental to the determination of the structure of decisions in politics.

The suddenness of the emergence of new dimensions of conflict is often related to shifts in general understandings of the nature of politics, such as between a "prisoner's dilemma" scenario and an "assurance" scenario. Shifts in such understandings among a few often cause "cascades" as such understandings are communicated to others. Such cascades are denoted as "mobilizations" or "conflict expansions" by political scientists.

Political institutions serve to "fix" attentiveness on a limited number of dimensions of evaluation. These are "structure-induced equilibria" because their stability is dependent on the structure of institutions. Such local equilibria characterize policy subsystems, which in our terms are arrangements that incorporate the interested and ignore the possible preferences and interests of the unconcerned.

Because of the "fixing" of attention on a limited number of dimensions of evaluation, democratic policymaking is "path dependent"; that is, it continues to build on the limited perspective introduced in the past. Path dependency in policy solutions leads almost invariably to drift from optimum performance except on the dimension that has been structured into the policy arrangement. In effect, the subsystem adjusts to a policy "niche," which is quite secure until the niche is disrupted by outside forces (perhaps brought in by "losers" in a local policy dispute, as occurs in conflict expansion models). If we compare the *pluralist policy equilibrium,* which is the hypothetical sum of the policies enacted in parallel policy subsystems, with the *populist policy equilibrium,* which is the hypothetical match between citizen preferences and overall policy outputs, we will find considerable differences at any one time.

The interjection of new dimensions of conflict may disrupt structure-induced equilibria, thereby injecting an instability in even the most open and democratic politics. This more or less continual disruption interposed on path-dependent policy arrangements means that the pluralist policy equilibrium is subject to continual destabilizations. These destabilizations are democratizing and can act to bring the pluralist policy equilibrium toward the populist policy equilibrium.

When mobilizations occur, the normal parallel processing of issues is shifted momentarily to the serial processing apparatus (the president and leadership structures in Congress). Media interest is heightened, and parties organize conflict. This system-level serial shift is analogous to the serial shift in individual decision-making and is primarily driven by it.

Serial shifting at the collective level allows a policymaking system to "leap" from a suboptimum local maximum to a better performance "peak," but it may also allow the "leaping" to an inferior local maximum. There are no guarantees that policy leaps are adaptive. We can say that path-dependent local equilibria are likely to drift away from optimal performance and that it will be extremely difficult to alter the situation in the absence of such a shift.

Let us turn briefly to a few of the more important implications of the model summarized above. First, I discuss the implications of the model for preference aggregation. Then I turn to the issues raised by viewing episodic, nonincremental shifts as fundamental to political decision-making. Finally, I discuss the implications of such a model of systems-level decision-making for democratic, adaptable policymaking.

The Aggregation of Attention

The responsiveness of government to citizen preferences has been a primary theme in normative analyses of democratic government. It turns out that the "counting" of preferences in any democratically based decision-making institution is not straightforward. I have argued here that preference activation and issue expansion from elites to masses are just as critical to the understanding of the operation of democracies as is the problem of aggregation. Governments are active creatures themselves, not just vessels for some sort of counting up of the preferences of citizens.

The strong influence of the shift in focus in policy debates is why any empirical examination of the responsiveness of government must take account of both attention and preferences. Empirical work suggests that democratic governments are responsive through policy outcomes when changes in citizen preferences are sufficient (Page and Shapiro 1983; Hartley and Russett 1992). The limited analysis of defense spending presented in chapter 4 suggested that citizen preferences about defense spending and citizen attentiveness to the issues of defense and foreign affairs combine to produce a responsive outcome. We need to understand how political systems aggregate attention as much as we need to know how they aggregate preferences. As suggestive and useful as they are, the "black-box" models that political scientists use to explain policy outputs (which I used in chap. 4) can point us in the right direction, but they cannot tell us *how* attentiveness affects the policy process.

However things are aggregated, it is clear that politicians are a critical key to aggregation. It has been argued that democratic politicians adopt simple maximizing rules that incorporate only one dimension. Their preferences, at base, are simple: to get into office and, once there, to stay there. That means one ought simply to please one's constituency. "One's constituency" in formal models of representation is not infrequently conceived as the "median voter"—that is, the voter at the median of the prevailing dimension of conflict. In one-dimensional situations, this is the position that dominates—that is, it cannot be defeated by any other position. In effect, the problem of the comprehensive utility function is defined away as the serial shift is eliminated as a problem (because if there exists only one dimension, then there is nothing to shift to). There are no conflicts between wanting to get rich and stay in power, or between the legislator's policy aims and his constituents, or between the wishes of constituents and of nationally organized interest groups.

Normally the response to any of these objections is that legislators successfully factor decisions; they may not kowtow to constituencies when the constituencies are not paying attention.

Even if we do allow this one-dimensional approach to politicians to stand, it will not obviate the serial shift. First, so long as one's constituency consists of some mixture of the attentive and the inattentive, it seems necessary to figure out what part of the constituency is attentive to what. Second, the notion of a one-dimensional evaluative framework that constituents use to structure politics has long ago been discredited. Multiple attributes underlie the policy debate. Different frames can be used by different parts of the constituency. Moreover, it can happen that the constituency, or some critical part of it, shifts *en masse* to a new focus. Then the serial shift will affect the maximizing politician quite directly, even though he or she may harbor preferences that are not themselves affected. Finally, if the constituency so shifts, it can render the politician's decisional factoring wrong. He or she may have to scramble to address the new reality, hence looking inconsistent in the process. So the simple assumption of maximizing politicians cannot alone lead to any kind of overall equilibrium.

The Futility of a Marginalist Politics

Even within the operation of liberal democracies, new framings of issues emerge that destabilize old equilibria of active interests. Yet the major approaches political scientists have used to study politics in democratic societies tend to be marginalist. Group theory, incremental decision-making, representation of interests in Congress, the stability of bureaucratic decision rules—all imply not only marginal adjustment from an implied equilibrium but also the incorporation of an analytic (as opposed to a synthetic) approach to understanding politics. Objections to the prevailing approaches have been raised: in the study of partisan realignments; in the study of policy agendas, where new ideas "break through"; in theoretical analyses of state building and political development. Nevertheless, our understandings of the workings of democracy have tended toward the marginalist and the analytical.

Political scientists do not always recognize that their marginalist and analytical approach is quite compatible with theories of economics that extend economic analysis to social life. People are purposive; they face costs and benefits; they will invest in the activities that bring them the highest rate of return in terms of the broad goals they harbor. University of Chicago Nobel Laureate economist Gary Becker has been the most forceful advocate of this point of view, arguing that stable preferences, maximizing behavior, and market equilibrium are conditions that affect social life (and, presumably, politics). In this book, I have questioned some of these assumptions. When decisions, particularly political decisions involving collective goods and nonvoluntary choices, are examined across time, one must question the assumption of stable preferences. Empirical choices seem too inconsistent, and one's arguments to the contrary become too elaborate and rarefied to be persuasive. One may keep the concept of very general preferences that Becker and his colleague George Stigler advocate if one is willing to allow attentiveness to those preferences to vary over time. This means that any choice situation rests on both active and latent preferences. Shifts from currently active to latent preferences are disjointed, episodic events and can wreak havoc on a previously well behaved choice situation. This implies that the "market" is not at equilibrium and that marginalist adjustment in choice situations is at least occasionally not possible. So I argue that people can and do maximize, but only on the dimensions of preference that are currently active in a decision-making situation.

Alfred Marshall was a leading figure in the marginalist school of economics. He developed a conception of economics based on continuity and marginal adjustment that was appropriate to the use of the maximization techniques of the calculus. In the first edition of his *Principles of Economics,* published in 1890, Marshall stressed the principle of continuity as fundamental. First, things categorized separately often graded into one another. Second, things transformed gradually rather than abruptly. Marshall at first seems to have in mind a general theory of choice: economics, he writes, "is a study of men in the ordinary business of life." Then he qualifies: "But it concerns itself chiefly with those motives which affect, most powerfully and most steadily, man's conduct in the business part of life" (Marshall 1961: 14).

The fundamental application of the principle of continuity is "the general equilibrium of demand and supply" (p. viii). Continuity will allow analytical decomposition and bracketing presumed extraneous variables in the infamous ceteris paribus clause. And continuity will allow marginalist analysis: "Our observations of nature, in the moral as in the physical world, relate not so much to aggregate quantities, as to increments of quantities, and that in particular the demand for a thing is a continuous function, of which the 'marginal' increment is, in stable equilibrium, balanced against the corresponding increment of its cost of production" (p. x). So Marshall's approach, which is mirrored in today's economic analyses, was both analytical and marginalist. And it would seem to be quite a general model of decision-making, not one just associated with economic decisions.

Scarcity is such a normal part of "the business of everyday life" that it is easy to see why today's political economists would depict a political world in which the principle of continuity holds, and marginalist analysis is the path of scientific progress. In response to William Riker's (1980) claim that equilibria in politics do not exist (discussed in chap. 4 of this book), Peter Ordeshook defended the mainstream: "Riker's conclusions call into question the objectives and methodologies of most students of politics . . . most of us do share, knowingly or unknowingly, a common goal: to search for political equilibria" (Ordeshook 1980: 447).[1]

In the eighth edition of his book, published in 1920, Marshall had become more circumspect with regard to the nature of change. "Economic evolution is gradual. Its progress is sometimes arrested or reversed by *political* catastrophes; but its forward movements are never sudden" (p. xiii, italics added). He distinguishes between orderly events of nature, which may be observed and which are the foundations of change, for which "the motto *Natura non facit saltum* is specially appropriate," and those events that are "spasmodic, infrequent, and difficult of observation" (p. xiii). The former are quite appropriate topics for marginalist analysis. But "normal action falls into the background . . . *when communities of interest are being made and unmade*" (p. xiv, italics added).[2] Much of politics, however, is about the making and unmaking of communities of interest—about how fresh definitions of issues cause people to become active in politics. This process is essentially noncontinuous; it is about a fundamental shift in attentiveness to the very defining characteristics of communities of interest. Analytical decomposition will not work (at least used alone) to isolate the circumstances when communities of interest are emerging; these processes are based on positive feedback systems that are not decomposable.

Hence it seems that a study of politics based solely on analytical decomposition, maximization, and marginality is bound to fail. Only an understanding of how limited equilibrium processes are in politics will lead to the appropriate conception of government as a complex system adapting to contradictory imperatives. Indeed, if adaptive government has anything to do with openness to new frames, then a nonmarginalist approach would be far superior to one that insists on Becker's "maximizing behavior, market equilibrium, and stable preferences."

1. Ordeshook's defense of the search for equilibria is sophisticated; he concedes the existence of multiple equilibria and notes that the existence of equilibria does not necessarily imply predictability. He is not, however, sufficiently sensitive to interequilibrium dynamics.

2. Marshall is mostly concerned here about attempts to control markets.

Three Issues of Democratic Performance

Generally, we think of democracies as having a lot to do with the ability of people to express their policy preferences and to have government respond to those preferences. Shifting the focus from preference satisfaction to a combination of preference and attention moves us somewhat away from a preference-satisfaction approach to democratic governance and toward a problem-solving perspective on democratic performance. So the standard of performance for democracy includes the identification and solution of problems as well as the satisfaction of preferences. While this role of democracy has been often noted, its relevance to the policymaking process has received less analysis by political scientists using the tools of modern social science. But an intriguing body of evidence is accumulating that democracies allocate attention to problems in a superior manner: democracies, for example, don't fight each other (although they are quite capable of waging war) (Mintz and Geva 1993), and they don't have famines—even poor democracies don't have famines (Sen 1993). We want to be cautious, of course, about inferring too much about how democracies operate from such tentative empirical observations. But it seems probable that the seemingly better performance of democracies on at least some measures has something to do with *both* the molding of values and preferences (for example, the respect for the individual) *and* the allocation of attention to the most pressing problems facing the political system.

Incorporating problem identification as well as preference satisfaction highlights three performance issues in democratic policymaking:

1. Does the "attentiveness heuristic" impair decision-makers? Lindblom (1991) points to the role of adaptive learning in political systems. He notes that much of democratic politics deals with overcoming "impairment"—such as racial and sexual discrimination and myopic views of policy problems and solutions. Lindblom's impairment approach is based on a model of choice that stresses changing preferences, which, I have argued, happens mostly in the longer run. What about more immediate decisions? Whatever their current preference structures, would decision-makers make better decisions if they could learn to integrate domains, that is, if they could formulate consistent comprehensive utility functions?

I believe the answer is yes, but only a partial yes. Because the terms of the discourse change so rapidly in politics, it would seem fruitful if decision-makers could better anticipate and deal with such changes rather than become locked into one-dimensional (path-dependent) policy responses, hence being "blind-sided" by new issues. What is important is openness to new issue-definitions rather than maintaining some locked-in predefinition.

I have argued in this book that serial shifting at the individual level is a result of "cognitive limitations." But this phrase is somewhat misleading. Attention is clearly a result of limits in cognitive processing when compared to some sort of global information-processing system. But shifts in attention may be the result *either* of weakness in the ability to develop cognitive frames *or* of a sensitivity to the changing nature of incoming information. Many students of voting behavior have treated the lack of ideology, one aspect of which is the lack of fixed cognitive frames, as a limitation in mass publics. But does one really want rigidity in mass decision-making? That is, the opposite end of the supposedly weak political cognitive frames in mass publics is the fixity of the ideologue, rigid and unrepentant in a changing world. Good decision-making would seem to require reasonably fixed frames that are "used but not believed." It would mean an openness to new frames, with a balanced mix of readiness to "jump" with a "standing decision" to "check," in Margolis's terms. So the term *cognitive limitations* must be used advisedly when discussing the changes in selective attention that I have termed the serial shift.

2. How do attention-directing structures operate? How is attention aggregated in a democratic system (in comparison to the aggregation of preferences)? "Paying attention to attention" allows us to judge democratic institutions according to how they direct attention to emergent problems and concerns, not just according to how they respond to preferences. A major principle is decentralization: a decentralized structure is far better at nurturing fresh policy perspectives than a centralized one. A centralized policy apparatus will almost certainly fall prey to path dependency. Of course, a completely decentralized structure may lead to local path dependency and gridlock through mutual noninterference. Hence continual interference with the decentralized policymaking system by central authorities can break the local path dependency of policy subsystems.

3. Is the policy serial shift adaptive—that is, does it break up suboptimal (path-dependent) policy subsystems, offering a superior approach? Or is it maladaptive, by causing blind leaps to worse options?

The answer is that "it depends." Partly it depends on what "fitness function" we try to define for democratic policymaking. The only thing that is certain is that, because of path dependence in the development of policy solutions, marginal adjustment often cannot work. It is true that the serial shift is often related to the activation of new participants in a previously closed process. E. E. Schattschneider believed that there exists a critical connection between conflict expansion and democratic policymaking. So, not infrequently, the serial shift is associated with mobilization and democratization. Moreover, while the preference activation approach that is implied by shifts in selective attention could be employed to understand "representation," it would be more useful in the study of conflict expansion. Elite appeal to mass publics often acts to stimulate attention to previously ignored dimensions of conflict, and thereby to activate groups of citizens who were previously inattentive to the policy process more generally. Hence more closed methods of decision-making can fall when mass preferences are activated.

Whether the actions by government resulting from this process of mobilization are "good" public policy, however, is a distinctly different matter. What is evident is that path-dependent subsystem policies that are never subject to disruption by the intrusion of democratic forces will tend to become oligarchical, operating at considerable distance from the "populist policy equilibrium."

Nobel Laureate economist Robert Fogel, in his book *Time on the Cross,* argued theoretically and empirically that slavery was an economically efficient institution (Fogel 1974). At the time, considerable outrage was expressed over the book. But a fresh look would lead us to appreciate economic efficiency as but one of several criteria by which we ought to judge political and social institutions; otherwise we would come to the conclusion that slavery, being efficient, was desirable. Economic efficiency alone is not sufficient to conclude that an institution or particular public policy is optimal. Similarly, democratic mobilization may or may not result in desirable outcomes. It is a mistake to judge outcomes in democracies *solely* by the standard of preference satisfaction. That is why I have been at great pains in this book to distinguish between democratic mobilization via conflict expansion and the adaptability of political systems. No single "fitness function" can be used to judge outcomes in liberal democracies.

Institutional Design

In this book, I have adopted an adaptive systems framework to try to understand the nexus between human capacities to make political decisions and the operation of democratic political systems. At both levels, information processing is a critical component; both decision-making (at the individual level) and policymaking (at the system level) are affected by the "bottleneck of attention" and the fixing of attention on limited evaluative aspects of a complex political reality. An adaptive systems framework, however, fails to factor in the possibility of *institutional de-sign,* the conscious construction of institutions to achieve purposes. In several major respects, however, the adaptive systems approach can guide the design of political institutions. First, institutions may be de-signed to achieve but one aim, and when they confront the contradictory demands that are part and parcel of governance, they may fail. Schneider and Teske (1993) show how policymaking in local governments may be destabilized by shifts in frames of reference from efficiency in service provision to equity in access. Designing institutions explicitly to maximize efficiency may cause other legitimate purposes to be ignored, perhaps leading to larger policy disruptions in the long run. Second, what might be termed *the fallacy of hierarchical control* affects all large adaptive systems. That is, policymakers can attend only to se-lected aspects of the organizations they have constructed to implement their policies. Yet subparts of the organization will always be adjusting to aspects of the local environment out of the limelight of the central policy apparatus. The more open and fluid the system, the more this will happen. Hierarchical institutions that are designed to rely over-much on central control are bound to fail where open and relatively democratic systems of policymaking interact with changing, fluid environments.

Most metropolitan areas consist of numerous overlapping govern-mental units, from municipalities (generally a central city and numerous suburbs), through school districts, to special purpose districts. County governments and other units are also superimposed on the metropolitan arena. Local governments thus interacting approximate a market, be-cause citizen-consumers as well as businesses have a great deal of choice in where to locate (Schneider 1989). If local governments were allowed to operate without any interference from higher levels of government, they would probably act to maximize their attractiveness to citizens and businesses that could bring the greatest wealth to the community, thereby maximizing the tax base. But they don't have complete freedom; indeed, there are numerous policy mandates from state governments and even from the federal government. So the local forces never have com-plete control of their destinies; rather, they are subject to periodic "exog-enous shocks" as some aspect of local governance or another gets on the agenda of state policymaking bodies.

No institutional design, from the hierarchical "principal-agent" mod-els to the decentralized "political economy" scenarios, is going to solve the problems of governance once and for all. Only when we become aware of the adaptive nature of political systems are we going to become comfortable with systems of policymaking in which a process of *dis-*

jointed disruption is fundamental—that is, in which policymaking is mostly decentralized but in which central authorities intervene sporadically to institute major corrections in direction. The key to democratic government, I have come to believe, is to allow and even encourage disruption at a moderate scale, but to deflect it at both the small and large scales of political action. If one waits too long to disrupt, the consequences for the entire political system can be disastrous. If one acts too quickly, then nothing can be accomplished, because no settlement will last.

In general, decentralized policymaking systems "at the edge of chaos" will provide the most effective processing of information. If the system is too structured, it will be subject to great disruptions. If it is decentralized and disorderly, it will process information (and consequently be most effective in isolating problems). But it will adjust mostly to local forces and will reach local equilibria that can be quite out of tune with the populist policy equilibrium. Under such a system, national institutions will require considerable agreement to achieve major changes. Even then, a policy leap can be quite maladaptive, but the probability is lessened.

Individual Choice and Policy Agendas

We end as we began: by noting that both individuals and collectivities, such as entire political systems, make choices. Individuals make decisions; collectivities make policies. How the two are connected is an empirical issue; that is, it is not to be taken for granted that the policies of a collectivity are neatly connected to the choices of the individuals composing the collectivity. Assuming that certain democratic institutions such as majority rule automatically link individual and collective choice is not warranted.

The traditional manner of examining the connection between choice and policies has involved comparing policy outcomes with the preferences of citizens. This tradition has its roots in the utilitarianism of Adam Smith and James Mill. The utilitarians distrusted government because it too often fell prey to the "conspiracies" of interest associations, allowing them to impose their preferences on the public through the use of public coercion. A comparison of what I have termed the *populist policy equilibrium* and what I have termed the *pluralist policy equilibrium* would show substantial divergence for the utilitarians. Open government allowing free association invariably leads to such divergence.

The problem with this pessimistic approach is that it fails to appreciate the information-processing role of both individuals and political systems. In chapter 2, we noted that marginalist models of decision-making stress the acquisition of information until it is no longer cost-effective. But information is processed by humans in serial fashion; hence attentiveness plays a critical component in information processing. Shifts in attentiveness imply shifts in decision framing. Incoming information either can be put into existing frames (hence acting in accordance with the marginalist model) or can force a shift in evaluative focus. Because people have contradictory preferences and because they process information serially, they have a strong tendency to "cognitive twoness"— that is, to focus on one evaluative dimension at a time, sometimes shifting back and forth between two foci but seldom fully integrating them.

Political systems also display such shifting in the policies they enact. Such abrupt policy changes, called *agenda shifts*, are associated with changes from negative to positive feedback and are often disruptive of standard ways of doing things. Just as in the case of individuals, policymaking branches are information-processing systems; just as in the case of individuals, incoming information has the potential either of being incorporated into existing issue-frames or of disrupting current understandings. Both individual and system choices are subject to the "bottleneck" of serial processing. At the systems level, these shifts are generally democratizing, mobilizing participants who were previously disinterested and forcing the pluralist policy equilibrium toward the populist policy equilibrium.

Because mobilizations tend to occur on an issue-by-issue basis in American politics, it is unlikely that the pluralist and populist equilibria would ever correspond. The tendency toward path dependency in policy subsystems is too powerful. But in the long run, the mobilizations associated with the policy serial shift probably keep the dynamic pluralist equilibrium in bounds.

Scientific understanding of information-processing systems is in its infancy, but the direction of thought is clear. It is moving away from an emphasis on central control toward an adaptive systems approach that stresses the difficulty of control when complex systems interact with complex environments (Holland 1992). Similarly, the study of political decisions ought to move away from an exclusive focus on preference satisfaction to a conception of decisions based on an interaction between preferences and attention to the context of decision. And the study of government and politics ought to move away from a preference-satisfaction approach toward a problem-solving conception—although clearly both are important. The ideal approach would deemphasize the issue of preference aggregation and highlight the aggregation of attentiveness—how policymaking systems define the problems they choose to address. Individual choice and policymaking in political systems are linked through information processing—the requirement that information be addressed serially. The serial shift links the dynamics of individual decision-making with the dynamics of policymaking.

APPENDIX
Spatial Choice Theory and Attentional Dynamics

Because the rational choice model has been developed axiomatically, it has a geometric analogue: spatial choice theory. Chapters 2 and 4 illustrated how the approach developed here may be described in the language of spatial choice, without being overly formal. Here I discuss the attentional dynamics developed in this book in somewhat more formal terms, and show how one might begin to assess dynamics within formal models. Then I point to some problems in empirical approaches to the recovery of underlying dimensions of evaluation from observed choices where the salience of dimensions varies.

The Basic Spatial Model

The spatial approach hinges on the assumption that choices may be represented in geometric space and that the distance between the individual's preferred (or ideal) position and the choices that are actually offered is inversely related to that individual's preference for the choice. Most commonly, a Euclidean distance function is employed, although any distance function that maintains monotonocity between preferences and distances may be used. A decision-maker prefers outcome a to outcome b if and only if the distance between the decision-maker's ideal point and a is less than the distance between the ideal point and b. If we assume Euclidean distances in two-dimensional space, and let the ideal point be located at (y_{1i}, y_{2i}), and a policy alternative, p, located at (y_{1p}, y_{2p}), then the preference function will be defined by

$$P = -D = \{a_{11}(Y_{1i} - Y_{1p})^2 + a_{22}(Y_{2i} - Y_{2p})^2$$
$$+ 2a_{12}(Y_{1i} - Y_{1p})(Y_{2i} - Y_{2p})\}^{1/2} \tag{1}$$
$$P = -D = [y'Ay]^{1/2}.$$

The Parameters of the Spatial Model

The spatial model, in essence, has two components: the distance function and the parameters governing the relationship of the distance function to the primary axes of choice. The distance function is assessed by the y vectors, whereas the parameters are represented at the matrix A in equation 1.

The coefficients a_{11} and a_{22} assess the sensitivity of the decision-maker to the basic dimensions of choice by weighting the dimensions Y_1 and Y_2. The larger the coefficient, the more relevant that dimension to the choice (Ordeshook 1986: 25). The coefficients denoted as a_{12} indicate the correlations between the basic dimensions (Enelow and Hinich 1983).

We have seen D as a distance from a decision-maker's ideal point to a choice option located at (y_{2p}, y_{1p}). We may also allow D to be an arbitrary distance and letting the point p vary. The result is an ellipse with its center at the ideal point. All points on the ellipse would be policies that the decision-maker would prefer equally; that is, they would fall along one of the decision-maker's indifference curves. If $a_{11} = a_{22} = 1$, and $a_{12} = 0$, then the result is a circle with radius D centered on the ideal point. If the correlations are zero and the attention coefficients are positive, then the result is an ellipse whose axes are parallel to the underlying dimensions (see fig. 2.2).

In this book, I have assumed that the correlations between the dimensions are zero but that the attention coefficients a_{11} and a_{22} can vary across time. This incorporates the assumption that underlying preferences are contradictory. The assumption that there is no correlation between dimensions implies that preferences are separable, that is, that preferences on one dimension are not affected by preferences on the second.

The approach to decision-making developed here stresses (1) the attributes that underlie choice and (2) serial shifting between these attributes. Serial shifting attenuated the problem of connectivity between the underlying attributes (which is now what must be seen as connected), because the decision-maker normally finds it difficult to focus on more than one attribute at a time. Hence the coefficient matrix for the Euclidean distance metric assumes the form

$$\begin{bmatrix} a_{11} & 0 \\ 0 & a_{22} \end{bmatrix}.$$

But the coefficients are not constant; they can vary over time in response to changing circumstances. They thus assess attention to context and do not affect the location of the ideal point (which represents preferences). The assumption of constant, separable preferences for decision-makers is crucial to the development of the theory of structure-induced equilibria, in which issues are voted on separately within committees in a legislature (or other institution that imposes factoring on the decision-making process). If legislators have constant, separable preferences and if the institution factors, then the problem of issue cycling is avoided. Now, if attentiveness is allowed to vary episodically across time, then the result could be the periodic destruction of structure-induced equilibria or policy monopolies, as argued in this book.

The second assumption, that of separable preferences, has also been questioned. Hinich (1986: 181) feels that the assumption of independent preferences is unwarranted and that, if it fails, the problem of issue cycling will be reintroduced. In effect, the institutional factoring will fail, because trying to hold legislators to one dimension of voting will invariably affect their voting preferences on other dimensions. This *correlated preference* problem is one reason that subsystems are linked; if one is affected, others will also be affected. The deregulation movement that affected several regulatory subsystems is an example of the manner in which correlated preferences can spill over into numerous subsystems, affecting all of them.

It seems that one ought to consider both changes in attention and correlated preferences in analyzing policy subsystems and structure-induced equilibria. If one allows for a dynamic on both the attention and correlation parameters, then one may have a situation where structure-induced equilibria are disturbed or destroyed, as in the punctuated equilibria theory (Baumgartner and Jones 1993). But one might also observe the destabilization of other structure-induced equilibria as the domains spilled over into one another. This is what seems to happen when major mobilizations occur. A model incorporating dynamics on both kinds of coefficients seems most appropriate (but more difficult).

Assessing Dynamics

Viewing changes in political choice as a function of shifting attention to standard dimensions of conflict implies that dynamics are every bit as important to study as equilibria. But what are the "moving parts" of the models that ought to be studied? Let us return to the shifting ellipses that characterize changes in attention. Ellipses are characterized by two axes, one in the x-dimension, one in the y-dimension. Should these axes be equal, then the "ellipse" becomes a curve. For indifference curves around an i-point, the axes must always be parallel to the two dimensions. Hence we may form a ratio of the two axes of an arbitrary indifference curve at a given point in time:

$$R(i,t) = (y_{2t} - y_{1t}) / (x_{2t} - x_{1t}) ,$$

where $R(i,t)$ is the ratio (at the fixed ideal point at time t), and y and x are the axes. Because the i-point is in the center of the indifference ellipse, the ratio may be reduced to

$$R(i,t) = r_{y,t} / r_{x,t} ,$$

where $r_{y,t}$ is the radius of the indifference ellipse in the y-dimension and $r_{x,t}$ is the radius of the ellipse in the x- dimension. The ratio may be interpreted as the attention that is being paid to conflict dimension y relative to conflict dimension x. Because the width of an indifference curve is inversely proportional to the sensitivity with which a dimension is viewed, the ratio is actually an assessment of *inattention* to y relative to x, or a direct measure of the attention of x relative to y.

$R(i,t)$ may also be interpreted as a trigonometric identity, as can be seen in figure A. 1. Note that the axes of the indifference ellipse form a right triangle whose hypotenuse is the line connecting the points at which the axes meet the indifference ellipse. $R(i,t)$ is the *tangent* of the angle made by the x-axis and the hypotenuse, which is angle Q in figure A.1.

The tangent function suggests discordant, rapid shifts in the ratio,

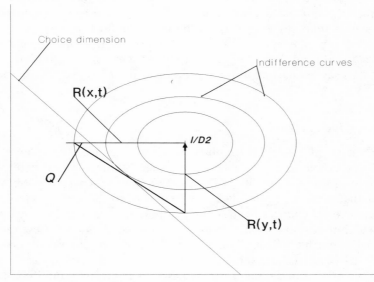

Fig. A.1. Assessing attentional dynamics.

quite unlike the sine and cosine functions, which are smooth-changing waves. This would imply the absence of self-righting cycles, for example, which might be modeled by the sine function. Because there is no reason to expect that attention shifts from axis to axis according to the tangent function, one would not want to make too much of this. It is interesting that we have been able to derive a tangent identity, however, because it would lead away from self-generating cycles as explanations of political change.

Problems in Recovering Dimensions of Evaluation

Considerable effort has been expended in trying to recover the basic evaluative dimensions of conflict from observed choices. That is, given that we observe a set of particular choices, what are the dimensions of evaluation that the decision-makers are using? One empirical approach to the study of the structure of evaluative dimensions in legislative conflict is to examine roll-call voting patterns to discern the emergence of new dimensions of conflict. There may, however, be a substantial problem with current approaches to dimensioning of roll-call voting if the salience of dimensions varies. Koford (1991) has suggested that problems can occur in dimensioning studies that assume constant salience to dimensions of conflict across legislators. Let us also consider the situation where the dimensions of conflict change in their salience across time for the same legislators. In a 100-member legislature, a vote like that on the supercollider could be represented as follows:

		Vote at time 2		
		Yes	No	
Vote at time 1	Yes	40	20	60
	No	0	40	40
		40	60	100

These data would probably look one-dimensional when subjected to empirical analysis. They would form a cumulative (Guttman) scale. The Pearsonian correlation would be 0.663. The prediction equation would be $Y = 0.333 + 0.667X$. In the situation where *all* legislators became attentive to the second dimension, the correlation would be perfectly negative and the votes would be at opposite ends of the same continuum—even though the voting content was exactly the same. But *context* had changed.

Poole and Rosenthal (1991) warn that how issues get defined on the basic dimensions of conflict is problematic. Yet it is possible that the issue-definition process can foul empirical attempts to recover underlying policy dimensions. It quite depends on the model of choice that we suppose influences the observed voting choices. If the voters or legislators are subject to serial shifting, then studying the observed choices alone to try to recover the underlying dimensions of choice can potentially be seriously misleading.

BIBLIOGRAPHY

Allport, Alan. 1989. Visual Attention. In Michael I. Posner, ed., *Foundations of Cognitive Science*. Cambridge, Mass.: MIT Press.

Anton, Thomas. 1989. *American Federalism and Public Policy*. Philadelphia: Temple University Press.

Arthur, W. Brian. 1988. Self-Reinforcing Mechanisms in Economics. In Philip W. Anderson, Kenneth J. Arrow, and David Pines, eds., *The Economy as an Evolving Complex System*. Reading, Mass.: Addison-Wesley.

———. 1989. Competing Technologies, Increasing Returns, and Lock-in by Historical Events. *Economic Journal* 99:116–31.

———. 1990. Positive Feedbacks in the Economy. *Scientific American*, February, pp. 92–99.

Arthur, W. Brian, Yu M. Ermoliev, and Yu M. Kaniovski. 1987. Path-Dependent Processes and the Emergence of Macro-Structure. *European Journal of Operational Research* 30:294–303.

Axelrod, Robert. 1984. *The Evolution of Cooperation*. New York: Basic Books.

Bachrach, Peter, and Morton Baratz. 1962. The Two Faces of Power. *American Political Science Review* 56:947–52.

Bak, Peter, and Kan Chen. 1991. Self-Organized Criticality. *Scientific American* 264 (January): 46–53.

Barrett, Paul. 1990. Moving On: Though the Drug War Isn't Over, Spotlight Turns to Other Issues. *Wall Street Journal*, November 11.

Baumgartner, Frank R. 1987. Parliament's Capacity to Expand Political Controversy in France. *Legislative Studies Quarterly* 12:33–54.

Baumgartner, Frank R. 1989. *Conflict and Rhetoric in French Policymaking*. Pittsburgh: University of Pittsburgh Press.

Baumgartner, Frank R., and Bryan D. Jones. 1990. Toward the Quantitative Study of Agenda Setting. Paper presented at the annual meeting of the American Political Science Association, San Francisco, Calif., August 29–September 2.

———. 1991. Agenda Dynamics and Policy Subsystems. *Journal of Politics* 53:1044–74.

———. 1993. *Agendas and Instability in American Politics*. Chicago: University of Chicago Press.

Bauer, Raymond. 1966. *Social Indicators.* Cambridge, Mass.: MIT Press.

Becker, Gary S. 1976. *The Economic Approach to Human Behavior.* Chicago: University of Chicago Press.

———. 1986. "The Economic Approach to Human Behavior." In Jon Elster, ed., *Rational Choice,* pp. 108–22. New York: New York University Press.

Beecher, Janice A., Robert J. Lineberry, and Michael J. Rich. 1981. Political Power, the Urban Agenda, and Crime Policies. *Social Science Quarterly* 62:630–43.

Beer, Samuel. 1976. The Adoption of General Revenue Sharing: A Case Study of Public Sector Politics. *Public Policy* 24:127–95.

———. 1977. Political Overload and Federalism. *Policy* 10:5–17.

———. 1978. Federalism, Nationalism, and Democracy in America. *American Political Science Review* 72:9–22.

Bendor, Jonathan. 1985. *Parallel Systems: Redundancy in Government.* Berkeley: University of California Press.

Bendor, Jonathan, and Thomas Hammond. 1992. Rethinking Allison's Models. *American Political Science Review* 86:301–22.

Bendor, Jonathan, and Terry M. Moe. 1985. An Adaptive Model of Bureaucratic Politics. *American Political Science Review* 79:756–74.

———. 1986. Agenda Control, Committee Capture, and the Dynamics of Institutional Politics. *American Political Science Review* 80:1187–1207.

Bennett, Linda M., and Stephen Bennett. 1990. *Living with Leviathan.* Lawrence: University Press of Kansas.

Berlyne, D. E. 1960. *Conflict Arousal and Curiosity.* New York: McGraw-Hill.

———. 1974. Attention. In Edward C. Carterette and Morton P. Friedman, eds., *Handbook of Perception.* New York: Academic.

Bernstein, Robert. 1989. *Elections, Representation, and Congressional Voting Behavior.* Englewood Cliffs, N.J.: Prentice-Hall.

Best, Joel. 1990. *Threatened Children: Rhetoric and Concern about Child-Victims.* Chicago: University of Chicago Press.

Blau, Peter. 1964. *Exchange and Power in Social Life.* New York: John Wiley.

Bosso, Christopher J. 1987. *Pesticides and Politics: The Life Cycle of a Public Issue.* Pittsburgh: University of Pittsburgh Press.

———. 1989. Setting the Agenda: Mass Media and the Discovery of Famine in Ethiopia. In Michael Margolis and Gary Mauser, eds., *Manipulating Public Opinion.* Monterey, Calif.: Brooks-Cole.

———. 1991. Adaptation and Change in the Environmental Movement. In Allan J. Cigler and Burdett A. Loomis, eds., *Interest Group Poli-*

tics, 3d ed., pp. 151–76. Washington, D.C.: Congressional Quarterly Inc.

Boulding, Kenneth. 1956. *The Image.* Ann Arbor: University of Michigan Press.

Brady, Henry E., and Stephen Ansolabehere. 1989. On the Nature of Utility Functions. *American Political Science Review* 83:143–63.

Broadbent, D. E. 1958. *Perception and Communication.* Oxford: Pergamon.

X Brown, JoAnne. 1990. The Social Construction of Invisible Danger: Two Historical Examples. In Andrew Kirby, ed., *Nothing to Fear: Risks and Hazards in American Society.* Tucson: University of Arizona Press.

Campbell, Angus, Phillip Converse, Warren Miller, and Donald Stokes. 1960. *The American Voter.* New York: Wiley

Carmines, Edward G., and James A. Stimson. 1986. On the Structure and Sequence of Issue Evolution. *American Political Science Review* 80:901–20.

———. 1989. *Issue Evolution: Race and the Transformation of American Politics.* Princeton, N.J.: Princeton University Press.

Casstevens, Thomas. 1980. Birth and Death Processes of Governmental Bureaus in the United States. *Behavioral Science* 25:161–65.

Cater, Douglass. 1964. *Power in Washington.* New York: Random House.

Chong, Dennis. 1991. *Collective Action and the Civil Rights Movement.* Chicago: University of Chicago Press.

Chubb, John E. 1985. The Political Economy of Federalism. *American Political Science Review* 79:994–1015.

Church, Thomas, and Robert T. Nakamura. 1993. *Cleaning Up the Mess.* Washington, D.C.: Brookings.

Clausen, Aage. 1967. Longitudinal Analysis of Legislative Voting. *American Political Science Review* 61:1020–35.

———. 1973. *How Congressmen Decide: A Policy Focus.* New York: St. Martin's.

Clemens, Elisabeth S. 1986. Of Asteroids and Dinosaurs: The Role of the Press in the Shaping of Scientific Debate. *Social Studies of Science* 16:421–56.

Clayton, William. 1992. House-Senate Conferees Vote More Money to Revive Collider. *Houston Chronicle,* September 16.

Cobb, Roger W., and Charles D. Elder. 1983. *Participation in American Politics: The Dynamics of Agenda-Building.* Baltimore: Johns Hopkins University Press.

Cobb, Roger W., and David Rochefort, eds. 1994. *The Politics of Issue Definition.* Lawrence: University Press of Kansas. In Press.

Cobb, Roger W., Jeannie-Keith Ross, and Marc Howard Ross. 1976. Agenda Building as a Comparative Political Process. *American Political Science Review* 70:126–38.

Cohen, Bernard. 1981. Nuclear Journalism: Lies, Damned Lies, and News Reports. *Policy Review,* pp. 70–74.

Cohen, Michael, and Robert Axelrod. 1984. Coping with Complexity: The Adaptive Value of Changing Utility. *American Economic Review* 74:30–42.

Cohen, Michael, and James March. 1986. *Leadership and Ambiguity,* 2d ed. Boston: Harvard Business School.

Cohen, Michael, James G. March, and Johan P. Olsen. 1972. A Garbage Can Theory of Organizational Choice. *Administrative Science Quarterly* 17:1–25.

Congressional Information Service, Inc. Annual. *CIS/Annual: Abstracts of Congressional Publications and Legislative History Citations.* Washington, D.C.: CIS.

Conover, Pamela J., and Stanley Feldman. 1984. How People Organize the Political World: A Schematic Model. *American Journal of Political Science* 28:95–126.

————. 1991. Where Is the Schema: Critiques. *American Political Science Review* 85:1364–69.

Converse, Phillip. 1964. The Nature of Belief Systems in Mass Publics. In David Apter, ed., *Ideology and Discontent.* New York: Free Press.

Cook, Fay Lomax, and Wesley G. Skogan. 1989. Agenda Setting: Convergent and Divergent Voice Models of the Rise and Fall of Policy Issues. Unpublished paper.

Cook, Fay Lomax, T. R. Tyler, E. G. Goetz, Margaret T. Gordon, Donna R. Leff, and Harvey L. Molotch. 1983. Media and Agenda-Setting: Effects on the Public, Interest Group Leaders, Policy Makers, and Policy. *Public Opinion Quarterly* 57:16–35.

Cook, Karen Schweers, and Margaret Levy, eds. 1990. *The Limits of Rationality.* Chicago: University of Chicago Press.

Coughlin, P. and M. Hinich. 1984. Necessary and Sufficient Conditions for Single-Peakedness in Public Economic Models. *Journal of Public Economics* 25:161–79.

Crecine, John P. 1969. *Government Problem-Solving.* Chicago: Rand McNally.

Crenson, Matthew A. 1971. *The Unpolitics of Air Pollution.* Baltimore: Johns Hopkins University Press.

Cyert, Richard M., and James G. March. 1963. *A Behavioral Theory of the Firm.* Englewood Cliffs, N.J.: Prentice-Hall.

Dahl, Robert. 1961. *Who Governs?* New Haven, Conn.: Yale University Press.

―――. 1963. *Modern Political Analysis.* Englewood Cliffs, N.J.: Prentice-Hall.

Davidson, Roger H. 1989. Multiple Referral of Legislation in the U.S. Senate. *Legislative Studies Quarterly* 14:375–92.

Davidson, Roger H., Walter J. Oleszek, and Thomas Kephart. 1988. One Bill, Many Committees: Multiple Referrals in the U.S. House of Representatives. *Legislative Studies Quarterly* 13:3–28.

Davis, Otto A., M. A. H. Dempster, and Aaron Wildavsky. 1974. Toward a Predictive Theory of the Federal Budgetary Process. *British Journal of Political Science* 4:419–52.

Davis, Otto A., Melvin J. Hinich, and Peter Ordeshook. 1970. An Expository Development of a Mathematical Model of the Electoral Process. *American Political Science Review* 64:426–48.

Dawkins, Richard. 1986. *The Blind Watchmaker.* New York: Norton.

DeAngelis, Donald L., Wilfred M. Post, and Curtis C. Travis. 1986. *Positive Feedback in Natural Systems.* Berlin: Springer-Verlag.

Del Sesto, Steven L. 1980. Conflicting Ideologies of Nuclear Power: Congressional Testimony on Nuclear Reactor Safety. *Public Policy* 28:39–70.

Dodd, Lawrence. 1991. Congress, the Presidency, and the American Experience: A Transformational Perspective. In James A. Thurber, ed., *Divided Democracy.* Washington, D.C.: Congressional Quarterly Press.

―――. 1992. Transformational Politics: The American Experience Reconsidered. Paper delivered at the Conference on the Dynamics of American Politics, Department of Political Science, University of Colorado, Boulder. February 20–22.

Dodd, Lawrence, and Richard Schott. 1979. *Congress and the Administrative State.* New York: Wiley.

Downs, Anthony. 1972. Up and Down with Ecology—The Issue Attention Cycle. *Public Interest* 28:38– 50.

Dunlap, Thomas. 1981. *DDT: Scientists, Citizens, and Public Policy.* Princeton, N.J.: Princeton University Press.

Durant, Robert F., and Paul F. Diehl. 1989. Agendas, Alternatives, and Public Policy: Lessons from the U.S. Foreign Policy Arena. *Journal of Public Policy* 9:179–205.

Edelman, Murray. 1964. *The Symbolic Uses of Politics.* Urbana: University of Illinois Press.

―――. 1989. *Constructing the Political Spectacle.* Chicago: University of Chicago Press.

Edwards, George C. 1989. *At the Margins: Presidential Leadership of Congress.* New Haven: Yale University Press.

Edwards, George C., III, William Mitchell, and Reed Welch. 1992. Explaining Presidential Approval: The Significance of Issue Salience. An Occasional Paper. Center for Presidential Studies, Texas A&M University.

Elder, Charles D., and Roger W. Cobb. 1983. *The Political Uses of Symbols.* New York: Longman.

Eldredge, Niles. 1985. *Time Frames.* Princeton, N.J.: Princeton University Press.

Eldredge, Niles, and Stephen Jay Gould. 1972. Punctuated Equilibria: An Alternative to Phyletic Gradualism. In Thomas J. M. Schopf, ed., *Models in Paleobiology,* pp. 82–115. San Francisco: Freeman, Cooper.

Elster, Jon. 1979. *Ulysses and the Sirens.* Cambridge: Cambridge University Press.

Enelow, James M. 1984. A Generalized Model of Voting One Issue at a Time with Applications to Congress. *American Journal of Political Science* 28:587–97.

Enelow, James M., and Melvin J. Hinich. 1983. Voting One Issue at a Time. *American Political Science Review* 77:435–45.

———. 1990. The Theory of Predictive Mappings. In James M. Enelow and Melvin J. Hinich, eds., *Advances in the Spatial Theory of Voting.* Cambridge: Cambridge University Press.

Eyestone, Robert. 1978. *From Social Issues to Public Policy.* New York: Wiley.

Farkas, Steve, Robert Y. Shapiro, and Benjamin I. Page. 1990. The Dynamics of Public Opinion and Policy. Paper presented at the annual meeting of the American Association for Public Opinion Research, May 17–20, Lancaster, Pa.

Fingarette, Herbert. 1988. *Heavy Drinking: The Myth of Alcoholism as a Disease.* Berkeley: University of California Press.

Fiorina, Morris P. 1990. Information and Rationality in Elections. In John A. Ferejohn and James H. Kuklinski, eds., *Information and Democratic Processes,* pp. 329–42. Urbana: University of Illinois Press.

Fiorina, Morris P., and Kenneth A. Shepsle. 1989. Formal Theories of Leadership: Agents, Agenda Setters, and Entrepreneurs. In Bryan D. Jones, ed., *Leadership and Politics.* Lawrence: University Press of Kansas.

Fiske, Susan T., and Shelly E. Taylor. 1984. *Social Cognition.* New York: Addison-Wesley.

————. 1992. *Social Cognition*, 2d ed. New York: Addison-Wesley.

Fitch-Hauser, Margaret. 1990. Making Sense of Data: Constructs, Schemas, and Concepts. In Robert N. Bostrum, ed., *Listening Behavior: Measurement and Application*, pp. 76–90. New York: Guilford Press.

Fogel, Robert. 1974. *Time on the Cross*. Boston: Little, Brown.

Foley, Michael W. 1991. Agenda for Mobilization: The Agrarian Question and Popular Mobilization in Contemporary Mexico. *Latin American Research Review* 26:39–74.

Foster, Mary Lecron. 1977. Speaking of Energy. Berkeley, Calif.: Department of Anthropology, University of California, Berkeley. Unpublished paper.

Free, Lloyd, and Hadley Cantril. 1967. *The Political Beliefs of Americans*. New York: Free Press.

Friedman, Milton. 1953. *Essays in Positive Economics*. Chicago: University of Chicago Press.

Friedman, Sharon M., Carole M. Gorney, and Brenda P. Egolf. 1987. Reporting on Radiation: A Content Analysis of Chernobyl Coverage. *Journal of Communication* 37:58–79.

Frisch, Deborah. 1993. Reasons for Framing Effects. *Organizational Behavior and Human Decision Processes* 54:399–429.

Fukuyama, Francis. 1992. *The End of History and the Last Man*. New York: Free Press.

Funkhouser, G. Ray. 1973. Trends in Media Coverage of the Issues of the '60s. *Journalism Quarterly* 50:533–38.

Gould, Stephen Jay. 1980. *The Panda's Thumb*. New York: Norton.

Greenberg, Michael R., David B. Sachsman, Peter M. Sandman, and Kandice L. Salomone. 1989. Risk, Drama and Geography in Coverage of Environmental Risk by Network TV. *Journalism Quarterly* 66:267–76.

Gusfield, Joseph. 1963. *Symbolic Crusade: Status Politics and the American Temperance Movement*. Urbana: University of Illinois Press.

————. 1981. *The Culture of Public Problems: Drinking-Driving and the Symbolic Order*. Chicago: University of Chicago Press.

Hall, Richard L. 1987. Participation and Purpose in Committee Decision Making. *American Political Science Review* 81:105–28.

Hall, Richard L., and C. Lawrence Evans. 1990. The Power of Subcommittees. *Journal of Politics* 52:335–55.

Hall, Richard L., and Bernard Grofman. 1990. The Committee Assignment Process and the Conditional Nature of Committee Bias. *American Political Science Review* 84:1149–66.

Hall, Richard L., and Frank Wayman. 1990. Buying Time: Moneyed Interests and the Mobilization of Bias in Congressional Committees. *American Political Science Review* 84:797–820.

Hammond, Thomas H., and Jack H. Knott. 1992. Presidential Power, Congressional Dominance, and Bureaucratic Autonomy in a Model of Multi-Institutional Policymaking. East Lansing: Department of Political Science, Michigan State University. Unpublished ms.

Hammond, Thomas H., and Gary J. Miller. 1987. The Core of the Constitution. *American Political Science Review* 81:1155–74.

Hartley, Thomas, and Bruce Russett. 1992. Public Opinion and the Common Defense: Who Governs Military Spending in the United States? *American Political Science Review* 86:905–15.

Heinz, John P., Edward O. Laumann, Robert L. Nelson, and Robert H. Salisbury. 1993. *The Hollow Core: Private Interests in National Policymaking.* Cambridge, Mass.: Harvard University Press.

Henriques, Diana. 1993. Big Agriculture Provides a Study in Raw Power. *New York Times*, October 12.

Herstein, John A. 1981. Keeping the Voter's Limits in Mind: A Cognitive Process Analysis of Decision-Making in Voting. *Journal of Personality and Social Psychology* 40:843–61.

Hilgartner, Stephen, and Charles L. Bosk. 1988. The Rise and Fall of Social Problems: A Public Arenas Model. *American Journal of Sociology* 94:53–78.

Hillis, W. Daniel. 1992. Co-Evolving Parasites Improve Simulated Evolution as an Optimization Procedure. In Christopher Langton et al., eds., *Artificial Life II*, pp. 313–24. Reading, Mass.: Addison-Wesley.

Hinich, Melvin J. 1986. Discussion of "The Positive Theory of Legislative Institutions." *Public Choice* 50:179–83.

Hinich, Melvin J., and Walker Pollard. 1981. A New Approach to the Spatial Theory of Electoral Competition. *American Journal of Political Science* 25:323–41.

Hochschild, Jennifer. 1981. *What's Fair? Americans' Beliefs about Distributive Justice.* Cambridge, Mass.: Harvard University Press.

Holland, John H. 1989. Using Classifier Systems to Study Adaptive Nonlinear Networks. In Daniel L. Stein, ed., *Lectures in the Sciences of Complexity.* Redwood City, Calif.: Addison-Wesley.

———. 1992 (1975). *Adaptation in Natural and Artificial Systems.* Cambridge, Mass.: MIT Press.

Hoppe, Layne. 1991. The Evolution and Usefulness of the Concept of Policy Agendas. Presentation at the annual meeting of the Southwest Social Science Association, San Antonio.

Huntington, Samuel P. 1981. *American Politics: The Promise of Disharmony.* Cambridge, Mass.: Harvard University Press.

Hurley, Patricia A. 1982. Collective Representation Reappraised. *Legislative Studies Quarterly* 7:119–36.

―――. 1989. Partisan Representation and the Failure of Realignment in the 1980's. *American Journal of Political Science* 33:240–61.

Hurley, Patricia A., and Rick K. Wilson. 1989. Partisan Voting Patterns in the U.S. Senate, 1877–1986. *Legislative Studies Quarterly* 14:225–50.

Inglehart, Ronald. 1990. *Culture Shift in Advanced Industrial Democracies.* Princeton, N.J.: Princeton University Press.

Iyengar, Shanto. 1990. Shortcuts to Political Knowledge: Selective Attention and the Accessibility Bias. In John Ferejohn and James Kuklinski, eds., *Information and the Democratic Process*, pp. 160–85. Urbana: University of Illinois Press.

―――. 1991. *Is Anyone Responsible? How Television Frames Political Issues.* Chicago: University of Chicago Press.

―――. 1993. Agenda Setting and Beyond: Television News and the Strength of Issues. In William H. Riker, ed., *Agenda Formation*, pp. 211–30. Ann Arbor: University of Michigan Press.

Iyengar, Shanto, and Donald Kinder. 1987. *News That Matters.* Chicago: University of Chicago Press.

Jackson, John E. 1983. The Systematic Beliefs of the Mass Public: Estimating Policy Preferences with Survey Data. *Journal of Politics* 45:840–65.

Jackson, John E., and John W. Kingdon. 1992. Ideology, Interest Group Scores, and Legislative Votes. *American Journal of Political Science* 36: 805–23.

Jacob, Herbert. 1988. *Silent Revolution.* Chicago: University of Chicago Press.

Jacobs, James. 1989. *Drunk Driving: An American Dilemma.* Chicago: University of Chicago Press.

Jenkins-Smith, Hank. 1988. Analytical Debates and Policy Learning: Analysis and Change in the Federal Bureaucracy. *Policy Science* 21:169–211.

Johnson, Eric J., and Amos Tversky. 1984. Representations of Perceptions of Risks. *Journal of Experimental Psychology* 113:55–70.

Jones, Bryan. 1973a. Competitiveness, Role Orientations, and Legislative Responsiveness. *Journal of Politics* 35:924–48.

―――. 1973b. Candidate Perceptions by Detroit-Area Actives. *Michigan Academician* 7:137–48.

―――. 1980. *Service Delivery in the City.* New York: Longman.

―――. 1983. *Governing Urban America: A Policy Focus.* Boston: Little, Brown.

————. 1985. *Governing Buildings and Building Government.* Tusca-
loosa: University of Alabama Press.

————. 1986. Government and Business: The Automobile Industry and
the Public Sector in Michigan. *Political Geography Quarterly*
5:369–84.

Jones, Bryan D., ed. 1989. *Leadership and Politics.* Lawrence: University
Press of Kansas.

Jones, Bryan D., and Lynn W. Bachelor. 1993. *The Sustaining Hand,* 2d
revised ed. Lawrence: University Press of Kansas.

Jones, Bryan D., and Frank R. Baumgartner. 1989. Changing Images and
Venues of Nuclear Power in the United States. Paper presented at
the annual meeting of the Midwest Political Science Association,
Chicago.

Jones, Bryan D., Frank R. Baumgartner, and Jeffrey Talbert. 1993. The
Destruction of Issue Monopolies in Congress. *American Political
Science Review* 87:657–71.

Jones, Charles O. 1975. *Clean Air.* Pittsburgh: University of Pittsburgh
Press.

Jones, Charles O., and Randall Strahan. 1985. The Effect of Energy Politics on Congressional and Executive Organization in the 1970's. *Legislative Studies Quarterly* 10:151–79.

Jones, Edward E., and Harold B. Gerard. 1967. *Foundations of Social
Psychology.* New York: John Wiley.

Kahneman, Daniel. 1973. *Attention and Effort.* Englewood Cliffs, N.J.:
Prentice-Hall.

Kahneman, Daniel, and Amos Tversky. 1985. Prospect Theory: An Analysis of Decision-Making under Risk. *Econometrica* 47:263–91.

Kauffman, Arnold. 1968. *The Science of Decision-Making.* New York:
World University Library.

Kauffman, Stuart A. 1993. *The Origins of Order.* New York: Oxford University Press.

Kauffman, Stuart A., and Sonke Johnsen. 1992. Co-Evolution to the
Edge of Chaos: Coupled Fitness Landscapes, Poised States, and Co-
Evolutionary Avalanches. In Christopher G. Langton et al., eds., *Ar-
tificial Life II.* Redwood City, Calif.: Addison-Wesley.

Key, V. O. 1949. *Southern Politics, State and Nation.* New York: Knopf.

King, David C. 1991. Congressional Committee Jurisdictions and the
Consequences of Reforms. Paper presented at the annual meeting
of the Midwest Political Science Association, Chicago.

————. 1994. The Nature of Congressional Committee Jurisdictions.
American Political Science Review 88:48–62.

Kingdon, John W. 1984. *Agendas, Alternatives, and Public Policies.* Boston: Little, Brown.

Kirby, Andrew, ed. 1990. *Nothing to Fear: Risks and Hazards in American Society.* Tucson: University of Arizona Press.

Koford, Kenneth. 1989. Dimensions in Congressional Voting. *American Political Science Review* 83:59–82.

—————. 1991. Dimensionalizing Roll Call Voting. *American Political Science Review* 85:960–75.

Krasner, Stephen. 1984. Approaches to the State: Alternative Conceptions and Historical Dynamics. *Comparative Politics* 16:223–46.

Krauss, Clifford. 1992. Senate Endorses Further Spending on Supercollider. *New York Times,* August 4.

Krehbiel, Keith. 1990. Are Congressional Committees Composed of Preference Outliers? *American Political Science Review* 84:149–63.

—————. 1991. *Information and Legislative Organization.* Ann Arbor: University of Michigan Press.

Kuklinski, James, Robert C. Luskin, and John Bolland. 1991. Where Is the Schema? Going Beyond the "S" Word in Political Psychology. *American Political Science Review* 85:1341–56.

Lane, Robert E. 1969. *Political Man.* New York: Free Press.

—————. 1991. *The Market Experience.* Cambridge: Cambridge University Press.

Langton, Christopher G. 1989. Artificial Life. In Christopher G. Langton, ed., *Artificial Life.* Redwood City, Calif.: Addison-Wesley.

Lanouette, William. 1990. How Atomic Agency Managed the News in Early Years. *Newsletter of the National Association of Science Writers* 38:1–3.

Larson, Stephanie, and David Grier. 1990. Agenda Setting and AIDS. Paper prepared for presentation at the American Political Science Association meeting, San Francisco, Calif., August 29–September 2.

Laumann, Edward O., and David Knoke. 1987. *The Organizational State.* Madison: University of Wisconsin Press.

Leff, Donna R., David L. Protess, and S. Brooks. 1986. Changing Public Attitudes and Policymaking Agendas. *Public Opinion Quarterly* 36:300–314.

Leogrande, William, and Philip Brenner. 1993. The House Divided: Ideological Polarization over Aid to the Nicaraguan "Contras." *Legislative Studies Quarterly* 18:105–36.

Levine, Charles H., and James A. Thurber. 1986. Reagan and the Intergovernmental Lobby: Iron Triangles, Cozy Subsystems, and Political Conflict. In Allan J. Cigler and Burdett A. Loomis, eds.,

Interest Group Politics. Washington, D.C.: Congressional Quarterly.

Levy, Frank, Arnold Meltsner, and Aaron Wildavsky. 1974. *Urban Outcomes.* Berkeley: University of California Press.

Levy, Steven. 1992. *Artificial Life.* New York: Pantheon.

Light, Paul. 1991. *The President's Agenda,* rev. ed. Baltimore: Johns Hopkins University Press.

Lindblom, Charles E. 1959. The Science of "Muddling Through." *Public Administration Review* 18:79–88.

―――. 1977. *Politics and Markets.* New York: Basic Books.

―――. 1991. *Inquiry and Change.* New Haven: Yale University Press.

Lindgren, Kristen. 1992. Evolutionary Phenomena in Simple Dynamics. In Christopher G. Langton et al., eds., *Artificial Life II.* Redwood City, Calif.: Addison-Wesley.

Lodge, Milton, and Kathleen McGraw. 1991. Where Is the Schema? Critiques. *American Political Science Review* 85:1357–64.

Lowenstein, George, and Jon Elster. 1992. *Choice over Time.* New York: Russell Sage Foundation.

Lowi, Theodore. 1979. *The End of Liberalism.* New York: Norton.

Luce, R. Duncan, and Howard Raffia. 1990. Utility Theory. In Paul K. Moser, ed., *Rationality in Action.* Cambridge: Cambridge University Press.

MacDonald, Stuart Elaine, and George Rabinowitz. 1987. The Dynamics of Structural Realignment. *American Political Science Review* 81:775–96.

Majone, Giandomenico. 1989. *Evidence, Argument, and Persuasion in the Policy Process.* New Haven: Yale University Press.

Manheim, Jarrold B. 1987. A Model of Agenda Dynamics. In Margaret L. McLaughlin, ed., *Communication Yearbook 10,* pp. 499–516. Newbury Park, Calif.: Sage.

Mansbridge, Jane, ed. 1990. *Beyond Self Interest.* Chicago: University of Chicago Press.

March, James G. 1978. Bounded Rationality, Ambiguity, and the Engineering of Choice. *Bell Journal of Economics* 9:578–608.

March, James G., and Johan P. Olsen. 1989. *Rediscovering Institutions.* New York: Free Press.

Marcus, George E., and Michael B. MacKuen. 1993. Anxiety, Enthusiasm, and the Vote: The Emotional Underpinnings of Learning and Involvement during Presidential Campaigns. *American Political Science Review* 87:672–85.

Margolis, Howard. 1987. *Patterns, Thinking, and Cognition.* Chicago: University of Chicago Press.

Marshall, Alfred. 1961. *Principles of Economics,* 9th (Variorum) ed. London: Macmillan.

May, Robert, and George Oster. 1976. Bifurcations and Dynamic Complexity in Simple Ecological Models. *American Naturalist* 110:573–99.

Mayer, William G. 1992. *The Changing American Mind.* Ann Arbor: University of Michigan Press.

Mayhew, David. 1991. *Divided We Govern.* New Haven: Yale University Press.

Maynard-Smith, J. 1982. *Evolution and the Theory of Games.* Cambridge: Cambridge University Press.

Mazur, Allan. 1981a. *The Dynamics of Technical Controversy.* Washington, D.C.: Communications Press.

———. 1981b. Media Coverage and Public Opinion on Scientific Controversies. *Journal of Communication* 31:106–16.

McCleary, Richard, and Richard Hay. 1980. *Applied Time Series Analysis for the Social Sciences.* Beverly Hills, Calif.: Sage.

McCombs, Maxwell E. 1981. The Agenda Setting Approach. In Dan Nimmo and Keith R. Sanders, eds., *Handbook of Political Communication.* Beverly Hills, Calif.: Sage.

McCubbins, Matthew D., and Thomas Schwartz. 1984. Congressional Oversight Overlooked: Police Patrols versus Fire Alarms. *American Journal of Political Science* 28:165–79.

McCurdy, Karen M. 1990. Environmental Legislation as Viewed from Different Committees: A Comparison of Committee Membership and Decisions. Paper presented at the annual meeting of the Midwest Political Science Association, Chicago.

McFarland, Andrew S. 1991. Interest Groups and Political Time: Cycles in America. *British Journal of Political Science* 21:257–84.

McGowan, Alan H. 1986. Science and the Media: The Vital Connection. *Technology in Society* 7:353–60.

McKelvey, Richard D., and Peter C. Ordeshook. A Decade of Experimental Research on Spatial Models. In James M. Enelow and Melvin J. Hinich, eds., *Advances in the Spatial Theory of Voting,* pp. 99–144. Cambridge: Cambridge University Press.

Meltsner, Arnold. 1971. *The Politics of City Revenue.* Berkeley: University of California Press.

Meltzer, Allan H., and Scott F. Richard. 1978. Why Government Grows (and Grows) in a Democracy. *Public Interest* 52 (Summer).

Milbrath, Lester W., and M. L. Goel. 1977. *Political Participation,* 2d ed. Chicago: Rand McNally.

Miller, Arthur H. 1991. Where Is the Schema? Critiques. *American Political Science Review* 85:1369–76.

Miller, Arthur H., Edie N. Goldenberg, and Lutz Erbring. 1979. Type-Set Politics: Impact of Newspapers on Public Confidence. *American Political Science Review* 73:67–84.

Miller, Gary J., and Thomas H. Hammond. 1990. Committees and the Core of the Constitution. *Public Choice* 66:201–27.

Miller, Warren E., and Donald E. Stokes. 1963. Constituency Influence in Congress. *American Political Science Review* 57:45–56.

Mills, Mike. 1993. Super Collider Backers Cave after Pivotal House Vote. *Congressional Quarterly* 51 (October 23): 2866–69.

Milward, H. Brinton, and Wendy Laird. 1990. Where Does Policy Come From? Paper presented at annual meeting of the Western Political Science Association, Newport Beach, California, March 23–25.

Mintz, Alex. 1993. The Decision to Attack Iraq: A Non-Compensatory Theory of Decision-Making. *Journal of Conflict Resolution* 37: 595–618.

Mintz, Alex, and Nehemia Geva. 1993. Why Don't Democracies Fight Each Other? An Experimental Study. *Journal of Conflict Resolution* 37:484–503.

Moe, Terry M. 1985. Control and Feedback in Economic Regulation: The Case of the NLRB. *American Political Science Review* 79:1094–1116.

———. 1987. Interests, Institutions, and Positive Theory: The Politics of the NLRB. In Karen Orren and Stephen Skowronek, eds., *Studies in American Political Development*, vol. 2. New Haven: Yale University Press.

Molotch, Harvey, and Marilyn Lester. 1974. News as Purposive Behavior: On the Strategic Uses of Routine Events, Accidents, and Scandals. *American Sociological Review* 39:101–12.

Moray, Neville. 1970. *Attention: Selective Processes in Vision and Hearing.* New York: Academic.

Nardulli, Peter F. 1993. Beyond the "End of Realignment": The Concept of a Critical Realignment, Electoral Behavior, and Political Change. Urbana: Department of Political Science, University of Illinois. Unpublished ms.

National Institute on Drug Abuse. 1989. *Annual Data 1988: Data from the Drug Abuse Warning Network.* Washington, D.C.: U.S. Department of Health and Human Services, Public Health Service.

Neisser, Ulric. 1967. *Cognitive Psychology.* New York: Appleton.

———. 1976. *Cognition and Reality.* San Francisco: W. H. Freeman.

Nelkin, Dorothy. 1971. *Nuclear Power and Its Critics.* Ithaca, N.Y.: Cornell University Press.

―――. 1987. *Selling Science.* New York: W. H. Freeman.

Nelkin, Dorothy, ed. 1984. *Controversy: The Politics of Technical Decisions.* London: Sage.

Nelkin, Dorothy, and Susan Fallows. 1978. The Evolution of the Nuclear Debate: The Role of Public Participation. *Annual Review of Energy* 3:275–312.

Nelkin, Dorothy, and Michael Pollak. 1981. *The Atom Besieged: Extra Parliamentary Dissent in France and Germany.* Cambridge, Mass.: MIT Press.

Nelson, Barbara J. 1984. *Making an Issue of Child Abuse: Political Agenda Setting for Social Problems.* Chicago: University of Chicago Press.

New York Times. 1993. Governor Assails NRA for Opposing Gun Limits for Teen-Agers. September 8.

North, Douglass. 1990. *Institutions, Institutional Change and Economic Performance.* New York: Cambridge University Press.

O'Connor, James. 1973. *The Fiscal Crisis of the State.* New York: St. Martin's.

Olson, Mancur. 1965. *The Logic of Collective Action.* Cambridge, Mass.: Harvard University Press.

―――. 1982. *The Rise and Decline of Nations.* New Haven: Yale University Press.

Ordeshook, Peter. 1980. Response to Riker. *American Political Science Review* 74:447–49.

―――. 1986. *Game Theory and Political Theory: An Introduction.* New York: Cambridge University Press.

Ostrom, Charles W., Jr., and Robin F. Marra. 1986. U.S. Defense Spending and the Sarit Estimate. *American Political Science Review* 80:819–41.

Ostrom, Charles W., Jr., and Dennis M. Simon. 1985. Promise and Performance: A Dynamic Model of Presidential Popularity. *American Political Science Review* 79:334–58.

Packard, Norman. 1989. Evolving Bugs in a Simulated Ecosystem. In Christopher Langton, ed., *Artificial Life.* Redwood City, Calif.: Addison-Wesley.

Page, Benjamin, and Robert Shapiro. 1983. Effects of Public Opinion on Policy. *American Political Science Review* 77:23–43.

―――. 1992. *The Rational Public.* Chicago: University of Chicago Press.

Payne, J. W. 1976. Task Complexity and Contingent Processing in Decision-Making. *Organizational Behavior and Human Performance* 16:366–87.

Perrow, Charles. 1979. *Complex Organizations: A Critical Essay*, 2d ed. Glenview, Ill.: Scott, Foresman.

Peters, B. Guy, and Brian W. Hogwood. 1985. In Search of the Issue-Attention Cycle. *Journal of Politics* 47:239–53.

Peterson, Iver. 1993. New Jersey's Gun Control Fight Rewrites the Rules. *New York Times,* April 3.

Peterson, Paul. 1980. *City Limits.* Chicago: University of Chicago Press.

Polsby, Nelson W. 1984. *Policy Innovation in America: The Politics of Policy Initiation.* New Haven: Yale University Press.

Popkin, Samuel. 1991. *The Reasoning Voter.* Chicago: University of Chicago Press.

Poole, Keith T., and Howard Rosenthal. 1984. U.S. Presidential Elections, 1968–80: A Spatial Analysis. *American Journal of Political Science* 28:282–312.

———. 1991. Patterns of Congressional Voting. *American Journal of Political Science* 35:228–78.

———. 1993. Spatial Realignment and the Mapping of Issues in U.S. History: The Evidence from Roll Call Voting. In William H. Riker, ed., *Agenda Formation,* pp. 13–41. Ann Arbor: University of Michigan Press.

Protess, David L., Fay Lomax Cook, Thomas R. Curtin, Margaret T. Gordon, Donna R. Leff, Maxwell E. McCombs, and Peter Miller. 1987. The Impact of Investigative Reporting on Public Opinion and Policymaking: Targeting Toxic Waste. *Public Opinion Quarterly* 51:166–85.

Protess, David L., Donna R. Leff, S. C. Brooks, and Margaret T. Gordon. 1985. Uncovering Rape: The Watchdog Press and the Limits of Agenda-Setting. *Public Opinion Quarterly* 49:19–37.

Quattrone, George A., and Amos Tversky. 1988. Contrasting Rational and Psychological Analyses of Political Choice. *American Political Science Review* 83:720–36.

Rabinowitz, George. 1978. On the Nature of Political Issues: Insights from a Spatial Analysis. *American Journal of Political Science* 22:793–817.

Rabinowitz, George, and Stuart Elaine MacDonald. 1989. A Directional Theory of Voting. *American Political Science Review* 83:93–121.

Rabinowitz, George, James W. Prothro, and William Jacoby. 1982. Salience as a Factor in the Impact of Issues on Candidate Evaluation. *Journal of Politics* 44:41–63.

Radner, Roy. 1964. Mathematical Specification of Goals for Decision Problems. In Maynard W. Shelly II and Glenn L. Bryan, eds., *Human Judgments and Optimality*, pp. 178–216. New York: John Wiley.

Raup, David. 1991. *Extinction: Bad Genes or Bad Luck?* New York: Norton.

Ray, Thomas. 1992. An Approach to the Synthesis of Life. In Christopher G. Langton et al., eds., *Artificial Life II*. Reading, Mass.: Addison-Wesley.

Redford, Emmette. 1969. *Democracy in the Administrative State*. New York: Oxford University Press.

Reitman, Walter R. 1964. Heuristic Decision Procedures, Open Constraints, and the Structure of Ill-Defined Problems. In Maynard W. Shelly II and Glenn L. Bryan, eds., *Human Judgments and Optimality*, pp. 282–315. New York: John Wiley.

Ricks, Thomas E. 1993. With Cold War Over, the Military-Industrial Complex Is Dissolving. *Wall Street Journal*, May 20.

Riker, William H. 1980. Implications from the Disequilibrium of Majority Rule for the Study of Institutions. *American Political Science Review* 74:432–46.

———. 1982. *Liberalism against Populism*. Prospect Heights, Ill.: Waveland Press.

———. 1983. Political Theory and the Art of Heresthetics. In Ada Finifter, ed., *Political Science: The State of the Discipline*. Washington, D.C.: American Political Science Association.

———. 1984. The Heresthetics of Constitution-Making: The Presidency in 1787, with Comments on Determinism and Rational Choice. *American Political Science Review* 78:1–16.

———. 1986. *The Art of Political Manipulation*. New Haven: Yale University Press.

———. 1990. Heresthetic and Rhetoric in the Spatial Model. In James M. Enelow and Melvin J. Hinich, eds., *Advances in the Spatial Theory of Voting*, pp. 46–65. Cambridge: Cambridge University Press.

———. 1993. Rhetorical Interaction in the Ratification Campaigns. In William H. Riker, ed., *Agenda Formation*, pp. 81–126. Ann Arbor: University of Michigan Press.

Rimer, Sara. 1993. In Shift, Massachusetts Governor Backs Gun Law. *New York Times*, October 1.

Rogers, Everett M., and James W. Dearing. 1988. Agendas and Agenda Research: Where Has It Been, Where Is It Going? In James A. Anderson, ed., *Communication Yearbook 11*. Beverly Hills, Calif.: Sage.

Rosenthal, Andrew. 1992. White House Fight on Collider Deal. *New York Times*, September 26.

Rothman, Stanley, and S. Robert Lichter. 1982. The Nuclear Energy Debate: Scientists, the Media, and the Public. *Public Opinion* 5:47–52.

———. 1987. Elite Ideology and Risk Perception in Nuclear Energy Policy. *American Political Science Review* 81:383–404.

Rubin, David M. 1987. How the News Media Reported on Three Mile Island and Chernobyl. *Journal of Communication* 37:42–57.

Rushefsky, Mark E. 1991. Testing Models of Agenda Building. Paper presented at the annual meeting of the American Political Science Association, Washington, D. C., August 29–September 1.

Rusk, Jerrold, and Herbert Weisberg. 1972. Perceptions of Presidential Candidates: Implications for Electoral Change. *Midwest Journal of Political Science* 16:388–410.

Sabatier, Paul A. 1987. Knowledge, Policy-Oriented Learning, and Policy Change. *Knowledge: Creation, Diffusion, Utilization* 8:649–92.

———. 1988. An Advocacy Coalition Framework of Policy Change and the Role of Policy-Oriented Learning Therein. *Policy Sciences* 21:129–68.

Sabatier, Paul A., and Susan Hunter. 1989. The Incorporation of Causal Perception into Models of Elite Belief Systems. *Western Political Quarterly* 42:229–61.

Sandler, Todd. 1992. *Collective Action: Theory and Applications.* Ann Arbor: University of Michigan Press.

Schacter, Daniel L. 1989. Memory. In Michael I. Posner, ed., *Foundations of Cognitive Science.* Cambridge, Mass.: MIT Press.

Schattschneider, E. E. 1935. *Politics, Pressures, and the Tariff.* New York: Prentice-Hall.

———. 1960. *The Semi-Sovereign People.* New York: Holt, Rinehart and Winston.

Schelling, Thomas. 1978. *Micromotives and Macrobehavior.* New York: Norton.

Schlesinger, Arthur M. 1986. *The Cycles of American History.* Boston: Houghton Mifflin.

Schneider, Judy. 1980. Multiple Referrals and Jurisdictional Overlaps, House of Representatives, 94th and 95th Congress. In U.S. Congress, House Select Committee on Committees, *Final Report.* H. Rept. 96–866. 96th Congress, 2d session. Washington, D.C.: Government Printing Office.

Schneider, Mark. 1989. *The Contested City.* Pittsburgh: University of Pittsburgh Press.

Schneider, Mark, and Paul Teske. 1992. Toward a Theory of the Political

Entrepreneur: Evidence from Local Government. *American Political Science Review* 86:737–47.

———. 1993. Public Entrepreneurs: Identifying Agents for Change in the Local Market for Public Goods. Unpublished ms.

Schoenfeld, A. Clay, Robert F. Meier, and Robert J. Griffin. 1979. Constructing a Social Problem: The Press and the Environment. *Social Problems* 27:38–61.

Scholz, John T., Jim Twombly, and Barbara Headrick. 1991. Street-Level Political Control over Federal Bureaucracy. *American Political Science Review* 85:829–50.

Schubert, Glendon. 1985. *Evolutionary Politics.* Carbondale: Southern Illinois University Press.

Schulman, Paul R. 1980. *Large-Scale Policy Making.* New York: Elsevier and North Holland.

———. 1988. The Politics of Ideational Policy. *Journal of Politics* 50:263–91.

Schumpeter, Joseph A. 1950. *Capitalism, Socialism, and Democracy.* New York: Harpers.

Sen, Amaryta. 1973. Behavior and the Concept of Preference. *Economica* 40:241–59.

———. 1991. *The Political Economy of Hunger.* New York: Oxford University Press.

Sharp, Elaine B. 1991. Interest Groups and Symbolic Policy Formation: The Case of Anti-Drug Policy. Paper presented at the annual meeting of the American Political Science Association, Washington, D. C., August 29–September 1.

———. N. d. Agenda Setting and Policy Results: Lessons from Three Drug Policy Episodes. Unpublished manuscript.

Shefter, Martin. 1985. *Political Crisis/Fiscal Crisis.* New York: Basic Books.

Shepsle, Kenneth A. 1979. Institutional Arrangements and Equilibrium in Multidimensional Voting Models. *American Journal of Political Science* 23:27–59.

Shepsle, Kenneth A., and Barry R. Weingast. 1987. Why Are Congressional Committees Powerful? *American Political Science Review* 81:85–104.

Simon, Donald. 1977a. *Senator Kennedy and the Civil Aeronautics Board: Part I.* Cambridge, Mass.: Kennedy School of Government, Harvard University.

———. 1977b. *Senator Kennedy and the Civil Aeronautics Board: Part II.* Cambridge, Mass.: Kennedy School of Government, Harvard University.

Simon, Herbert A. 1977. The Logic of Heuristic Decision-Making. In R. S. Cohen and M. W. Wartofsky, eds., *Models of Discovery.* Boston: D. Reidel.

————. 1979. Rational Decision-Making in Business Organizations. *American Economic Review* 69:495–501.

————. 1981. *The Architecture of Complexity,* 2d ed. Cambridge, Mass.: MIT Press.

————. 1983. *Reason in Human Affairs.* Stanford, Calif.: Stanford University Press.

————. 1985. Human Nature in Politics: The Dialogue of Psychology with Political Science. *American Political Science Review* 79:293–304.

Sinclair, Barbara. 1986. The Role of Committees in Agenda Setting in the U.S. Congress. *Legislative Studies Quarterly* 11:35–46.

Smith, Tom. 1985. The Polls: America's Most Important Problems. Part I: National and International. *Public Opinion Quarterly* 49 (Summer): 264–74.

Sniderman, Paul M., Richard A. Brody, and Philip E. Tetlock. 1991. *Reasoning and Choice.* Cambridge: Cambridge University Press.

Snyder, James M. 1992. Committee Power, Structure-Induced Equilibria, and Roll-Call Votes. *American Journal of Political Science* 36:1–30.

Somit, Albert, and Steven A. Peterson. 1989. *The Dynamics of Evolution.* Ithaca, N.Y.: Cornell University Press.

Specter, Michael. 1993. Sea Dumping Ban: Good Politics, But Not Necessarily Good Policy. *New York Times,* March 22, A1 and C8.

Spinks, John A., and David Siddle. 1983. The Functional Significance of the Orienting Response. In David Siddle, ed., *Orienting and Habituation,* pp. 237–314. Chichester: John Wiley.

Stigler, George J., and Gary S. Becker. 1977. De Gustibus Non Est Disputandum. *American Economic Review* 67:76–90.

Stimson, James A. 1991. *Public Opinion in America: Moods, Cycles, and Swings.* Boulder, Colo.: Westview Press.

Stoker, Robert. 1992. *Reluctant Partners: Implementing Federal Policy.* Pittsburgh: University of Pittsburgh Press.

Stokes, Donald. 1963. Spatial Models of Party Competition. *American Political Science Review* 57:368–77.

Stokey, Edith, and Richard Zeckhauser. 1978. *A Primer for Policy Analysis.* New York: W. W. Norton.

Stone, Clarence. 1980. Systemic Power in Community Decision-Making. *American Political Science Review* 74:978–90.

————. 1989. *Regime Politics.* Lawrence: University Press of Kansas.

————. 1993. Urban Regimes and the Capacity to Govern: A Political Economy Approach. *Journal of Urban Affairs* 15:1–28.

————. 1992. Group Politics Reexamined: From Pluralism to Political Economy. Paper presented at the Dynamics of American Politics Conference, Boulder, Colo., February 20–22.

Stone, Deborah A. 1988. *Policy Paradox and Political Reason.* Glenview, Ill.: Scott, Foresman.

————. 1989. Causal Stories and the Formation of Policy Agendas. *Political Science Quarterly* 104:281–300.

Studlar, Donley, and Zig Layton-Henry. 1990. Nonwhite Minority Access to the Political Agenda in Britain. *Policy Studies Review* 9:273–93.

Summary of Comparative Data on the U.S. House of Representatives. 1991. *Congressional Record, House,* pp. 15–18. Washington, D.C.: Government Printing Office. 3 January.

Talbert, Jeffrey, Bryan Jones, and Frank Baumgartner. 1994. The Legislative Use of Non-Legislative Hearings. Paper presented at the annual meeting of the Midwest Political Science Association, Chicago, April 12–15.

Thaler, Richard H. 1991. *Quasi-Rational Economics.* New York: Russell Sage.

Thom, René. 1975. *Structural Stability and Morphogenesis.* Reading, Mass.: Addison-Wesley.

Thorngate, Warren. 1988. On Paying Attention. In William J. Baker, L. P. Moos, and H. J. Stam, eds., *Recent Trends in Theoretical Psychology.* New York: Springer-Verlag.

Treaster, Joseph. 1991. Cocaine Use Found on the Way Down among U.S. Youths. *New York Times,* January 25.

Treisman, A. M. 1964. Verbal Cues, Language, and Meaning in Selective Attention. *American Journal of Psychology* 77:206–19.

Truman, David. 1951. *The Governmental Process.* New York: Knopf.

Tversky, Amos. 1972. Elimination by Aspects: A Theory of Choice. *Psychological Review* 79:281–99.

Tversky, Amos, and Daniel Kahneman. 1981. The Framing of Decisions and the Psychology of Choice. *Science* 211 (January 30): 435–58.

————. 1986. Rational Choice and the Framing of Decisions. *Journal of Business* 59:251–78.

Tversky, Amos, Shmuel Sattath, and Paul Slovic. 1988. Contingent Weighting in Judgment and Choice. *Psychological Review* 95:371–84.

Tyler, T. R., and Fay Lomax Cook. 1984. The Mass Media and Judgments of Risk: Distinguishing Impact on Personal and Societal Level Judgments. *Journal of Personality and Social Psychology* 47:693–708.

VanLehn, Kurt. 1989. Problem Solving and Cognitive Skill Acquisition. In Michael I. Posner, ed., *Cognitive Science*. Cambridge, Mass.: MIT Press.

Veblen, Eric P. 1981. Liberalism and National Newspaper Coverage of Members of Congress. *Polity* 14:153–59.

Vogel, David. 1989. *Fluctuating Fortunes: The Political Power of Business in America*. New York: Basic Books.

Waldrop, M. Mitchell. 1992. *Complexity*. New York: Simon & Schuster.

Walker, Jack L., Jr. 1977. Setting the Agenda in the U.S. Senate. *British Journal of Political Science* 7:423–45.

Waste, Robert. 1989. *The Ecology of City Policymaking*. New York: Oxford University Press.

Weart, Spencer. 1988. *Nuclear Fear: A History of Images*. Cambridge, Mass.: Harvard University Press.

Weingast, Barry R. 1984. The Congressional-Bureaucratic System: A Principal-Agent Perspective with Applications to the SEC. *Public Choice* 44:147–91.

Weingast, Barry R., and Mark J. Moran. 1983. Bureaucratic Discretion or Congressional Control? Regulatory Policy Making by the Federal Trade Commission. *Journal of Political Economy* 91:765–800.

Weisberg, Herbert, and Jerrold Rusk. 1970. Dimensions of Candidate Evaluation. *American Political Science Review* 64:1167–85.

Weissberg, Robert. 1978. Collective versus Dyadic Representation in Congress. *American Political Science Review* 80:567–88.

Wildavsky, Aaron. 1979. *Speaking Truth to Power*. Boston: Little, Brown.

———. 1984. *The Politics of the Budgetary Process*. New York: Little, Brown.

———. 1988. *Searching for Safety*. New Brunswick, N.J.: Transaction Books.

Wilson, James Q. 1973. *Political Organizations*. New York: Basic Books.

———. 1980. *The Politics of Regulation*. New York: Basic Books.

Wlezien, Christopher. 1993. The Public Thermostat: Preferences for Spending and Budgetary Policy. Houston: Department of Political Science, University of Houston. Unpublished ms.

Wood, B. Dan. 1988. Principals, Bureaucrats, and Responsiveness in Clean Air Enforcements. *American Political Science Review* 82:213–34.

———. 1991. Federalism and Policy Responsiveness: The Clean Air Case. *Journal of Politics* 53:851–59.

Wood, B. Dan, and James E. Anderson. 1993. The Politics of U.S. Antitrust Regulation. *American Journal of Political Science* 37:1–39.

Wood, B. Dan, and Richard Waterman. 1991. The Dynamics of Political Control of the Bureaucracy. *American Political Science Review* 85:801–28.

Wooley, John T. 1993. Conflict among Regulators and the Hypothesis of Congressional Dominance. *Journal of Politics* 55:92–114.

Zaller, John, and Stanley Feldman. 1992. A Simple Theory of Survey Response: Answering Questions versus Revealing Preferences. *American Journal of Political Science* 36:579–616.

INDEX